W9-DEU-521

Teach Your Child to Manage Money

Teach Your Child to Manage Money

by Catherine Crook de Camp and
the Editors of U.S.News & World Report Books

Joseph Newman—Directing Editor
U.S.NEWS & WORLD REPORT BOOKS

A division of U.S.News & World Report, Inc.
WASHINGTON, D.C.

Copyright © 1974
by U.S.News & World Report, Inc.
2300 N Street, N.W., Washington, D.C. 20037

ISBN 0-89193-413-8

First Printing, 1974
Second Printing, Revised, 1976
Third Printing, Revised, 1977

All rights reserved, including the right to reproduce this book
or portions thereof in any form.

Trade Distribution by Simon and Schuster
New York, New York 10020
ISBN 0-671-22970-2

Library of Congress Catalog Card Number 74-18911

Printed in the United States of America

Contents

Illustrations

Other Illustrations

Acknowledgments

Catherine Crook de Camp and the Editors of *U.S.News & World Report Books* wish to thank Dr. W. Peter Sax and Dr. Milton Brutten for reading and commenting on the early chapters of this work.

They are grateful to Mrs. Phoebe Resnick, specialist in consumer education, and to Dorothy Crook, long-time economics editor at the *Voice of America,* for reading the completed manuscript.

Roslyn Grant edited the manuscript and coordinated the editorial work, assisted by Barbara Clark.

Money is important. But only because it enables you to buy the things that are more important than money.

DEAR ABBY

CHAPTER 1

Money,
Money,
Money

Money came into use about three thousand years ago. And money in one form or another will be in use until the last fires of civilization flicker out. Yet, strangely enough, few American children are thoughtfully educated in the use and management of money.

Until the second quarter of the twentieth century, managing money was a relatively simple matter. People either had money or they had none. If they did not have the cash, they got along without the goods. Except to finance a house, most families had little access to credit of any kind. They managed without many things which people now consider essential; but they knew where they stood financially, and they seldom went bankrupt.

In the past fifty years, it has become increasingly difficult to manage money wisely. For one thing, rich and poor alike are being offered almost unlimited credit by means of credit cards, charge accounts, finance company loans, and even checking accounts with instant loan provisions. So great is the change that it might be called a credit revolution.

Wide use of credit is encouraged by television advertisers who endlessly stimulate desires for material things. Buying with borrowed money is also encouraged by galloping inflation which spurs consumers to make purchases before prices rise higher.

For half of America's families, the old adage "save, then spend" has been replaced by the new concept "borrow to buy." A rising tide of personal bankruptcies points up the danger of always living one jump ahead of a paycheck.

The cashless, checkless society

The credit revolution is far from over. Modern computers have made possible future developments which sound like science fiction. Soon, experts believe, salaries will no longer be paid by cash or check. Instead, money due will go directly into the wage earner's bank account. Regular outlays, such as mortgage payments or telephone and electric bills, will automatically be deducted from the account. If the account runs low, the computer will credit it with a loan, charge interest, and deduct repayments from future deposits. All this is being done today on a small scale in some communities.

To operate a cashless, checkless society, it will be necessary to have complete credit data on every adult in the United States. All sorts of information about a person's background, education, work record, family composition, and credit status will have to be instantly available to those who sell goods and services on credit. Master credit files are now in operation in connection with bank credit card plans. They cover more than 50 million individuals, and names are rapidly being added to the list.

Whether we like it or not, credit and credit cards are here to stay. The cashless, checkless method of doing business is just around the corner. We cannot return to the days when the cookie jar served as a bank and a friendly clerk filled the grocery order at the general store.

Credit buying offers convenience and flexibility. But there are dangers, too. Computers make mistakes, and their mistakes are difficult to correct. Credit cards get lost or stolen. Most importantly, people who buy on credit tend to forget that they are spending real dollar bills. They often overspend and then find "easy credit" can be "hard credit" indeed.

Fight fire with fire

Faced with the complexities of this credit-oriented society, its tantalizing array of merchandise, and screaming advertisements, how can young, inexperienced buyers hope for success? The answer is that they cannot—unless they receive a thorough education in all aspects of money management.

By and large, schools have not begun to meet this need, although all states have initiated some experimental consumer education programs, and a federal law, passed in 1965 and amended in 1972, has begun to set in motion better consumer education. Until such programs reach every community and prove their worth—and that will take a dozen years or so—what can parents do?

Parents can interest themselves in promoting sound legislation to protect the consumer at local, state, and national levels while combating unworkable plans to overregulate the consumer. Parents can demand that schools offer meaningful courses in personal finance. Best of all, parents themselves can give their children training in money management. This book is designed to help them with their task.

*This time, like all times, is a very good one
if we but know what to do with it.*

EMERSON

CHAPTER 2

Pennies, Nickels, and Dimes

When Mary was two and a half, her tease of an uncle set out on the dining table a crisp new dollar bill, a half-dollar, a quarter, a dime, a nickel, and a newly minted penny. He told her that she could have her choice. Mary hesitated not a moment but picked up the shiny penny. After enjoying its glow in the candlelight, she reached for the greenback and asked, "Please, may I have that piece of paper to wrap my present in?"

Very little children have no way of judging the value of money. Except as something to bite on or to put in one's pocket, coins have little worth. Paper money has no use at all.

Parents must often wonder how to begin a child's education about money. To gain a perspective on the problem, it might be useful to consider some findings of researchers in child development. Dr. Benjamin S. Bloom of the University of Chicago has pointed out that, by the age of four years, as much as 50 percent of a person's intelligence has become fixed.

Dr. Burton L. White, wishing to find out how to recognize and develop intellectual competence, set up a research program called the Harvard Pre-School Project. For two years he and his assistants studied the activities of forty mothers and their children. They made a surprising discovery: In the life of the average child, the period between the age of ten months and eighteen months is of crucial importance.

Dr. White found that children who became outstandingly successful with their peers, with their school work, and with adult relationships enjoyed a specific kind of mothering. He wrote: "You don't need an awful lot of resources to do a good job with a child at that age—not even a marvelous marriage!"

What makes a child superior?

A superior child has superior mothering during those crucial months. To do an outstanding job of mothering, a mother (or a mother substitute) needs some knowledge of how a baby's mind develops, a vast reserve of energy, and some practical guidelines for education.

A superior mother fills the world of the ten-to-eighteen-month-old child with small, visually detailed objects—either toys or household utensils—and big boxes or similar objects to climb on or push about. This mother is not a meticulous housekeeper who places lots of fascinating things out of bounds or pens up the eager toddler for long hours at a time.

A superior mother need not always drop her own work to attend to the child's requests, but she should respond most of the time with cheerful help and friendly attention. Following the child's interests of the moment, she should stimulate him to do things well or suggest a related task or game to promote further development. On the other hand, she must not teach too much nor push the child beyond his capacities to the point of frustration.

Every mother should talk to her child a great deal even before she is certain that the child can understand. And she should smile. Children who are fondled, smiled at, talked to, sung to, rocked, and helped when they cry develop the ability to interact with other people. They develop basic trust. They begin to sense their own identity. A child cannot grow away from infantile dependence unless he has a trustworthy mother to grow away from.

Finally, if something goes wrong and the child begins to fall behind his peers, either because of a lack of early mothering or because of some physical defect, a good mother does not wait for him to grow out of it but seeks help right away. She has the child's hearing tested if he does not seem to heed commands. If the child seems exceptionally slow at learning things, or emotionally disturbed, or clumsy, or unmanageable, she does not punish him but takes him to a neurologist. He may be one of the estimated 7.5 million children in America who suffer from dyslexia—a little-understood group of related physiological problems called learning disabilities, which are discussed at length in Dr. Milton Brutten's book *Something's Wrong With My Child.*

Dr. Peter Neubauer, director of the Child Development Center in New York, believes that retardation of personality or of intellectual development is increasingly difficult to overcome after the age of three, although it is by no means impossible if parents understand the importance of prompt and continuing medical help.

What has all this to do with money? A great deal. Children who have love and understanding, good physical care, and intellectual stimulation during their earliest years tend to shine in school and later are likely to succeed in their chosen business or profession, to handle their finances sensibly and unemotionally, and to find satisfaction in their personal lives.

Concept development and the infant consumer

Mothers who have done their homework in the field of child development know that even the youngest child learns while he plays. With help or without it, each child must master one developmental task after another, and the child who is assisted with the job gets an emotional and intellectual headstart in life.

Adults have only recently begun to understand the step-by-step way that concepts are developed. Some tasks are easy, others difficult. Simple concepts must be grasped before more difficult ones can be understood. A child has to learn about the names of things, the differences in shapes and colors, the feel of things that are heavy or light, hard or soft, solid or fluid, rigid or pliable. He has to learn to sort things by similarity, size, and number. He has to develop motor control so that he can tie his shoelaces, button his clothing, and play simple games.

A child has to understand about symbols—drawings that represent animals, letters that make up words, sounds that recall the "moo" of a cow or the "whoosh" of a passing car. He needs to imitate other people; he needs to pretend to be an airplane, a lawn mower, a boat, a bird. He needs practice in understanding concepts like over and under, above and below, right and left, high and low.

The older preschooler needs to know how to count, how to add and subtract in a simple way, how to tell time in hours, how to divide things in halves, quarters, and other fractions. The concepts before and after, beginning, middle, and end, and month and year are among the most difficult ideas the young child has to master. Even grade-school children have little sense of time.

Many of the concepts that the young child has to learn can be taught while he is being given an understanding of money and its management. This integrated approach to education is of the utmost importance if the child is to become an educated consumer in later years. An alert mother can teach "pairing" with pennies or cereal boxes, letters and words from the labels on packages or from television commercials, counting with dimes or cookies or cans of soup.

Setting the table for Mommy teaches spatial relations; finding things on grocery store shelves develops the concepts of nearer or farther, higher or lower. Playing with pots and pans shows that some things are larger, others smaller. Pies can be cut in halves or other fractions. Children can grasp the sequence of events by planning a trip to the store with Mommy, bringing home the purchases, and putting them away.

The possibilities are endless. The job is not as difficult as it sounds. The child whose mother works with him and explains

things to him amasses without effort a tremendous amount of knowledge by the time he reaches nursery school. The child who is isolated in crib or playpen hour after hour is like Thursday's child in the old jingle: He has far to go on a slow and uphill road.

Teaching the toddler "thine" and "mine"

Babies do not distinguish between themselves and the person who mothers them. Their small world revolves around their own bodies, and parents are expected to attend to their needs as if they were an extension of the child himself. Although during their early months babies do learn to recognize the confines of their own bodies, they continue to be egocentric in the extreme. What they need or want, they cry for. What is there is theirs to use.

It takes some time, and not a little patience, to teach a small child that some things are his, other things belong to all members of the family, and still other things are the personal property of those around him. Usually, by the time he is three, a child understands that there are things he may look at but not touch, things of his own that he may offer or withhold, and things that others may share with him or not, as they choose.

Only when he has gained a sense of his own identity and his own possessions can a child begin to understand that people buy the things they need or want and that money is something you hand over when you wish to acquire some article.

Playing the money game

Young children often watch with interest as their parents hand over pieces of green paper in order to get groceries or other items. Sometimes, before they can talk very well, children will spontaneously play the money game. They hand Mommy or Daddy a slip of paper and expect to receive some object in return. This is a good game to encourage because it gives the child practice for his role as a consumer.

A little later, when there is less danger of swallowing a coin, this game can be played with real money. Coins for the game should be scrubbed or boiled and a new dollar bill procured, for money is, in a very real sense, "filthy lucre." One pretty purse filled with these special coins and several things to "buy" or "sell"—spools of thread, a small ball, a pad of paper, a toy animal—might be kept together and brought out once in a while as a special treat.

By the age of four, the set of coins might be doubled or tripled to teach the concept of two or three. Parents, however, should not worry if a small son or daughter does not adhere to this or any other developmental timetable. Children are individuals and maturate at their own pace.

Until the average child is five or six, it is not possible to explain meaningfully that five pennies are equal to a nickel or that two nickels are worth a dime. To help the child grasp such concepts, use the terms "five-cent piece," "ten-cent piece," "twenty-five-cent piece," and "fifty-cent piece."

Little jingles can be sung or repeated to begin the counting process:

> One, two, three, four, five, six, seven,
> Eight, nine, ten, and one makes eleven.
> Twelve, thirteen, and fourteen, too,
> Fifteen, sixteen. We're almost through.
> Seventeen, eighteen, nineteen, twenty—
> I would say that this is plenty.

Saving is spending deferred

When Joey was five, his grandmother gave him a half dollar. She told him to put it away and never, never spend it. He held out the coin in his chubby hand and said, "But, Grandma, if I can't spend it, I don't want it. It's no good to me."

Joey was right. What Grandma should have said was, "Here is a fifty-cent piece. Put it away carefully and save it until you find something that you want with all your heart. Then this coin may help you to get your heart's desire."

A child must learn that saving is spending deferred. It involves putting off some satisfaction, not denying it. The worst feature of a piggy bank is the fact that there is no proper way to retrieve a coin from it. Much better for the kindergarten set—and for older children as well—is a tiny replica of a safe with a combination lock. This the owner may open at will to count his wealth while keeping it out of the hands of playmates or siblings.

Children must be taught when to save and when to spend. If a young person took seriously the admonition never to spend money, he would become a miser. He would, in present-day society, suffer the pangs of frustration at every turn, for getting and spending are necessary functions of modern life.

Five-year-old Kevin did obey when his uncle told him not to spend his allowance. Being a serious, literal-minded child, he paid close attention because grown-ups seemed so big and wise. Thereafter he watched the other children eating ice-cream cones and stood forlornly clutching the coin he never dared to spend. Today, as a middle-aged man, he still feels the deprivation of those early years and asks for ice cream with nearly every evening meal.

To spend or not to spend

Little ones need to be taught not only when to spend but also how to make the best use of their allowances. Take the four- or five-year-old to a dime store—although nothing much can be bought for a dime these days. Be sure that he knows in advance just how much he has to spend. Walk about with him, letting him handle the things that catch his fancy. When he sees something that is within his means (please, no cheating by indulgent parents who would like to pay the difference), hold the object for him while he looks a little further. When he decides that he would rather have this object than keep the money to spend tomorrow, help him through the check-out counter while he hands the clerk his money.

Another way to familiarize the young child with the use and value of money is to allow him to pay for some small household purchase with money supplied by the parent. The sum involved must be pennies, nickels, or dimes—coins that he can comprehend. If the transaction involves large coins or dollar bills, he will go through the motions without any understanding of the nature of the transaction. If he hands

over a dollar, he might learn a very strange lesson indeed: Sometimes when he hands the clerk a piece of green paper, she will hand back many valuable coins. He will be puzzled to discover that when he hands over an even prettier piece of pink or blue paper, the magic no longer works. He will receive neither goods nor change.

Security and consistency are necessary for learning to take place. Situations where the rules work erratically confuse and sometimes upset a child.

Money and emotion

It is far more important that parents live within their means than that they lavish gifts upon a child or try to keep up with the Joneses. A child can accept the fact that his family has less money to spend than some of the other families on the block. He seldom notices whether the neighbors' houses have handsomer furniture or better carpets than his home. But he quickly notices whether his mother welcomes his playmates to his yard and serves them milk and cookies once in a while. He knows whether children like to visit him.

Most homes can provide this warm environment as long as there is a steady income, some harmony in the family, and an understanding of the emotional needs of the child. A sense of security through affection and kindness makes the poorest home as rich as a palace.

The play *I Remember Mama* tells how a courageous widow brought up her children with this essential sense of security. Mama was the breadwinner for a large family of Norwegian immigrants who lived in San Francisco at the turn of the century. Mama worked long hours every day and then came home to wash, scrub, cook, cuddle little ones, and help older ones with their home work. When a child became seriously ill or some other disaster threatened to engulf the little family, the children would suggest that Mama dip into the money in the savings bank. They all knew about the savings account because Mama had shown them the passbook before locking it up in her little tin box. Fortunately, each time the money ran low, she or one of the teen-agers managed to find a little extra work; so the savings lay untouched.

The years went by. Most of the children were happily married, and the youngest was earning his own way. Mama was tired and worn—as well she might be—and the children urged her to take a vacation. This, they said, was the rainy day for which she had saved so long.

Mama silently handed one of her daughters the key to the little tin box. The daughter opened the box in which the passbook lay, took a look at the balance, and gasped. There were five dollars in the account—the same five dollars Mama had deposited twenty years before when she opened the account that had made the family feel secure during all those lean years.

Money matters—but not at dinnertime

A generation or two ago, ladies and gentlemen never discussed money in the presence of children. Today's parents realize that the subject of money management is as genteel as any other subject and rather more important than most. In fact, financial planning is really a family affair, and older children should know that money is limited and that plans must be made before it is spent.

But what about the little ones, the toddlers and kindergarteners? Should they be in on discussions about checkbooks, living costs, and shortages of cash?

Christopher was nearly four when his father decided to join the country club and move into a house as large as those of the other executives in the advertising agency where he worked. Christopher's mother had worked her way through school and felt that, instead of moving, they should put a large sum of money into Christopher's college fund. Battle was joined. Voices rose in anger. Finally the mother wailed, "But John, you'll have us in the poorhouse with those big ideas of yours!"

Christopher stopped cowering in the playroom. He knew what he must do to save the day. He went to his bedroom, smashed the piggy bank, and brought his mother his entire fortune of $3.27.

"Now we won't have to go to the poorhouse, Mommy," he said. His parents looked at each other for a long time; then his mother said gravely, "Thank you, dear. Everything's going to be all right now."

Christopher had taught his parents a valuable lesson before he trotted off to play. Tension and anger over finances can harm the young child by dissipating the sense of security that is his birthright. Even when angry words are not said in the small child's hearing, he can sense fury, frustration, or fear by the set of a parent's jaw and the way he holds his shoulders.

Money is regarded as just a simple medium of exchange by the nursery-schooler brought up to understand how to use it in a dispassionate way. But if parental emotions get mixed up with the handling of money—if the young child associates money with fear, or anger, or hate—money no longer remains a simple medium of exchange.

Being laughed at by parents or peers who think his inexperience in money matters is funny or cute makes a tot timid about going to the store. Feeling unloved creates misers whether a person is three years old or seventy-three. Hate creates compulsive gamblers.

Bobby had parents who squabbled constantly over family finances. His father was a selfish, dominating person who had little time for his son. His mother was overly protective, playing the roles of father and mother as well as she could. Bobby hoped that someday he could give his mother the things she wanted to make her happy. He secretly hated his father for being so demanding and so mean about money.

As Bobby grew older, he began to make bets with the other boys. As a teen-ager, he played poker and went to the racetrack day after day. By the time he was nineteen, Bobby had become a compulsive gambler—wanting to win to prove that he was a good and worthy person, wanting to lose to erase the guilt he felt over his hatred of his father.

Mixing money and emotion can cruelly wound the unfolding personality. And these wounds leave scars that last a lifetime.

Money and the stroller set

The child needs his parents' help to grow from helpless infancy through toddlerhood feeling loved and secure. He needs to have a chance to see, hear, smell, taste, and touch in order to comprehend the little world of home and neighborhood so that one day he will understand the greater world beyond it.

He needs to learn about pennies, nickels, and dimes and the many good uses to which they can be put by playing games, buying gifts, and going with Mommy on shopping trips. He must discover that nobody has all the money he would like to have, that the people he admires can cope with limited finances, and that everyone can count on having some of the things that money can buy. He ought to have some money of his own in order to learn that money he does not need today can be saved to use tomorrow. He should learn the joy of giving.

But the child under six should be sheltered from the strong emotions so often aroused by talk of family finances. He must be shielded as much as possible from family members who indulge in destructive uses of money—people who punish others by wild spending or by withholding cash, people who use money as a bribe to try to buy love or good behavior. The child has a big enough job in growing from babyhood to school age without being distressed over matters about which he can understand little but feel a great deal.

Ah, search the wide world wherever you can,
There is no open door for the moneyless man!

HENRY THOMPSON STANTON

CHAPTER 3

Quarters and Half-Dollars

While some understanding of money can be taught at the pre-school level, a child is not ready to begin his education in money management until he is six years old. Consumer education during the grade-school years is very important. This is the family's big opportunity to develop sound attitudes about money and to teach the concepts and skills which the child can later develop into consumer competence.

To begin with, parents should examine rather carefully their own philosophy of getting and spending, for what they teach their children depends a great deal on how they feel about the value and use of money.

It is to be hoped that every parent who reads this book agrees with three propositions:

- Money is simply a medium of exchange—a tool for living.
- The management of money involves a series of choices by

which the individual hopes to gain maximum satisfaction for every penny spent.

• Money, time, and energy are the most important resources that people can use or misuse.

Everyone remembers the juggler in the circus who tosses three balls into the air and catches them in rotation. Each of us is like that juggler; we need a quick hand and a steady eye to juggle money, time, and energy without losing sight of any one of them. Moreover, it takes patience and good humor to impart these juggler's skills to the younger generation. But the job can be done and should be done.

Why do we need money?

Harriet looked at the two quarters in her hand and asked, "Why do we have to have money?"

"A long, long time ago," her mother explained, "when people lived in caves or little farming villages, there was no such thing as money. If someone needed a pot to carry water, he either made it himself or went to the local potter and offered to trade one of his possessions for a pot.

"The act of trading one article for another is called 'barter.' Barter is a slow and clumsy way to buy or sell things. It doesn't work very well because making some articles requires a great deal of time, skill, effort, and hard-to-get materials, while other articles can be made quickly and easily out of plentiful materials. The easily-made articles are, therefore, less valuable—even though they are often equally useful. Value depends on time, skill, effort, and materials—and on how much people want a particular article.

"The people of Lydia and Greece were famous traders. They invented metal coins to make it easier to trade one article for another. Coins can be made of rare metals like silver or gold, or of common metals like copper and nickel. Coins can be made large, like a silver dollar, or small, like a penny. Coins can be carried about conveniently. With coins of various values, a person can buy what he needs whether it is worth a penny or many dollars."

"But money itself isn't valuable," said Harriet. "It's nothing I can eat or wear or work with."

"Money is valuable in a very special way," replied her mother. "It serves as a medium of exchange. That is, we get money for the things we sell and give money for the things we buy. You can't very well divide up a toy that you want to get rid of, but you can divide a dollar bill into quarters, dimes, and nickels."

"You forgot pennies and half-dollars, Mommy," said Harriet.

"So I did. Now, paper money was invented in China. Paper money—like our dollar bills—has no value in itself. It merely states that the government of the country will give coins or valuable metal to the person who holds the bill. If the government cannot, or will not, give the holder coins when he asks for them, paper money becomes worthless. That happened to the Confederate dollars after the South lost the Civil War."

"Wouldn't it be nice if we could print our own money?" asked Bobby, who had been listening to his little sister's questions with more interest than he would care to admit.

"In a way we do, you know," said his mother with a smile, "every time we write a check. Bank drafts came into use among the merchants of European countries about three hundred years ago, while early settlers were coming to America. They are safer to carry around than either coins or paper money if the person who draws the check has the money in his bank.

"And recently a new medium of exchange has become popular. It is called 'installment credit.' People who use installment credit pay each month a part of the cost of a new washing machine, or refrigerator, or car. They also pay a high fee for the use of money that belongs to a bank, a finance company, or a department store. But that's another story."

An income for the roller-skate set

A dollar bill changes hands five times on an average day. A small child, watching his mother trade dollars for food or clothing, eventually begins to wonder why he cannot have all the money he wants to spend.

This is the time to explain that nobody ever has all the money he could use. Money is in limited supply for every

family, and every family must plan to use it to good advantage.

Still, just as parents need a relatively steady source of income, the schoolchild needs an income, too. There are several sources of income for the roller-skate set: gifts on birthdays and holidays, handouts from parents, money earned by the child, and an allowance. From an educational standpoint, which is best for the child from age six to nine?

Gifts of cash

If benign grandparents give large sums of money toward the child's future education, this money will, of course, have to be put in the bank or invested. But small gifts of cash should be considered the child's to use as he wishes. Even if he spends the money foolishly, adults should not bully or scold. A gentle suggestion might help him make a better choice the next time; but seeing for himself that a toy was too easily broken is the best lesson of all.

Catherine, aged seven, got a ten-dollar bill from her aunt and a trip to a big toy store. The money was burning a hole in her pocket as she moved, starry-eyed, from counter to counter. Then she saw it—a walking, talking doll. The salesman demonstrated how well it walked.

Catherine, enchanted, held out the ten dollars. Her aunt asked, "Don't you want to pick up the doll and look it over before you buy it?"

No, Catherine was impatient to own the wonderful doll. She handed over the money and then pulled up the doll's dress to see her underwear. To Catherine's horror, the doll had no chest, no stomach, just a big hole covered with wire netting behind which the voice box was installed. Catherine was sick with revulsion and asked for her ten dollars back.

The clerk refused. Catherine left in tears without the ugly doll. But she learned a lesson that has stood her in good stead for four decades: Examine the merchandise carefully; then stop and think before you buy. Strong emotion has no place at the cash register. That ten-dollar lesson, so costly on that bitter day, has proved to be a bargain in the intervening years.

Earning and the six-to-nines

Some parents, anxious to help a child develop a responsible attitude toward work, substitute payments for allowances. Whether the job is a real one or a "make-work" project, they pay quarter after quarter, week after week.

While the parent's goal is good, the method of achieving it falls short. The child lives behind an outstretched palm. He equates worth with cash and grows disgruntled when the constant flow is halted. He fails to learn the important fact that to win love a person must perceive the needs of those about him and help them willingly.

And yet it is important for boys and girls to have the experience of being paid in order to understand money in terms of time, effort, and skill. The wise parent sets certain household chores for the child as his contribution to family living—chores within his capabilities, such as emptying trash baskets every day, making his bed, drying dishes, sweeping the front steps, or mowing the lawn.

Then, in addition, there should be other, optional jobs that the child may undertake for pay. These should be jobs for which outside help might otherwise be hired: baby-sitting, dog-walking, car-washing, gardening, and, perhaps, preparing a simple meal for a tired or busy mother.

Be wary about permitting the grade-school child to accept a job outside the home. It is important that he has time for study, friends, family responsibilities, and rest. If he works for a neighbor, make sure that the work is safe and the employer responsible. If he tires of the job, encourage him to quit. He was brave to undertake it in the first place; do not make him feel a failure because the work was too hard or too confining.

Some parents help a youngster with his outside job. In one family, the two boys run a newspaper route. Whenever the weather is bad or the work load extra heavy, their father drives them along the route. True, the father has to get up very early to assist them; but the boys earn a significant addition to the family income, and they receive in return the comradeship of an affectionate father—something they will never forget.

If a child does start working part-time outside the home, be sure he learns to record his earnings. It is an excellent time to encourage an excellent habit.

Managing on an allowance

While gifts and earnings may provide the youngster with extra money and early work experience, no child should be without that steady source of income: an allowance. An allowance is money given on a regular basis to cover necessary expenses. An allowance gives a child the opportunity to plan his spending, make important choices, live within his income, save for a large purchase—in short to manage money in a sensible, adult way.

Contrast this with the handout system of providing money for a young person. Handouts make the child dependent on the whims or convenience of the giver. He cannot plan his spending because he never knows what money he can count on. He either learns to play the miser, or fecklessly spends whatever he receives, relying on another handout tomorrow.

In some families, where the wage earner's income is irregular, a week-by-week allowance may seem a burden. However, if the child's weekly or monthly budget has been worked out realistically, his expenses will be obvious and should not be ignored. Wise parents will set aside money from peak income periods to make possible a regular allowance in lean times.

An allowance is not an award

Money should not be used as a fine or a punishment, nor as a reward or a bribe. Cash awards for good behavior or high grades teach the child that everything has its price. For a less successful sister or brother, the lesson is equally unfortunate; he or she learns that kindness, effort, or willingness are of no avail. Parental money and love are reserved for those who are docile, smart, or lucky.

Fines, likewise, tinge money with emotion. If the allowance that is being reduced or withheld is essential for school activities, contributions, or other necessities, the child learns to associate such unhappy emotions as frustration and disappointment with the person who withholds the cash. Frequent use of fines as punishment negates the training value of an allowance.

How much allowance?

No longer are weekly quarters and half-dollars enough for youngsters aged six to nine. Inflation has hit them, too.

To arrive at a realistic figure to cover the schoolchild's needs and wants, help him to draw up a mini-budget. Explain that there are three kinds of expenses in everyone's budget. Foremost are *fixed expenses,* those which occur week after week, month after month. They cover the necessities of life, things like school lunches, stationery supplies, and contributions to religious organizations.

Flexible expenses occur at irregular intervals. They involve things for which various amounts are paid. Everyone must plan and save for these expenditures because some money will be needed for them sooner or later. Children's flexible, or variable, expenses might include money for gifts, for a school outing, for books and magazines, and for sports equipment.

Finally, there are the *fun expenses,* called by adults *optional expenses.* The money set aside for this spending covers desires, not needs. People sometimes have to do without the things they want when funds run low. Children's optional expenses might include an occasional trip to the candy store, the hobby shop, or the movie theater.

Making a mini-budget

Johnny's parents understood that in today's society "there is no open door for the moneyless man." They realized that always being short of cash could permanently damage his self-image. They knew that the child whose funds are never adequate is likely to be scorned or pitied and left out of social activities by his classmates. Feeling inferior, he may become timid and lonely. If the family is obviously well-off, he will rightly resent his enforced poverty and those who are so callous about his financial needs.

So, on Johnny's seventh birthday, his parents gave him a wonderful birthday present—some financial independence and a chance to learn about budgets. They explained that they would give him a regular allowance of $2.50 on Wednesdays and Sundays, even though this money might sometimes be hard for them to raise because grown-ups' money is limited, too. His father helped Johnny to write down the things on which he spent his money, listing them under the headings "Fixed," "Flexible," and "Fun." Mother helped Johnny decide which items were necessary on a regular basis, which could be saved for, and which could be omitted if money ran short. (See page 39.)

At first Johnny's father thought this was an enormous sum to hand over to a seven-year-old, but Johnny's mother pointed out that their son was already getting the money. The only difference was that she had been doling it out quarter by quarter. So the budget was approved.

With his first allowance, Johnny received a copy of his budget, a folding change purse to fit in his pants pocket, and three small manila envelopes marked "Gifts," "Baseball Glove," and "Records or Toys." He also got a box with a lock and key in which to keep the envelopes. Each time his father gave him an allowance, his mother helped him to tuck the savings into the proper envelopes and put the spare money in his bureau drawer. Johnny never carried more than a dollar's worth of change to school at any time.

Later on, when he reached eight, Johnny's parents planned to show him how to record his expenses. In the meanwhile, Johnny was learning to divide his income among his expenses, to save for future needs, and to handle money intelligently. Besides, with his parents' help, it was almost like a game.

Eloise was not so fortunate. Her parents picked a figure out of the air when they set up her allowance. A dollar a week, they said, was enough for a child in second grade. Nobody bothered to find out what her expenses really were, even when she told them that lunch cost fifty cents a day and that her teacher had set up a "savings bank project" in the classroom with a bank teller, deposit slips, and passbooks, and that each pupil was depositing ten cents a week toward a forthcoming class outing. Eloise went without lunches for a month and became pale and listless before the teacher spotted the problem and explained the child's financial plight to her parents.

Adeline's situation was worst of all. Although her family could afford a nice home on a half-acre lot and ran two automobiles, they always seemed to have money troubles and worried aloud. They did not budget their income and never thought of planning their daughter's spending money. When Adeline tried to explain her need for a larger allowance, her mother replied irritably, "What's the matter with you? Do you think money grows on trees?"

One day the twenty dollars that Adeline's grandfather gave her at Christmas disappeared from her bureau drawer. Her mother explained that she had borrowed it to pay the cleaning woman and would replace it. But she forgot to do so.

Adeline hated to ask for her money when Mommy and Daddy were so terribly poor. One day at school, after the dismissal bell had rung and the other children had left the classroom, Adeline thought of a way to help her family. Her teacher had stopped to write some words on the blackboard for the next day's spelling class. Her teacher's purse stood open on the desk, so Adeline reached in and pulled out a five-dollar bill. Just then the teacher turned around.

That afternoon there was a conference in the principal's office. Although the teacher was understanding and explained that the child needed more pocket money, Adeline's mother was furious and called her daughter a thief and said she would be spanked when she got home. Adeline's eyes went wide with amazement. She had only tried to help poor Mommy by taking money when it was needed, just the way Mommy had done.

What did Adeline learn from these two experiences with money? That adults are illogical people who do one thing and say another? That it is all right to take money if you take it from a child? That Mommy spanks you for trying to be helpful? She surely did not learn that money belongs to one individual until it is handed over to another, or that taking money which has not been given or earned is stealing, no matter who does it or why.

Revamping the allowance

No matter how carefully a youngster's expenses are figured when an allowance is set up, there is bound to be a need for

Johnny's Weekly Spending Plan

Fixed Expenses
  School lunches $2.50
  School Supplies   .50
  Sunday School Contribution   .25
  Telephone Calls to Home   .10
                          Total $ 3.35 $3.35

Flexible Expenses
  Presents for the family   .50
  Saving for a Base Ball Glove   .25
  Set-asides for Buying
     Records or toys   .50
                          Total $ 1.25   1.25

Fun or Optional Expenses
  Candy or Bubble Gum   .20
  Snacks   .20
                          Total $ .40   .40
                                            $ 5.00

I am to get $2.50 in quarters and half-
dollars every Wednesday and every Sunday.

periodic reviews. The original allowance may prove too small to meet the child's expenses. After a month or two, the budget may have to be modified. The child grows older and his needs increase. He may require carfare or money to pursue some hobby that has educational value.

Two nine-year-old girls took some lessons in quilting and found themselves so delighted with the pillows and pictures they created that they plan to make all their Christmas presents. They will need money for supplies. A boy who learned a few carpenter's skills in a shop class at school decided to make and sell bird feeders and little two-step stools to enable short people to reach an upper closet shelf. Such worthy activities deserve assistance even if nothing comes of them beyond an increased interest in creative handicraft.

As children grow older and prove able to handle sizable sums of money, they might be given the responsibility of buying some of their clothing. Then, of course, their income would have to be increased. Children mature at different ages; no two are alike. Parents have to use judgment and tailor responsibility to fit the child.

Special problems will inevitably arise. No schoolchild's weekly allowance can cover expensive purchases such as ice skates and cameras. Nor should a child be asked to save for years for some hobby or sports equipment that he needs now. Still, before taking the youngster shopping for costly articles, parents can discuss the wisdom of the purchase, the probable cost of the item, and how it is to be paid for.

An allowance for a working child

Some parents ask whether they should stop allowances when an older child begins to earn substantial amounts of spending money. The answer is that this would be most unfair, except in cases where poverty is an overriding factor. First of all, no schoolchild can be certain of his source of income. A heavier work load or a new, more distant school might make it impossible to continue holding the job. Secondly, the older child needs increasingly larger sums of money with which to finance his business and social life. Thirdly, if the parents' aim is to teach good attitudes toward money, it is unwise to penalize an industrious child while subsidizing a lazy sibling.

It is suggested, therefore, that families continue to supply the working child with money for necessities while allowing the money he earns to be saved or spent for the extra things the child may want. If a young person develops the work ethic, he is most unlikely to lean on parents for more money than he requires.

Some parents think that penny-pinching is good training for the young. Others feel that their obligations do not include the gift of childhood happiness.

Alan ran a paper route when he was twelve. A thin and anxious boy, he tried hard to please his stern, adoptive parents. He was making about eight dollars a week when his father cut off his allowance. "From now on," he told Alan, "you're on your own."

Alan worked at odd jobs all through high school and had little time or energy for fun. At eighteen he entered the Air Force until, a year later, he developed multiple sclerosis. Now Alan is confined to a wheelchair in a veterans' hospital. Each month his parents receive over $700—Alan's entire disability compensation. Perhaps, too late, they regret having denied Alan the few dollars that would have made his childhood years a pleasant memory for him now.

Savings accounts for the bicycle crowd

It soon becomes obvious to anyone who tries to plan expenses that a safe place to keep set-aside money is essential. The little locked box in a bureau drawer is fine for dollars which will be spent in a few weeks. It is not a good place for the larger number of dollars that are being gathered for more sizable expenditures.

When a child masters the idea of saving money for future outlays, and when he is old enough to sign his name legibly— that is, between the ages of seven and eight—he is ready to be introduced to the thrill of having an account at a savings bank.

Parents should choose a savings bank conveniently near home. Make sure that the bank is a member of the Federal

Deposit Insurance Corporation (FDIC) or the Federal Savings and Loan Insurance Corporation (FSLIC). Deposits insured by either of these government agencies are covered up to $40,000 should the bank ever have to close its doors.

Opening a savings account is fun. Even a very young child may have an account in his own name. The bank teller asks the new depositor's full name, address, age, and birth date. Then the teller helps him to sign the passbook in a special, invisible ink so that no one can copy his signature. Most children readily understand that the number entered in the passbook is the number of dollars in the account and that by signing a withdrawal slip they can obtain this money whenever they wish.

A somewhat older, or more sophisticated, child will want to know why interest is paid on the balance in his account. You can explain the theory of interest this way: The bankers who accept depositors' money do not keep all of it in the bank vault. They lend it to people who wish to borrow money for a few weeks, months, or years. In time, these people pay back the dollars they borrowed. Just as at a roller-skating rink a child pays to borrow a pair of skates, so the people who borrow from the bank pay for the privilege of using money that does not belong to them. This rental fee is called interest. Every so often the bankers divide the interest among the depositors whose money is in their charge, after setting some aside to run the bank.

Encourage your child to make regular deposits. Teach him to fill out the slips. When he decides to withdraw his money, never deny him access to the bank, even though the money is going to be spent foolishly. It is a poor idea to direct every step of your child's spending. Self-confidence cannot grow under nagging supervision.

It is all right to offer suggestions; but do not expect them always to be acted upon. Grieve with your child if he makes a poor choice, but never say, "I told you so." After all, it was the child's money that went into the bank, and it is his privilege to spend it as he sees fit. Learning is a trial-and-error process. Acquiring wisdom in the use of money is no exception to this rule.

Saving under the Gifts to Minors Acts

Many families begin early in a child's life to set aside large sums of money for the child's higher education or for the purchase of a car when he is old enough to drive. Such a savings account was not, of course, under discussion in the preceding section.

If a large-scale savings program is undertaken, parents should know that there are state laws covering gifts to minors that work to the advantage of thrifty parents. A savings account may be set up, or stocks and bonds may be bought, in the name of the parent as custodian for the child. The custodian has the right to use the money for the expenses of the child other than those for which the parent is legally responsible. Custodian account earnings are considered the child's income and are taxed by the federal government only when the child's annual earnings exceed the exemption for a single taxpayer.

Once the custodian account has been organized, parents, grandparents, or others may add annual gifts. The custodian may, at will, make withdrawals for the child's benefit, deposit income, and buy or sell securities for the account.

Under federal tax laws, no donor may give more than $3,000 a year tax-free to a single recipient. Two parents may each give this amount, and so may two grandparents. Because of the limitation placed on annual gifts, it is wise to begin the capital accumulation program as early as possible.

It must be noted, however, that when the child reaches his majority—and in many states a child becomes an adult at eighteen instead of twenty-one—bank accounts and other property held in his name become legally his. Parents cannot compel the new adult to use his money as they had planned if he chooses to disregard their advice. However, parents who teach their children how to manage money have good reason to expect them to demonstrate excellent judgment about the care and spending of their capital when they become adults.

*The direction in which education starts
a man will determine his future life.*

PLATO

CHAPTER 4

Dollars and the Preteens

"Where does your family's money come from?" Mrs. Bennett asked her fourth-grade class. Nearly all the boys and girls shouted, "It comes from the bank." But only one or two knew how it got into the bank in the first place.

That evening, Helen saw her father writing checks. She threw her arm across his shoulders and repeated her teacher's question. Her father smiled. "You know I go to work every day in the city. I work in a big office with lots of other men and women, selling stocks and bonds. Every two weeks I get a check, like this, from the people I work for, and I put it into this checking account. And that's the money we use for food and clothes, and light and heat. It's as simple as that."

Of course, the concept was not simple at all. Helen found it especially hard to understand that the piece of pale pink paper her father called a check was the same thing as green dollar bills. Two years before, Helen had handed the teller at the bank a piece of pink paper and the teller had laughed and given her a lollipop instead of money.

Helen's parents, the Eliots, began to realize that, while Helen had already grasped many facts about spending and saving her allowance, there were many more concepts to be learned about the use of money in modern America. Smart as she was, Helen had been just a small frog in a tiny puddle. Now it was time to make that puddle into a pond.

So, the next day Helen and her mother rode the commuter train into town. They inspected Mr. Eliot's office with its rows of desks and clanging telephones. Then they all went out to lunch. Thereafter, Helen could imagine her father at work in the vast, brightly lit room; but it would require many visits to stores, factories, artists' studios, and repair shops before she could understand the various ways that people earn the money they spend.

Building a spending plan

A few days after Christmas 1976 the Eliots decided that the time had come to let Helen see how they planned to spend the income they expected to receive in the coming year.

They began this annual job by making a list of all anticipated income from Mr. Eliot's salary, stocks and bonds, and the two trusts that he managed. Next they looked at the spending plan they had made a year before; for a previous plan, adjusted to allow for changing income and expenses, is an excellent foundation on which to build the plan for the year ahead.

When the Eliots took their spending plan for 1976 out of the file box in which it was kept, they discovered three newspaper clippings that they had filed with it in the course of the year. The first showed how the cost of living varies from place to place (see page 47). Helen, who had been studying the geography of the United States, was fascinated to learn that it cost over 56 percent more to live in Anchorage, Alaska, than in Austin, Texas. Philadelphia, where she lived, cost about 2 percent more than the national average.

Comparative Living Costs
In Various Localities
(Autumn 1975)

U.S. Urban Average Cost = 100

Area	80	90	100	110	120	130	140

Anchorage, Alaska
Honolulu, Hawaii
New York-Northeastern N.J.
Boston, Mass.
San Francisco-Oakland, Calif.
Buffalo, N.Y.
Milwaukee, Wis.
Washington, D.C.-Md.-Va.
Minneapolis-St. Paul, Minn.
Detroit, Mich.
Hartford, Conn.
Champaign-Urbana, Ill.
Philadelphia-N.J.
Los Angeles-Long Beach, Calif.
Chicago-Northwestern Ind.
Green Bay, Wis.
Seattle-Everett, Wash.
Baltimore, Md.
Cleveland, Ohio
Cedar Rapids, Iowa
San Diego, Calif.
Portland, Maine
Kansas City, Mo.-Kans.
Indianapolis, Ind.
Denver, Colo.
Saint Louis, Mo.-Ill.
Durham, N.C.
Lancaster, Pa.
Pittsburgh, Pa.
Northeast Nonmetro Areas
Wichita, Kans.
Dayton, Ohio
Cincinnati, Ohio-Ky.-Ind.
Atlanta, Ga.
Baton Rouge, La.
Dallas, Tex.
Houston, Tex.
Nashville, Tenn.
Bakersfield, Calif.
North-Central Nonmetro Areas
Orlando, Fla.
West Nonmetro Areas
Austin, Tex.
South Nonmetro Areas

Source: Bureau of Labor Statistics

Of more immediate interest to the Eliots were "Three Annual Budgets for a Four-Person Urban Family," updated to the autumn of 1975 and published by the Bureau of Labor Statistics (BLS) in 1976 (see page 49). Although the figures were already about 5 percent too low because of rapid inflation, the Eliots found it interesting to compare the higher budget for an imaginary typical family of four with their real budget for 1976.

That these three BLS budgets were not real budgets, the Eliots knew. They were, instead, spending plans based on the estimated cost of goods and services for an imaginary family living at three different economic levels. This family consisted of a thirty-eight-year-old fully employed man, his non-employed wife, a thirteen-year-old boy, and an eight-year-old girl. While no two families spend their money in exactly the same way, and while families vary greatly in numbers, ages, and incomes, the cost of three levels of living for this statistically typical family can be helpful to anyone making or revising a budget. The Bureau of Labor Statistics intends to readjust these figures each year to reflect current price levels and to release the revised budgets for publication in newspapers throughout the country.

The third clipping the Eliots had was a printout of a survey showing the difference in costs of consumption for families of various sizes, types, ages, and levels of income (see page 50). Since this survey was made in 1975, the figures were out-of-date; yet they clearly reflected the comparative costs of living for families of various sizes and ages.

The costs of consumption—that is, the costs of such necessities as food, housing, clothing, transportation, and medical services—vary greatly with the size and ages of the family. For example, a family with one child aged between six and fifteen, living on the higher budget in 1975, would have had to pay $13,230 to cover consumption costs. The "typical" two-child family would have had to pay $16,141. A family with three children would have had to pay $18,720 to maintain the same standard of consumption.

The Eliots were not a "typical" family; they had only one child. Therefore, they could live somewhat better than a four-

Three Annual Budgets
For a Four-Person Urban Family
(Autumn 1975)

	Lower Budget	Inter-mediate Budget	Higher Budget
Total Budget	$9,588	$15,318	$22,294
Total Family Consumption	**7,795**	**11,725**	**16,141**
Food	2,952	3,827	4,819
Housing	1,857	3,533	5,353
Transportation	702	1,279	1,658
Clothing	771	1,102	1,613
Personal Care	248	331	470
Medical Care	818	822	857
Other Family Consumption	447	831	1,371
Other Items	**436**	**701**	**1,182**
Taxes	**1,358**	**2,891**	**4,971**
Social Security and Disability	577	834	841
Personal Income Taxes	781	2,057	4,130

Note: Because of rounding, sums of individual items may not equal totals.

Source: Bureau of Labor Statistics

person family with preteen children; and their opportunity for saving and optional spending would be relatively greater.

Helen's parents studied the printout carefully. They saw that consumption costs rise rapidly when children reach adolescence. Because a college education is the second most expensive purchase a family ever makes, the Eliots decided to begin saving $125 every month in order to protect their standard of living during those costly college years. This would mean some belt-tightening now, especially in view of the rapid rate of inflation; but they thought that money for Helen's college education was a goal worth struggling to achieve.

Annual Consumption Costs
For Various Family Types
(Urban United States, Autumn 1975)

Family Size, Type, and Age	Lower Level	Inter- mediate Level	Higher Level
Single person, under 35 years	$ 2,730	$ 4,100	$ 5,650
Husband and wife, under 35 years:			
No children	3,820	5,740	7,910
1 child under 6	4,830	7,270	10,010
2 children, older under 6	5,610	8,440	11,620
Husband and wife, 35-54 years:			
1 child 6-15 years	6,390	9,610	13,230
2 children, older 6-15	7,795	11,725	16,141
3 children, oldest 6-15	9,040	13,600	18,720
Husband and wife, 65 years and over	3,980	5,980	8,230
Single person, 65 years and over	2,180	3,280	4,520

Source: Bureau of Labor Statistics

The budget revised

Having made this momentous decision, the Eliots sharpened their pencils and went to work. They discussed each item of the old budget while their daughter watched and listened. The mortgage payments had gone up somewhat because of an increase in real estate taxes. Fuel prices had soared. Food and medical costs were up sharply and headed higher. According to news reports, the overall cost of living had risen about 7 percent in 1975, another 5 percent in 1976, and a large additional increase was expected in 1977.

Luckily, the debt on the car had been paid off. They could spend their vacation at the shore with Grandma instead of putting up at a resort hotel. As her parents talked things over, Helen began to see how much planning and budget-trimming had to be done in order to stretch dollars to cover costs.

At last the revised budget was finished (see page 53). Helen, who had begun to doze in her father's armchair, woke up and looked at it. She was pleased to see that her allowance was listed under "Flexible Expenses"—expenses the family expected to meet, even though the amounts might vary from time to time. Then she spied the large sum that was to be put in the savings bank toward her college tuition.

"Daddy," she said, "it will be nine years before I go to college. If you put $1,500 in the bank for me every year, there will be $13,500 for me then. Isn't that right?"

"It will be more like $17,500, if interest rates remain at 5¼ percent or better," said Mr. Eliot. "Money put to work earns money. But that's something you will learn more about later on. Now, off to bed with you. You're a pretty sleepy financier."

"And by the way, Helen," her mother added, "remember that the family budget is a family secret—something we talk about only among ourselves."

Learning to shop

Shopping is the act of seeking out two or more similar articles, often located in different places, and comparing them from memory for various qualities such as size, grade, color, pattern, model, style, workmanship, and price. Shopping also involves deciding which new article will blend most harmoniously with all the other articles with which it must be used. Buying, on the other hand, is the simple act of gaining possession of an article by paying cash or arranging credit terms.

Although young children readily learn how to hand over money and receive a package containing their purchases, the skills of shopping require an apprenticeship of several years' duration.

Apprentices, in the days of the medieval guilds, learned

each step of their craft under the eagle eye of a master crafts-man. It is important to remember that they learned by doing. Twentieth-century children can become good shoppers only through preteen and teen-age shopping experience. They, too, must learn by doing.

Some parents belittle their children's attempts at shopping or wantonly overrule youthful decisions. Ten-year-old Sandra had earned eight dollars by dog-walking. She was visiting a new city just before the opening of school and wanted to bring home a memento of her travels. In the girls' clothing department of a famous store, she tried on slacks while her mother sat watching. Nothing seemed to fit her thin little figure. At last she found a pair of plaid slacks that were per-fect in size and cut. Sandra was ecstatic; but her mother ve-toed the purchase. She said, "I know you like green but I don't. When we get home we'll find something we both like."

Sandra pleaded in vain. She was not permitted to spend her own money on clothing that, to the woman who watched this little drama, appeared tasteful, well-fitting, and well-made.

What did Sandra learn that afternoon? That her mother's preferences are more important than hers? That it is a waste of time to earn money if one cannot have the pleasure of spending it in a reasonable manner? Whatever she learned, it was negative. She trailed her mother out of the store dis-consolately.

Patricia, also ten years old, was already on the way toward becoming a competent shopper. She entered the same girls' clothing department with a confident step, a benign grand-mother in tow. Patricia selected a coordinated set of slacks, shirt, and sweater in raspberry and navy blue, plus an outfit consisting of chocolate brown slacks and a matching sweater with a design in pumpkin and autumn gold. With just a little help, she checked the sizes and prices of all these garments and noted that they were drip-dry and wrinkle-resistant.

Both outfits looked so well on her that choice was next to impossible. Grandmother, delighted with Patricia's good taste and efficiency, bought both.

Young shoppers are bound to make mistakes from time to time. Mistakes are an inevitable part of developing compe-

The Eliots' Spending Plan for 1977

Expected Gross Income: $25,000.00 Annual Consumption Costs: $16,814.04
Expected Monthly: 2,083.33 College and Other Savings: 2,300.00

	Annual Average	Monthly Average	Annual Total	Monthly Total
FIXED EXPENSES				
Housing				
Mortgage Payments	$2,520.00	$210.00		
Electric and Gas	720.00	60.00		
Heating Oil	960.00	80.00		
Water	144.00	12.00		
Sewer Rental	99.96	8.33		
Telephone	360.00	30.00		
Estimated Repairs	400.08	33.34		
Furnishings and Garden Supplies	600.00	50.00		
Total Housing			$ 5,804.04	$ 483.67
Taxes				
Social Security	965.25	80.44		
State	499.92	41.66		
Federal	4,050.00	337.50		
Total Taxes			5,515.20	459.60
Life Insurance	480.00	40.00	480.00	40.00
Interest on Debts	.00	.00	.00	.00
FLEXIBLE EXPENSES				
Food and Household Supplies	3,600.00	300.00		
Clothing	1,519.80	126.65		
Personal Care	360.00	30.00		
Helen's Allowance	264.00	22.00		
Medical Care and Insurance	840.00	70.00		
Clubs and Dues	360.00	30.00		
Helen's College Fund	1,500.00	125.00		
Transportation	2,200.20	183.35		
Total Flexible Expenses			10,644.00	887.00
OPTIONAL EXPENSES				
Gifts and Contributions	480.00	40.00		
Vacations and Entertainment	600.00	50.00		
Savings and Investments	800.00	66.66		
Other and Unaccounted	676.76	56.40		
Total Optional Expenses			2,556.76	213.06
Totals			$25,000.00*	$2,083.33

*Rounded off.

tence. Parents should not sneer or scold when poor choices are made. After all, nobody berates a beginning skier who takes a fall. Nobody expects a neophyte golfer to break eighty the first time around the course. If the unfortunate purchase can be returned or exchanged, help the young shopper to rectify the error. If it cannot be returned, help the child to make use of it until it is outgrown or outworn.

Sizes, labels, and price tags

Helen was almost eleven when Mrs. Eliot decided that her daughter was old enough to try her shopping wings. She was to select her own school shoes, slacks, and a coat. Mrs. Eliot set aside $60.00 for these purchases and asked Helen which should be made first. Helen was anxious to look at coats until her mother pointed out that well-fitting, well-made shoes are essential for the comfort and health of growing feet. The shoes cost $14.95.

That left $45.05 for the slacks and coat. Helen headed for the coat department. Coats of many colors and styles hung on the racks, and even the group marked "Size 12" seemed to vary considerably in size.

"Mommy," Helen said, "I don't know where to begin."

"Well, let's begin by looking at the sales tags and the labels. Nowadays labels tell us the fiber content of the garment and whether it is washable or not. All-wool coats are warm and light, but so are these furry pile materials."

Helen found a beautiful jacket, but it cost $39.00. When she began to beg for it, her mother reminded her that grown-up shoppers often had to bypass lovely things they could not afford. Then she directed Helen to a rack of coats that had been reduced.

"They don't look old or anything," said Helen. "I wonder why they have been reduced."

Her mother explained that, since these coats were one of a kind, they might have been part of last year's stock, or a manufacturer might have closed out his line.

"This is a reliable store," said Helen's mother. "When things are on sale here, they are really reduced. See, the tag says 70 percent wool and 30 percent polyester. That should never wrinkle. It once cost $50.00. Now it is marked down to $29.00."

Helen tried on the navy blue coat. It fit her perfectly, and she loved its two rows of brass buttons. Soon the coat was packed, and the shoppers turned their attention to slacks.

Helen was attracted to a pair of pumpkin-colored slacks. But her mother asked her to think what she would look like in orange pants and a navy blue coat, and told her she could buy what she liked after she had pretended that she saw herself walking toward them down the aisle. Helen pretended, said, "Oh!" and looked for other slacks. Eventually, she selected well-fitting navy slacks at $9.95 and had enough money left for a red turtleneck T-shirt.

That evening she tried on all her new clothes. "You did a wonderful job of shopping," said her mother. "Tailored clothes are very becoming to you."

"You're a smart girl," said her father. "And pretty, too."

Helen felt very proud of herself. She had learned to read labels and price tags. She had learned that even when you cannot have some of the things you like, you can find something nice if you take time to hunt for it. And, although she did not know it, she had taken her first step toward developing a personal style of dress that would later become the delight of her friends and the envy of her enemies.

Shopping at the supermarket

Another day Helen's mother took her shopping at the local supermarket. Of course, Helen had been going to the market with her mother ever since she was a baby; but this time it was different. During her earlier visits she had ridden in a shopping cart or drifted along in a bored sort of way. Now she was going as a shopper. Buying the things on the list was her responsibility. Her mother would only push the cart and offer a few suggestions.

Helen soon discovered that choosing the best food at the lowest price took a great deal of skill. Mrs. Eliot had explained the importance of reading the labels on boxes and cans and then comparing the contents of two look-alikes. "Fortunately," she had told Helen, "a recent federal law has made it necessary for manufacturers and processors to list the ingredients in order of their greatest importance. If a can contains a large amount of sweetened water or packing oil, this now becomes obvious to anyone who takes the time to read."

Then there was the matter of weight or volume. Two cans or packages might seem equally full; but careful inspection of the small print showed Helen that one contained more soup, detergent, or cereal than the other. When her mother asked which of two cans of salmon was the better buy, Helen was stumped. One can contained 7¾ ounces and cost $1.39. The other contained 16 ounces and cost $2.69.

Helen started to divide the cost by the number of ounces; but it was almost impossible to do arithmetic in the busy aisle of a supermarket. Then Mrs. Eliot showed her that this market had posted the unit price of each brand on the edge of the shelf to assist shoppers. Helen saw that the price per ounce of the first can was almost 18 cents while the second was 16.8 cents.

But Helen still was not sure of the quality of the salmon in each can. She decided that the can with the least packing oil was probably better, penny for penny. Her mother agreed.

Mrs. Eliot next pointed out that the more expensive article was not necessarily the better buy. It might carry a higher price tag because it was constantly advertised on the radio or television. "Also," she said, "supermarket managers often place the less costly, but equally good, products on lower shelves and put the more expensive jars, cans, and boxes on easy-to-reach, eye-level shelves. The only way to judge value is to compare the labels on two or more brands and then to compare the unit prices of two brands that seem similar."

When Helen sighed, her mother added, "You check each product this way only once in a long while. When you have convinced yourself which brand is the better buy, you just reach for that brand each time you need a product of that particular kind. Another way to learn about quality at a price is to read magazines like *Consumer Reports*[1] and *Con-*

---

[1] Published by Consumers Union of the United States, 256 Washington Street, Mount Vernon, New York 10550

sumers' Research Magazine.[2] These magazines have saved me quite a lot of comparison shopping. They are especially helpful when you want to buy watches, cars, and other things too complicated to study for yourself."

That evening, when her father came home from work, Helen said, "I did the marketing today—with Mommy's help. I had no idea how hard a job it is to compare prices, and qualities, and quantities. It's decisions, decisions, decisions! And I used to think Mommy just grabbed things off the shelf while pushing a cart around."

"Careful food shopping is a big job and a very important one, too," her father replied. "Did you know that food costs our family more than one-sixth of our income after taxes are deducted? Families with less money spend an even larger fraction of their income on food and household supplies. Every dollar you and Mommy save on a bag of groceries is a dollar toward those dancing lessons you've been begging for."

Mrs. Eliot laughed. "I guess that means you've decided to let Helen start her lessons. Right?"

Helen glanced from her father to her mother. "Gee, Mommy, I'm glad you're such a good shopper. May I help you again next week?"

---

[2] Published by Consumers' Research, Inc., Washington, New Jersey 07882

The buyer needs a hundred eyes,
the seller not one.

GEORGE HERBERT

CHAPTER 5

How to
Be a
Supershopper

America's thirty million teen-agers earn or receive as allowances and gifts more than $21 billion each year. According to the Rand Youth Poll, the average boy aged between sixteen and nineteen spends $15.65 weekly, while the average girl in the same age group spends $16.85. This amounts to approximately $820 a year for the average older adolescent.

It has been reported that teen-agers buy 20 percent of all cars sold and 9 percent of all new cars. Teen-aged girls buy one-fifth of all women's clothing. Teen-agers spend more than $100 million each year for Mother's Day gifts and about $70 million for Father's Day.

Teen-agers buy half of all movie admission tickets, 55 percent of all soft drinks, 90 percent of all non-album records, 44 percent of all cameras, and 27 percent of all cosmetics. Moreover, they exert a considerable influence on the expenditures of their parents and of other children in their families.

Although the spending patterns of girls differ considerably from those of boys, as the table on page 61 indicates, all youngsters in their late teens need dollars in their jeans and smart spending habits to stretch those dollars.

Shortcuts to skillful shopping

Some people seem to be born superior shoppers. They know materials. They pay attention to cut, fit, color, and style. Their selections have that hard-to-define something that makes certain articles more pleasing to the eye than others of their class. They remember shades, shapes, and prices so clearly that they can compare something seen last week with something seen today.

Those who are less gifted or skilled can devise ways to jog their senses. They can carry a scrap of material clipped from the article they wish to match. They can measure the space they have for a chair, a picture, a record-player, or whatever, before they set out on a shopping expedition and can carry a tape to measure articles in shops. Large objects look smaller in a spacious showroom than they will look at home. Small rooms appear more spacious if the furniture in them is small in scale. An outsized sofa or table can dwarf the other furnishings in a room and create a very unpleasant effect. A photograph of the room with a notation of its dimensions often enables a good salesperson to help the inexperienced buyer make a sound selection.

Inexperienced shoppers should deal only with reputable stores that have a liberal refund policy. They should make sure that the merchant or the manufacturer will replace merchandise if it proves defective. Persons who lack intimate knowledge of the class of goods they are selecting should buy only in places where the merchant's reputation is impeccable.

Few people, for example, buy much jewelry. When they do have occasion to select a present for a graduate or a Mother's Day gift, it is better to patronize the best jeweler in town than to run the risk of being sold gold plate for gold or glass for precious stones. A good jeweler will gladly explain what makes one piece of silver or jewelry more costly than another.

How Older Teen-Agers Spend Their Money

	Boys	Girls
Food	32%	26%
Entertainment and Records	22%	11%
Sports	11%	6%
Books and School Supplies	7%	14%
Savings (Deferred Spending)	7%	9%
Clothing and Jewelry	7%	19%
Gas and Similar Expenses	4%	—
Grooming and Cosmetics	2%	7%
Other Spending	8%	8%
	100%	100%

Source: CUNA Mutual Insurance Society, Credit Union National Association

He will not rush a sale. He will, if requested, give a written guarantee to accept the piece for exchange if it does not suit the person for whom it was bought. The same is true of honest merchants who handle furs, audio equipment, and musical instruments.

It is most important to check out the reputation of dealers before buying unfamiliar merchandise, for some of the worst swindles occur in stores that sell expensive things about which most buyers know little.

Consumers, young and old, need to know how to stretch the dollars at their disposal. One good way is to shop at sales when these involve genuine reductions of price.

There are sales and "sales." Bona fide sales are held by reliable stores at the end of the season when the merchants wish to clear their shelves for new merchandise. Real bargains can be found at these sales, especially after the first of the year, when shelves must be cleared of fall and winter merchandise, and in mid-summer, when swim suits, summer clothes, and porch furniture no longer have much appeal.

Stores also hold traditional sales, such as those featuring linens in January and spring coats the week after Easter. If the buyer can wait for these periodic clearances, considerable savings may be realized in the large department stores. However, sales designed to stimulate business during slow periods do not guarantee the buyer real bargains. For these promotions, stores often buy irregular or slightly damaged goods to add to their regular merchandise. Sometimes articles of lower quality are mixed with the reduced stock. Some articles may carry a sale ticket because they are unpopular, poorly designed, or about to go out of style.

The sales shopper has to be familiar with the regular prices of goods of various qualities in order to spot a bargain when there is one. She must inspect sales merchandise with extreme care when the label says "irregular" or "imperfect." A sheet with an oil stain in one corner or a few thick threads in the cloth is just as useful as one labeled "perfect." But a sweater with a dropped stitch or a lipstick stain would have no value at all.

The sales shopper must also be able to judge style and gauge fashion trends. Items that are faddish and extreme today may be totally out of style by next year. Unless a person can alter them or have them remodeled, out-of-date garments, no matter how fine in quality, are no bargain at any price. Classic styles, on the other hand, continue to look right from year to year. They are well worth buying at clearance sale prices and storing until the seasons change.

More than a thing to wear

Sewing is a big dollar-stretcher, as a growing number of girls and women—and a not inconsiderable number of men— have discovered. Besides saving money on clothing, curtains, slipcovers, and the like, designing clothing and gifts gives the nimble-fingered a chance for creative expression.

One naval officer, annoyed at the high price demanded for a suit his wife liked, asserted that he could make one just like it for one-quarter the cost. He shopped with her for a pattern and material similar to that in the expensive suit. With his engineering training, he soon learned to operate his wife's sewing machine. He cut and fit the garment, faced the lapels and collar, and put in a lining. Then, one fine day, he and his wife returned to the store. To the amazement of the saleswoman who had challenged him to "just try it," the suit his wife wore was almost a duplicate and every bit as well made as the suit still hanging on the rack.

Another man, a toolmaker for an electrical manufacturer, runs a successful drapery and slipcover business in the evenings and on weekends. He sent three daughters through nursing school on the profits from his stitching.

Young girls who are handy with a needle can turn spare time into cash by altering hems for relatives and neighbors. With hand work so greatly in demand, people are willing to pay well for such services.

Buymanship and brand names

Products sold under brand names usually command a high price because they are widely advertised on television and radio. To meet the cost of this expensive advertising, manufacturers require quantity sales. So, in addition to selling their brand-name goods to smaller retailers at ordinary wholesale prices, they often sell at a considerable discount to large retailers, such as chain discount drugstores and supermarkets, which share the savings with their customers.

Toilet articles—such as cold cream, deodorants, aftershave lotions—and medicine-chest supplies—band-aids, cough syrup, aspirin, and such—are among the brand-name articles regularly bought by youngsters. By shopping in the discount outlets, they can obtain their toiletries for dimes or quarters less than the price printed on the package.

Even greater savings can be realized by buying equally good, but unadvertised, house brands. The trick is to read labels carefully and compare the listed ingredients on two or more packages. Take aspirin, for example. All aspirin tablets must meet the U.S. Pharmacopoeia (U.S.P.) standard. Yet some house brands sell for about one-third as much as heavily advertised brands. This is true of many pre-packaged medications used in every home.

Until recently the real cost of prescription medicines has been a well-kept secret between the drug companies and the pharmacists. In many states laws actually forbade public listing of drug prices. However, a federal law passed in 1976 encouraged pharmacies to advertise the prices of various prescription drugs so that consumers can shop more intelligently. Another federal law, effective July 1, 1977, further lowers the cost of medications. Thenceforth pharmacists may fill prescriptions with drugs sold under their actual or *generic* names instead of higher-priced brand-name drugs.

Labels on toiletries and cosmetics are less revealing because the manufacturers of these products are still permitted more secrecy than most other manufacturers of packaged goods. However, informed consumers know that inexpensive brands of lipstick, eye shadow, mascara, nail polish, and the like often come from the same factories that package the widely advertised, far more costly big-name brands. Cosmetics can safely be bought in dime stores and discount drugstores with one exception: hair dyes can be dangerous to the inexperienced user. Some contain chemicals that can damage the eyes or even cause blindness; some can destroy the texture of the hair or cause a rash on scalp and forehead.

If any cosmetic, regardless of cost, irritates the skin, stings the eyes, makes nails crack or peel, or causes any other allergic reaction, its use should immediately be discontinued. Fortunately for young people with allergies, many hypoallergenic preparations are available. Although the price of such special cosmetics may be above average, it never pays to cut corners where health is concerned.

Parents should never make light of a stubborn case of adolescent acne. The lesions may not be the result of simple acne at all but arise from a serious infection that can do permanent damage to the skin. Even if the difficulty is only a persistent case of acne arising out of temporary glandular imbalance, without corrective cleansing, diet, and medicated cover-up preparations, acne can damage a youngster's personality by eroding his self-confidence. The cost of a couple of visits to a dermatologist is a small price to pay for the improved self-image that follows the control of acne.

Shopping by mail

The Office of Consumer Affairs in Washington reports that second in number only to complaints about cars are the complaints about mail-order companies. Disgruntled letter writers state that they do not receive merchandise for which they have paid or that they do not receive a refund when they return goods to a company that "guaranteed" satisfaction.

Numerous young people are among the dissatisfied patrons of mail-order houses. Parents, therefore, should teach their children when and how to shop by mail.

There is no doubt whatever that it is best to shop in person. Goods displayed in bright colors on the pages of catalogs look enticingly better than they prove in reality. Size and fit simply cannot be assured without trying on clothing and testing sports equipment. There is no substitute for comparison shopping before one purchases any particularly personal or costly article; for price, style, comfort, and emotional reactions all play a part in the final choice a person makes.

If the buyer has absolutely no alternative to mail-order buying, there are some rules that will decrease the likelihood of disappointment. First, check whether the company is known to be reliable. In addition to asking experienced friends for their opinions, the would-be buyer can ask local or state consumer agencies whether they have records of complaints about the company. Better Business Bureaus (BBB) are now trying to upgrade their image as defenders of consumers as well as of their businessmen members. Upon request, the local BBB or chamber of commerce might contact its counterpart in the town where the mail-order house is situated and ascertain the reputation of the company. The potential buyer might also write for similar information to the Consumer Affairs Department, U.S. Postal Service, Washington, D.C. 20260.

Second, find out whether the company offers a written money-back guarantee. Even if the company should not live up to its promise, a written guarantee could serve as the basis for legal action. Check, also, to learn who pays the postage and insurance on the article being returned.

Third, always pay by check or money order; never send cash through the mail.

Fourth, keep a copy of the order, even if this means paying for a photocopy. If there are two order blanks in the catalog, a copy could be made by placing a carbon sheet between the two and pressing firmly with a ball-point pen. Also retain the mail-order company's catalog or advertisement until the purchase has been successfully concluded.

Finally, send the order by certified mail with a return receipt. Then there will be evidence that the order reached its destination.

If, despite these precautions, the item ordered does not arrive within two weeks, write to the president of the company (President, Careless Mail-Order Company, Anytown, U.S.A. 10000). State the problem, giving your full name and address, the date of the order, the catalog number and description of the merchandise, the type of payment sent, and similar data.

Should the article arrive in poor condition or seem a far cry from the item pictured in the catalog, return it carefully wrapped, insured, and with a return receipt to prove that the package arrived safely. Enclose with the package (at the cost of an additional letter-rate postage stamp) a note stating the reason for the return and asking for a refund. Be sure to keep a copy of this letter and the date on which the package was mailed.

If either of these procedures brings no response, try a second letter. If two letters do not resolve the problem, contact the Office of Consumer Affairs, Washington, D.C. 20201. Other organizations that might be of help are: Direct Mail Advertising Association, 230 Park Avenue, New York, New York 10017, which works with its 1,600 member firms to promote customer satisfaction; the consumer protection agency in your city or in the city in which the company is located; and the consumer column in your local newspaper.

Do not, however, count heavily on such assistance. If the company is fly-by-night or unethical in its dealings, the money you sent it is likely to be lost to you forever. That is why it is so very much wiser to hunt for the product locally or to deal only with one of the established mail-order houses.

Save pennies on postage

Most people spend a tidy sum each year sending greeting cards, letters, and packages through the U.S. Postal Service.

Smart shoppers know how to post the most mail for the least money.

Nowadays a regular stamp will carry letters weighing under an ounce anywhere in the United States and Canada. As a rule, letters traveling over 200 miles go by air. When the time element is important, letters can be sent by "priority mail" upon payment of additional postage. This may hasten by one day the delivery of letters going 600 miles or more. An additional special-delivery stamp insures delivery on the day the letter or package arrives at the destination post office. Because of this costly stamp, somebody's belated birthday card might arrive in time for the celebration. Foresight, however, is cheaper and surer.

Sometimes the sender must make certain that the mail arrives safely. If a letter contains nothing of monetary value, send it by certified mail and ask for a return receipt. Notification of the loss of a credit card, for instance, should be made by certified mail. But if the letter contains an irreplaceable document, use registered mail with a return receipt. Although registration is more expensive, it provides security and proof of delivery.

Never send cash through the mails, even by registered mail. Cash in letters is too easily lost or stolen. If a person has no checking account, he can buy a postal money order for a few cents and send that to the addressee.

Foreign letter rates depend on the country to which the letter is sent. Yet even here there are bargains for the asking. U.S. post offices sell pre-stamped air-letter forms at one cut-rate price to carry messages to the farthest corners of the globe.

Parcels sent by mail should be carefully wrapped and mailed well in advance of peak mailing periods, such as Christmas. To make sure the package arrives promptly, pay for a special-handling stamp. This will give the package priority over all other parcel post. A return receipt lets the sender know that the parcel arrived at its destination. Some people insure their packages for the minimum valuation because they believe that insured packages are somewhat less likely to be stolen en route to their destination. Placing large valuations on packages offers questionable protection. If a package is lost, it is difficult to prove its value, and it takes up to a year to settle a claim.

For books, manuscripts, and magazines, the Postal Service offers an inexpensive rate. Special handling is available even with these fourth-class rates. Letters may be included with ordinary and book-rate packages if the letter is declared and the postage for a first-class letter is added to the cost. People who try to include a letter and not pay for it are subject to stiff penalties. Supershoppers pay what they owe but no more than what they owe.

Santa's year-long helpers

Supershoppers do not wait until the frost is on the pumpkin to begin their Christmas shopping. They wake up on December 26, tell themselves that there are only 364 shopping days to Christmas, and lay plans for a prepaid celebration the following year.

On the day after Christmas, most people are so snowed under by torn wrappings, broken toys, and bills that they fail to notice that all Christmas decorations, cards, wrapping papers, ribbons, and tags are remaindered at half the original price. Prudent shoppers who have an attic or an extra closet shelf rush out early in the morning to stock up for another year. There is seldom anything left by eleven, so popular is this dollar-saving sale.

A sizable carton in a closet or attic can become a year-long workshop for each of Santa's helpers, large and small. Into each person's private carton go gifts bought as the months go by, each gift carefully noted on a pad. When Benjamin Brock was fourteen, he tucked the list shown on page 69 into the box containing his cache of future gifts. Next to each present he listed the cost, the retail value, and the date of purchase. In the last column, he placed a check mark when the gift was wrapped, beribboned, and tagged.

Smart shoppers know that in January home furnishings are marked down to stimulate bill-ridden consumers to re-enter the marketplace. Closeouts of lingerie come in July, and the sharp-eyed shopper, who had the foresight to tape a list

Benjamin Brock's
Christmas Present Cache

What and for Whom	Cost	Value	Date Bought	Wrapped
Cards, wrappings, ribbons, tags	$5.42	$10.84	Dec. 26ᵀᴴ, '73	
For Mom				
Nightie	8.00	12.95	July	✓
Needle threaders	.29	.29	September	
Sewing box with spool rack and felt-lined drawer (made in craft shop), materials cost	4.25	20.00?	Made in spring	
Dad				
Turtleneck sweater	9.95	14.99	March	
Billfold	3.95	5.00	August	
Pipe rack (made at shop), materials cost	3.69	18.00?	Made in fall	
Aunt Betty				
Evening bag	5.95	9.95	May	✓
Aunt Sally				
Silver earrings (bought at church fair)	3.50	12.00?	October	
Purse-sized folding raincoat	1.29	1.29	November	
Grandma				
Heating pad	4.99	6.98	April	
Fleece-lined gloves, size 6½	5.95	10.59	March	✓
Jimmy				
Watch	12.95	15.95	January	
Joey				
Record album	4.95	3.95	December	✓
	$75.13	$142.78		

of sizes atop his Santa box, can find lovely gifts at reductions of one-third or more.

Thrift shops, garage sales, and church bazaars abound in wonderful things that the owners or donors considered "white elephants." Dime stores carry useful and inexpensive gifts at all times. Nylon scarves in melting colors and fascinating prints sell there for half of what they cost in department stores. Unusual, personal gifts can be made in school or basement workshops or in knitting or quilting classes if the craftsman or craftswoman has enough time for the project.

If gift boxes are unavailable with items bought at sales, make a practice of asking for gift boxes when you make everyday purchases. Or glue gift-wrap paper to odd containers, such as cylindrical oatmeal boxes, to create highly attractive holiday packages.

Santa's helpers should never buy gifts they cannot readily afford. Nor should they buy shoddy, showy presents. It is far better to give a truly elegant pair of white cotton gloves costing five dollars than a poorly designed, cheaply made pocketbook for the same amount of money. The well-chosen gift should "look like" the recipient, whose taste may be entirely different from that of the giver. Ideally, it should be something the recipient would love but hesitates to buy for himself. And, if the purchase is made in November or December, it should be exchangeable when the sales slip is kept by the giver.

This year-long system of Christmas shopping enables a person to give presents worth much more than they cost. It allows the giver to substitute know-how for money. And after Thanksgiving, while most people scurry frantically through noisy, crowded stores, looking for something—anything—to buy, supershoppers can serenely tie bows on pretty packages, secure in the knowledge of a job well done.

Shoplifting is not a game

Shoplifters steal millions of dollars worth of merchandise each year. One Manhattan store estimates that this type of theft costs them sixty cents per customer per day. Surveys made by shadowing shoppers at random indicate that in

New York City, one out of twelve shoppers is a shoplifter; in Philadelphia, one in ten; and in Boston, one in twenty. And the numbers are rising rapidly.

Many young people fool themselves into believing that shoplifting is a game; that although they take goods, they would never steal money; that shopkeepers make enormous profits (they make an average of 4 percent on their operation); and that corporations are not people, and therefore taking things from them is not like stealing from a person. The truth is that shoplifting is stealing. It is a criminal act and can lead to serious consequences.

Parents cannot shield lawbreaking adolescents from the consequences of their illegal actions. Even if they do not serve a term in jail, convicted shoplifters have a police record that will follow them for the rest of their lives. It may surface when they apply for jobs, ask for visas to travel to foreign countries, or try to establish credit. If young people fully realized that a conviction would stain their reputations and jeopardize their economic lives, shoplifting as a game would certainly decrease.

Who are the shoplifters? Between 70 and 85 percent of adult shoplifters are women. Among adolescents, there are more male than female shoplifters. Pre-adolescent offenders are almost entirely boys. Although many younger shoplifters are economically and culturally deprived, a large majority of teen-aged and older shoplifters are middle-class individuals who steal for emotional gratification.

Dr. Donald Hayes Russell, in his article on "The Emotional Aspects of Shoplifting,"[1] points out that loneliness, depression, antiestablishment sentiments, or lack of parental affection and attention motivate a large percentage of cases.

Much shoplifting results from an ebbing tide of ethics and from modern merchandising techniques. Retail stores expose goods freely. Store displays and advertisements are deftly calculated to stimulate desires. The scarcity of clerks coupled with the encouragement of schoolmates puts a double strain on parental training in honesty.

---

[1] *Psychiatric Annals*, May, 1973, pp. 77-86.

Knowing these things, what preventive action can parents take? First, review the youngster's budget to make sure that allowances more than cover needs. Teach thrift, but not to the point where a child thinks it better to take than to spend. Money is a tool for living; something to be cared for until it is needed, then used. This, too, needs to be taught.

Check up on the attitudes about shoplifting held by your child's friends. If they are confirmed shoplifters, do something constructive. Take them to see a court in session. If possible, take them to see a correctional institution. If you cannot get permission to enter, just looking at the outside can be a sobering experience. Substitute some creative activity for aimless wandering through stores after school—sewing lessons, a nature club, a chance to earn some money.

One Girl Scout group developed a business which became so popular that the members carried on the activity for three years. They distributed flyers throughout the neighborhood offering to run errands, care for animals, rake lawns, read to the ill or the old, and do other chores for a dollar an hour. The girls worked in pairs and each banked her dollars. At the end of three years, their leader took the troop on a two-week tour of Europe. Nearly all the girls had saved enough to pay their way.

If, despite parental interest, worthwhile activities, and fair allowances, a child is tempted to pilfer, what should a parent do? Do not ignore the evidence; take prompt and positive action, no matter how embarrassing or painful it may be.

Arthur, aged nine, was interested in carpentry. One day while in a large hardware store, he acquired a screwdriver and a small box of assorted nails. His father realized immediately that the screwdriver with the yellow plastic handle had not come from his tool chest. Arthur said he had bought it, but his lunch money for the coming week was still in his pocket. Finally, Arthur confessed.

His father called the manager of the store and asked that he receive them even though it was past five o'clock. A thoroughly frightened Arthur met the solemn-faced manager and stammered that here were the tools he had forgotten to pay for. His father helped not at all but stood straight beside him through the ordeal. When they got back home, nothing more was said about the incident, but Arthur knew how it felt to be on his own outside the law. He never again took anything he did not pay for.

That fall, his father enrolled Arthur in the boys' woodworking class at the local art center. He made a bird feeder and a stool for his mother to use in reaching the upper shelves of her linen closet. He proved to be exceptionally gifted with his hands. Now an electronics engineer, his hobby is making small pieces of furniture and exquisite wooden toys for his children.

Shopping manners for minors

Many teen-aged consumers feel—and sometimes with reason—that they are victims of discrimination because of age. They say that store personnel eye them suspiciously when they examine merchandise. Snack-bar attendants urge them to move along before they have quite finished their sandwiches and soft drinks. They are sold poorly made or defective goods at prices higher than those charged adult consumers.

It is quite true that shopkeepers are on the defensive when large numbers of young people descend on them, fingering merchandise, talking loudly, elbowing other customers, sprinting along aisles, or chatting at lunch counters while hungry shoppers wait in line. Merchants know that shoplifting and vandalism have risen alarmingly. They also know that adult customers tend to avoid places that have become teen-age hangouts.

Some youthful complaints seem unjustified to adult shoppers. One boy, reprimanded for running down the stairs, said, "I wasn't running; I was just trying to keep up with my friends." He probably did not know about the seventeen-year-old who, a day earlier, raced her companion to the entrance of the store, put her foot through the plate glass, and suffered deep cuts on her leg.

A fifteen-year-old girl, who felt aggrieved at constant surveillance at a dime-store cosmetic counter, complained, "I just wanted to test the polish for color. But as I was touching

up one nail, the salesgirl came over, shouting, 'Don't you do that! Don't do it!' "

One teen-aged boy pointed to his friend's wrist rocket while the latter was taking pot-shots with pebbles at the sign above the store's plate-glass window. The boy reported, "They were charging $2.69 for that rocket the other day. Today they charged us $2.98."

One girl felt that stores discourage young people from careful shopping. "You walk into a store and everybody comes up asking, 'Can I help you?' Once you buy something, or if you are just looking, they want to get rid of you. They don't do that to grown-ups."

Other complaints have more merit. Nowadays, shoddy merchandise plagues all buyers, young and old. Records, which are among the most popular items teen-agers buy, occasionally do have scratches and other defects for which the merchants unfairly blame the youthful purchasers. The young and diffident often do wait while pushy adults are served ahead of them.

When a group of science-fiction fans rented a Philadelphia hotel ballroom for a convention, they found that the hotel personnel were deliberately rude in elevators, in the dining room, and even in the meeting room when asked to rearrange the chairs between sessions in accordance with agreements made with the manager. The fans, although well-behaved and intelligent young people, had antagonized the hotel employees with their imaginative garb and hair styles.

Rules to follow

Not all teen-aged consumers experience these difficulties. Two sixteen-year-old girls said, "We don't have any trouble when we go shopping. None of our friends do, either. That 'No bare feet' sign doesn't bother us; who'd want to go shopping in bare feet anyway? And if a clerk comes up and offers to help us, we're glad to save the time."

Yet, for many young shoppers, the problems do exist. Parents can help protect their children from suspicion of shoplifting and reduce the embarrassment that plagues teen-age shopping expeditions by teaching shopping manners. They can smooth their children's path into the marketplace by giving them rules to follow and by explaining the reasons for these rules:

1. Do not go shopping in a big group; the misbehavior of one member will reflect on everyone in the group.
2. Do not engage in horseplay in a store or in its parking lot, nor treat the premises less well than you would your own home.
3. Dress neatly when you go shopping, lest older people question your integrity because of your appearance.
4. Do not carry large bags, book packs, or purses into a store or finger merchandise that you have no intention of buying, for such practices draw suspicion to you, no matter how innocent your intent.
5. Do not sample nail polish, lipstick, or hair spray before you buy it. Once the seal has been broken, the contents can become a liability to the store.
6. When trying on clothes, handle them carefully. Put unwanted garments back on hangers and return them to the racks on which you found them.
7. Be courteous to those with whom you deal. Politeness encourages politeness.
8. Remember that the more theft and damage the merchant sustains, the more he is going to have to raise the prices of all the items he stocks.

The merchandising techniques Americans enjoy today—open racks and bins full of articles to see and touch and compare—did not exist fifty years ago. In those days a clerk would go into the storage room and bring out two or three garments for the customer to try on. Or, the buyer described the article he required, and one more or less like it was produced from behind the counter or from a showcase. Such person-to-person selling limited the buyer's choice and took a great deal of time. In most European stores, the seller still takes care of one customer while other customers wait and wait.

American department stores and supermarkets flaunting

their myriad wares can exist only because of an unwritten compact between the merchant and his customers that the shopper will be completely honest and responsible at all times. Young consumers who understand this tacit agreement and avoid even the appearance of breaking the rules will have fewer unpleasant experiences when they shop.

A fool and his money are soon parted.

OLD PROVERB

6

Thieves
With
Smiling
Faces

The con man has walked the streets from the day that the first city was built. Now, skilled in modern psychology, he has refined his ancient tricks. In stores, at doorsteps, by mail, and along the avenue, he preys on everyone, especially on the young, the old, the poor, the ignorant, and the unworldly. He reaps an estimated several billion dollars a year throughout the nation.

Sophisticated consumers are least likely to be taken in by the winning ways of the swindler. Most of his victims are credulous people who want to believe that there is a pot of gold at the end of every rainbow. They forget that no one has ever found the place where a rainbow ends.

Some swindlers are outright thieves; others operate on the thin edge of the law. Some of their tricks are so obvious that it is difficult to believe they can succeed. Yet the fact remains that millions of people are cheated year after year after year. In 1970, in Philadelphia alone, 10,000 complaints about frauds were filed in the district attorney's office. This figure is far below the number of frauds actually perpetrated, as most victims of swindles do not know where to turn, or they do not take time to report their losses, or they will not admit publicly that they behaved like a fool.

Parents can protect their children against being duped by teaching a few elementary facts about human psychology and the workings of the marketplace. They might say:

1. Look, dear, there is no Santa Claus. Nobody will ever give you something for nothing, except, perhaps, your parents.

2. The willing suspension of disbelief is fine when you are reading fairy tales or a science-fiction story. For the rest of the time, you must look reality straight in the eye, even when it hurts to do so.

3. Do not risk your money on the turn of a wheel, the cards of a fortune-teller, or the great American dream of making millions on a dime. If you must take chances, risk only what you can afford to lose.

4. The old Roman precept *caveat emptor* (let the buyer beware) is still the rule of the marketplace. The federal government has stepped up its efforts to provide some consumer protection, and state and local governments are beginning to move in the same direction. But Uncle Sam and the governors have a long, long way to go. Besides, a thousand new laws and a hundred consumer protection agencies could not save the ignorant and unwary from all the rackets, sales tricks, and con games that unscrupulous people devise.

5. Know yourself and how you react to people. Then learn to recognize your enemy, the thief with a thousand smiling faces. He will as readily play upon your kindness, trust, and fairness as upon your vanity, greed, and the universal feeling of immunity to the troubles that befall the rest of mankind.

6. Most people are fair in their dealings with others; some go out of their way to help or protect other human beings. Still, in today's impersonal, urban society there are enough

sly and dishonest operators to make it wise to know the tricks and watch out for them.

Parents and other educators know, of course, that words will not teach; actions will. Yet, obviously, no one wants to encourage a face-to-face confrontation with any swindler just for the sake of education.

The Stewarts came up with an answer to this problem. They began looking in the newspapers for cases where people had been swindled. They asked friends in other cities to clip similar reports. They even asked neighbors to remember and jot down episodes in which they had been involved with con men and women. Soon they had enough data for a little scrapbook.

Billy was fascinated. He decided to use the material in his eighth-grade social studies class, which was involved in a project about life in city and suburb. When he told his classmates that many young people are victims of swindlers and read some newspaper clippings to them, his friends decided to help him collect all the information they could on the subject.

Swindles in stores

The most often publicized swindle is the common merchandising trick called "bait and switch." The victim is lured into a store by a glowing advertisement or window display of desirable merchandise at an incredibly low price. Once in the store, the customer is greeted by a warm-voiced, friendly salesperson. Mrs. Hendrick, a newly married friend of the Stewarts, told Billy what happened to her.

"I was looking for a lounge chair for our den," she said. "The outlet store on Fourth Street advertised bargains that made the prices at The Washington Shop look ridiculous. Near the door of the outlet store, I saw just what I wanted and told the clerk to have it delivered to our home. She assured me that I had very good taste, but said that this particular chair had a defect in the upholstery which would never suit someone like me. If I was willing to wait six months, they would order another from the manufacturer. But if I wanted a chair now, she could show me a much finer chair that cost only $49.95 more.

"I couldn't afford to pay another $50.00. Besides, I couldn't see anything wrong with the chair I had selected, and I told the saleswoman so. She then called the manager. He said the chair was not for sale. When I pointed out the fact that it is against the law to put a price on something and then refuse to sell it, he practically ordered me out of the store.

"Luckily, in The Washington Shop, I found the same chair for only $9.00 more than the come-on in the Fourth Street store. Many people let themselves be switched to more expensive goods, instead of walking away to do some comparison shopping or to think things over."

The point of no returns
Another swindle worked in stores depends not so much on psychology as on downright cheating. The customer is allowed to handle, try on, or otherwise examine an article of superior quality. After the customer has made his decision and handed over his money, a dishonest salesperson takes the goods to a back room or behind a high counter, substitutes a similar but poorer quality item, wraps it, and hands the unsuspecting customer a surprise package.

Billy's cousin in Atlanta bought a pair of fine leather boots in a shoe store that had a "going out of business" sign splashed across its window. He paid cash and took home his prize only to discover that what he had was a cheap pair of plastic boots not at all like those he had selected. Since the sales check was stamped "all sales final," there was nothing he could do except report the fraud to the local Better Business Bureau.

Episodes of this type can be avoided if a person buys only at stores that have a good reputation and a liberal refund policy. Deal only with stores that permit returns or exchanges during a reasonable period of time, provided that the sales tags are attached and the sales checks are in order.

Skin games can be health hazards
Young consumers are often victimized by medical quack-

ery. Many who want to get rid of excess fat spend large sums of money on products that may be no more effective than the classic sugar-pill placebo. They buy garments that induce sweating, when sweating does not cause a permanent loss of weight. They buy over-the-counter medicines that are either ineffective or downright unsafe when used without medical supervision.

Sometimes they purchase fad items, such as copper bracelets that purport to ward off various illnesses, exercise machines that "guarantee" a bigger bosom or the muscles of a Tarzan, or dentrifices and shampoos that promise to make them popular overnight.

Worse yet, thinking to build their image as sophisticates, many young people—some as young as ten—smoke cigarettes, use pep pills, experiment with mind-altering drugs, or drink alcoholic beverages. Parents who wish to protect their children from these grave dangers to health and happiness are most likely to succeed if they limit their own use of these unhealthful substances, if they discourage their use in the home, and if they endow their children with such a strong sense of self-worth that they do not need these crutches for the ego.

Gas station cheats

In recent years motorists of all ages have been subjected to a number of dishonest practices. When several gas pumps stand in a row, attendants sometimes "accidentally" read the higher amount on the pump next to the one from which the car was filled. Once the hose is back on its hook, who can prove which pump dispensed the gas?

A dishonest attendant may, when checking under the hood, remove a small valve or other part. Then, for several dollars, the cheat will "repair" the defective motor by replacing the part. Sometimes many more than a few dollars are involved. Traveling motorists have reported that they were forced to stay overnight in some small town while a "part" was being obtained; then they were billed as much as a hundred dollars for putting the car in running order.

Occasionally, while checking the air pressure, an attendant

will deliberately slash a tire then innocently show that the tire is leaking and unsafe for the road. Naturally, the motorist is forced to purchase a new tire then and there.

To guard against gas station frauds, a sensible driver deals as much as possible with one well-regarded service station near his home. Regular customers are the backbone of a business, and any complaints they may have are bound to be listened to.

When a car must be serviced on the road, the motorist should always get out of the vehicle and stand beside the attendant as he pumps gas, looks under the hood, or checks the tire pressure. No one is likely to play any tricks under the driver's watchful eye.

Repair shop swindles

Plaguing most of the nation's car owners at the present time are the fraudulent practices of automobile repair shops. They recommend unnecessary work, charge for work that is not done, use secondhand parts and charge for new ones, or throw away good parts rather than take the time to clean and repair them.

Auto repair frauds are difficult to prove unless a mechanic inspects the vehicle immediately before and after the repairs have been made. Yet sometimes even the least experienced motorist can tell when he is being cheated.

Mrs. Springer brought her one-year-old car to a new gas station for its semiannual state inspection. She knew that her car was in perfect mechanical condition; it had traveled less than 8,000 miles and purred like a cat.

That evening when she went to pick up the vehicle, she was handed a bill for $104.50. Knowing that the state inspection costs $5.00, she asked what work had been done on the car. Among other things, the repairman said that he had found a hole in the muffler. She asked to see the old muffler; he had none to show. Furious, but afraid to leave the car while she tried to summon the police, she paid the bill.

How could Mrs. Springer, or any other motorist, have avoided this flagrant fraud? There is no sure answer to this question, as things stand today. Young people can study automobile maintenance so that they can make minor adjustments on their cars and check on the work done by a shop when major repairs are necessary.

People who have only a foggy notion of the machinery under the hood can limit their vulnerability to some extent. They should patronize a shop they know well. When they take a car to be repaired, they should get a written estimate of all work to be done. If parts are to be furnished, they should insist that the estimate state whether the parts are to be new or rebuilt. They should make it clear that only specified work will be paid for. If the work is badly done, they should report the fact to the local Better Business Bureau or Bureau of Consumer Affairs. Such action may not help the individual who has been cheated; but word gets around about firms against whom large numbers of complaints have been lodged, and their business drops off.

Motorists should also urge their state legislators to pass laws licensing auto repair shops and the mechanics who work in them. California already has a Bureau of Auto Repair. When every state sets up a similar bureau, motorists will have some recourse against unethical shops, and far fewer car owners will suffer Mrs. Springer's fate.

Swindles on the street

As Billy and his classmates discovered, many types of shady deals and outright con games are carried out on the street. Henry was asked by a pretty young woman to change a ten-dollar bill so that she might have money to make some telephone calls. He was delighted to be able to offer her a five-dollar bill, four ones, and a dollar's worth of change. She smiled so prettily that he scarcely noticed the crisp ten-dollar bill that she thrust at him before she disappeared into the crowd. Later he found it was a counterfeit bill, one of the several million passed off each year on the unsuspecting public.

That evening his father made Henry cut the bogus bill in half because he could face a jail sentence if he were caught using counterfeit money. His father told him, "You also have to be extra watchful when a salesclerk chatters while making change. This is an old trick used by people who want to short-change you or pass on a counterfeit bill or foreign coin." That is how Henry learned never to change bills for strangers nor to accept change in a store without paying strict attention to the matter at hand.

One day Henry's brother, Lee, was about to telephone from the station to ask his mother to give him a lift home. He had just pulled his wallet out of his hip pocket when a well-dressed man stepped up to tell him that the telephone was out of order. In the friendliest way, the stranger pointed out another telephone booth farther down the platform. Thanking the man, Lee proceeded to the other booth. When he got there, he reached for his wallet. It was gone. Lee had a long, cold walk home.

Lee's Uncle George later explained that a man should never put his wallet in an unbuttoned hip pocket. The left-hand pants pocket is the safest place to carry it. "When you are in a crowd," he said, "it is best not to display your wallet, especially if there are big bills in it. Don't use your wallet for a change purse, as many youngsters do. Instead, carry change for carfare and telephone calls in your right-hand pants or jacket pocket, so that pickpockets cannot readily locate the position of your wallet.

"Girls and women," Uncle George went on to say, "ought not to carry shoulder bags swinging out from a hip. When on a busy street or in a crowded store, they should clutch the bag against them."

The trickster well knows the art of diverting a person's attention so that he can give short change or remove something from his victim without being noticed. One man paid such close attention to a fellow who talked to him in a very low voice that he never felt his watch being removed from his wrist.

The stolen-goods racket

An old, old trick that still catches the unwary is the stolen-goods racket. A motorist may stop a car beside a youthful pedestrian and whisper that he has to unload a valuable stolen ring, or watch, or fur jacket. He names an incredible price: only ten or fifteen dollars; but the buyer must hurry, lest honking traffic force him to drive away.

It is surprising that this con game works at all, for no real thief would consider peddling stolen goods in such an open way. The merchandise is neither stolen nor valuable. If it were, the thief would go to a fence, a professional buyer of stolen goods, rather than risk a sale on a public thoroughfare.

Even if the goods were stolen and valuable, no sensible person would think of buying them. When the police eventually located the loot, grave suspicion would rest on the individual holding it. Moreover, stolen articles bought in good faith still belong to their true owner. So, although the buyer might prove himself innocent of wrong-doing, he would lose both his money and his purchase.

The pigeon drop

Some street swindles involve hundreds or thousands of dollars. Although they are so obvious, people continue to be duped by them with tragic consequences. One infamous flim-flam called "the pigeon drop" caught Marty, the exchange student from Denmark who was living near the Stewarts.

Marty was on her way to lunch when a couple of girls stopped her. They told her that she had just stepped over the long manila envelope they now held and that they felt she ought to share whatever was in it. Opening it, they displayed twelve $100 bills. "That's $400 for you. But," said the short, dark-haired girl, "to show good faith, you must take $400 out of your savings account to match it."

Marty's eyes shone. Instead of having to manage on a shoestring all year, she would now have plenty of pocket money. Excitedly, she led the two girls to the bank and drew out her money. They put her four big bills into the plump manila envelope—or seemed to—and gave her the envelope to hold. The blonde girl suddenly remembered that she had promised to phone her boyfriend before one o'clock.

"Just hold that envelope and wait; we'll be right back," she said. Marty waited, and waited, and waited. Finally, she opened the envelope and found to her horror that it contained only shredded newspaper.

One would think that such a trick once played would make the victim forever wary. But no! One clipping sent by Billy's great-aunt told of an elderly Philadelphia woman who had lost $2,000 in August, 1972, when she was the victim of a con game similar to the one played on Marty. Then, three months later, two "detectives" called at the woman's home to tell her that they thought they had located the women who had flim-flammed her in August.

The two men told the old woman that they needed her help to catch the criminals. They asked her to take $6,000 out of her bank account as bait. They drove her to the bank; she came out with an envelope containing the money and handed it to them. They took it, sealed it, and handed it back. Then, driving her home, they told her they would keep her house under surveillance until the women contacted her. That evening, when the old woman opened the envelope, it contained only scrap paper.

Billy added a footnote when he mounted this clipping. It read: "Don't carry large sums of money around with you. Don't listen to any stranger who asks you to draw money out of the bank for any purpose whatsoever. Don't try to play detective when your money is at stake."

Swindles on the doorstep

Billy Stewart and his classmates found that many con games are played on unsuspecting people's doorsteps or even right in their homes. One familiar trick is perpetrated by a young man or girl who sells magazines "to work my way through college." Almost invariably, the sympathetic house-wife invites the young salesperson in. The problem is to get him out again. He stays, unmindful of suggestions that he depart. Sometimes he stays for hours until at last, the dis-traught housewife buys magazines she does not want, at prices above the regular subscription rate, to win her free-dom from the unwanted visitor.

Door-to-door salesmen often sell things far more costly than magazines. Young couples with babies have been bullied into buying encyclopedias that cost hundreds of dollars and are sure to be out-of-date by the time their children are old enough to use them. One expectant mother complained to a newspaper columnist interested in consumer problems that a salesman talked to her steadily for three hours until she agreed to buy a crib that cost $125 and a high chair that cost $65.

Deal with door-to-door salesmen by never letting them into the house. Keep the chain on the door. Be rude. Slam the door in their faces. If they continue to annoy or alarm you, call the police.

If a salesman does induce some family member to sign a sales agreement that places a lien on his house or other property, the buyer has the legal right to cancel the contract if he notifies the seller in writing within three business days. It is important, therefore, to be sure of the name and address of the firm with which the deal was made and to send a registered letter with return receipt postmarked within the short period of time allowed. A copy of the letter must, of course, be saved. If the contract involves a sum above $100, it would be advisable to contact the family lawyer as well. Unfortunately, many consumers cannot get inexpensive, competent legal advice within three business days—if indeed they can get it at all.

Families should be suspicious of strangers who solicit for unheard-of charities. Official-looking persons who flash a card—any card—and push their way into the kitchen "to inspect the plumbing" or into the cellar "to check on the furnace" are likely to be participants in the growing "home improvement" racket. If a child is alone in the house, forbid him to admit any stranger, even though, as has happened, the stranger may later prove to be an irate repairman who had been duly hired but who had arrived earlier than expected.

Swindles with a postage stamp

Mail frauds wear many disguises and cost the unwary more than $500 million a year. While the U.S. Postal Service has statutes designed to deter illegal use of the mails, there is little a postmaster can do to help the individual victim of the swindler with a postage stamp.

Billy Stewart and his friends collected a large number of

letters that had a phony ring to them. One stated that a house-wife had won a free sewing machine. All she needed to do was select and pay for a cabinet. The winner of such a fake contest would probably pay more for the cabinet than the whole unit was worth.

One promoter told Billy's next-door neighbor that the family could have a free central vacuum-cleaning system. Al-though they would have to pay $800 to have it installed, they could earn a $50 commission each time they convinced a friend to buy one. The postal inspector investigating "chain referral schemes" such as this one discovered that the gullible householders seldom get even one other family to join them in their expensive folly and may even lose a friend by trying.

Charity begins at home

The mailing of unordered merchandise does not violate postal laws unless the goods are sent C.O.D. Articles such as cheap neckties, key chains, good-luck charms, and packets of notepaper often accompany appeals for gifts to individuals or organizations purporting to devote the money to worthy causes.

Families who receive such appeals and articles are often troubled by them. They feel obligated to pay for the items, no matter how useless the objects may be. They need not be con-cerned. They may write across an unopened package "Return to Sender" and put it back in the mail. If the package has been opened, they can either set it aside for a reasonable length of time in case the sender asks for its return, or treat it as an unconditional gift.

Appeals in the name of charity are legion; and charity by mail offers swindlers a chance for large-scale gains. One of the biggest rackets ever investigated by postal inspectors in-volved a professional fund-raising firm which circularized millions of persons throughout the country year after year, seeking funds to help cure a crippling disease. Of $22 million contributed by the public, over half was earmarked for salaries and expenses; and, in addition, the organizations that received the balance had to give illegal kickbacks to the fund-raisers.

Although many charities do make important contributions toward helping the handicapped, aiding orphans, and supporting medical research, families can make the most effective use of their charitable contributions if they restrict donations to causes and organizations with which they are familiar and ask for financial statements before contributing to organizations about which they know nothing.

Letters for the round file

Self-improvement courses are often offered by correspondence schools at prices ranging from $400 to $1,000. Many are fraudulent. They induce persons who are desperately trying to improve their economic position to sign contracts for a series of worthless lessons by "guaranteeing" them jobs in such fields as computer programming, airline mechanics, nursing, or the civil service. Before investing in any correspondence course, check with several employers in the field of your interest to determine the value of such a course. Then write the Bureau of Higher Education, U.S. Office of Education, Washington, D.C. 20202, for information about the school that you are considering.

Beware of anyone who offers to give you anything if you send him a sum such as one dollar, five dollars, or ten dollars. Sometimes the tricksters promise to help you to earn money at home. Many a young person has wasted his cash on expensive artist's supplies because he was led to believe that by following simple directions he could create pictures that were sure to sell.

One ingenious fellow, who claimed his parents' disapproval alone deterred him from using his infallible system of betting at the racetrack, offered to sell his foolproof idea to anyone who sent him "a ten-spot." Lest the recipient wonder what advantage he would have once everybody knew this system, the letter writer hastened to add that he wrote so slowly that few people would ever be given this opportunity to win.

One teen-ager who sent two dollars to a letter writer who promised to teach him to avoid being swindled by mail received an answer the following week. The message read, "Never answer letters like mine."

By the end of the school term, Billy Stewart and his class-mates had collected so many stories of swindlers at work that the class voted to give an assembly program called *Let the Buyer Beware* and afterward to present the scrapbook to the school library for the use of all the students. Mr. Smith, Billy's teacher, had a friend who was a reporter on the *Daily Chronicle*. He attended the program and then wrote a feature article under the headline "Gyps Revealed by Junior High School Students." Billy found his name in print.

*There can be no freedom or beauty about a
home life that depends on borrowing and debt.*

HENRIK IBSEN

CHAPTER 7

The
Cost of
Credit

In the horse-and-buggy days of seventy-five years ago, consumer credit was unavailable to most people of average means. Mortgage money could be obtained, but the terms were difficult for inexperienced people to meet. Each month the mortgagor, or borrower, was expected to pay interest on the loan, but was supposed also to set aside a portion of the principal for the day when the loan came due. Many a sad tale was told about widows and orphans who lost the family homestead because, on the due date, they lacked the cash to pay off the mortgage.

During the first quarter of the present century, some bright banker conceived the idea of amortizing loans—that is, paying off a portion of the principal, month by month, along with the interest. This made possible a much wider use of long-term credit.

Today consumer credit is available to almost everyone. People in all economic brackets are urged to buy, buy, buy on time. Opportunities to "fly now, pay later" tempt the readers of magazines and newspapers. "Play while you pay" advertisements show families cavorting in swimming pools, their debt to the builder happily forgotten. Car buyers are encouraged to make hasty purchases by offers of "easy credit" or "the fastest loans on wheels."

Long-term credit is never easy to repay despite the beguiling advertisements. Large numbers of people ruin their lives because they are ignorant about the safe use of borrowed money. Every young American, therefore, deserves a thorough education in the handling of credit; and parents can provide this education.

What is consumer credit?

Credit is an arrangement whereby one person obtains the right to use another person's money, goods, or services without immediate payment. Consumer credit is offered primarily for personal, family, household, or agricultural purposes.

It is important for young people to understand the difference between free short-term credit and costly long-term credit. Short-term credit is usually offered to responsible persons without additional expense. Most department stores, specialty shops, tradespeople, lawyers, and doctors extend credit to their customers or clients for as much as a month. Sometimes the purchaser of such costly items as a television set or a sewing machine is given the privilege of dividing his payments, interest free, over sixty or ninety days.

Such deferred-payment plans are not really "free" because the cost is included in the price of the article or service. Still, the price remains the same whether or not the buyer avails himself of this credit.

A person who has the resources to meet his bills should by all means make use of short-term credit. It saves carrying large sums of cash. It makes easy the exchange of merchandise that is defective or that loses its appeal between store and home. Monthly itemized bills give a permanent record of a person's larger purchases. Because bills must be met in full twenty or thirty days after billing, no one is likely to get deeply into debt with credit of this type.

Make the punishment fit the crime?

Teen-agers, of course, are not offered credit by a store without the backing of a parent, grandparent, or guardian. An invaluable Christmas or birthday gift to a cautious teen-ager would be a thirty-day charge account of his own. With a charge account, the young person would gain a sense of financial freedom, be able to make judicious purchases when goods are on sale, and learn to discipline his spending.

Should temptation lead to purchasing items that his allowance could not cover, it is true that the adult backer would be liable for the one-month's fling. But then, if the account were closed and the card destroyed until the young buyer gained more maturity in handling his affairs, he would learn a priceless lesson; for, once a person enjoys the pleasures of financial freedom, a return to economic dependence on even the kindest adult is punishment exquisitely well-fitted to the crime.

What credit costs

People who do not pay cash or settle their bills within the month, have to pay for the privilege of using money that does not belong to them. The cost of credit varies widely; yet many people, young and old, plunge into debt without ever considering the cost of borrowed money.

Aside from carrying a mortgage on their home, the Stewarts made very little use of long-term credit. Like 50 percent of all American families, they preferred to "save, then spend" rather than to "borrow to buy." They realized that the money debtors pay for interest and carrying charges can buy a debt-free family additional possessions, pleasures, and services. Still, as they knew, long-term credit plays an increasingly important role in the lives of many people; so one day they decided to teach their teen-agers how to use credit safely.

It all started when Mrs. Stewart came across a U.S. government chart comparing the annual percentage rates for the various types of consumer credit. She was amazed to discover that, in addition to repaying the original sum borrowed, some people pay for the use of money as little as 5 percent ($5 per $100) while others pay 1,200 percent ($1,200 per $100). Installment credit on appliances and used cars can be exorbitant, especially in states where rates are not regulated by law.

That evening at dinner Mrs. Stewart said, "Billy, you will be old enough for a car in three years, and Marilyn will soon be going off to college. Later on, you'll both want to furnish an apartment or even buy a house. Let's gather together all the information we can about the cost of credit."

"I'll be secretary and write down the most important points," volunteered Marilyn.

"Well," said Mr. Stewart, "let's start with the fact that credit costs money and that annual percentage rates run from the relatively low figure charged by the banks to the 1,000 percent or more charged by illegal lenders who prey upon the poor and ignorant."

"What does 'annual percentage rate' mean?" asked Billy.

Marilyn, who was taking a high-school course in consumer education, explained,"The annual percentage rate is the rate of interest plus other costs of borrowing, such as a service charge on the loan and insurance on the borrower's life while he is in debt. The annual percentage rate tells the borrower how many dollars he must pay to borrow $100 for one year. If he pays $8 for each $100 borrowed, he pays 8 percent." She wrote "8%" on her pad.

Billy studied the percent symbol closely. "Say, that percent symbol (%) has a one and two zeros. That makes it easy to remember the words *for each hundred*. Neat!"

Mr. Stewart smiled. "Before the Federal Consumer Credit Protection Act of 1968—which everybody calls the truth-in-lending law—went into effect, it was almost impossible for even the smartest shopper to figure out the cost of credit. Now, every lender has to tell the borrower, or the person buying on credit, two things: the *annual percentage rate* and the *dollar finance cost*—the number of dollars he will have to pay for the use of the borrowed money. With this information, we can shop for credit just as carefully as we shop for overcoats, or rugs, or anything else we buy."

"I don't get it," said Billy.

Mrs. Stewart thought a moment. "Shopping for credit is just like shopping for meat at the supermarket. You've watched me often. First I study the price per pound of a leg of lamb or a loin of pork to see which gives me the most meat per dollar. Then I look at the total cost to see if I can afford to spend so much money for meat. Just as the price per pound gives me the unit cost of the meat, so the annual percentage rate gives me the unit cost per $100 of credit. Just as the label also gives me the total dollars-and-cents cost of that particular roast, so the dollar finance charge states the total price of that particular credit arrangement. I need both figures to decide whether to buy one piece of meat or another, or whether to serve you all a can of beans. And if I were deciding whether to buy a certain washing machine on time, I'd want to know both the rate of interest and the number of dollars I'd have to pay for credit. If the price were too high, I'd shop for the washer in some other store. Or go to the laundromat until I'd saved up the cash."

"Mother's right," said Mr. Stewart. "Shopping for credit is the second-best way to stretch your spendable dollars. The best way is to use extended credit sparingly or not at all."

Cash for sale

The following evening Marilyn brought to the table the chart her mother had discovered. Everyone took a look at it (see page 100).

"I have to do a paper for consumer ed," said Marilyn, "and I'd like to write about the various kinds of credit a person can get. Is it good to borrow on your life insurance?"

"As you see from the chart," replied her father, "cash loans against life insurance carry a very low rate of interest. If the policy has built up sufficient cash values to support a loan— and it takes years of payments to build up these values—you can get a quick, inexpensive loan against your life insurance. Personally, I don't advise borrowing on life insurance, because as long as the money is out on loan, the face value of the policy is reduced by the amount of the loan. Say I borrow $2,000 on my $10,000 straight-life policy and then get run over by a car, my family would get only $8,000."

Comparison of Annual Percentage Rates
For Consumer Credit

Financing Agency or Type of Loan	Annual Percentage Rates (Interest Plus Other Finance Charges)	
	Common Rate in 1975	Approximate Range of Rates
CASH LOANS		
Borrowing on Life Insurance	5½ %	5-6%
Credit Unions	9	9-12
Commercial Banks—Secured Personal Loans	12	12-15
Commercial Banks—"Ready Credit" Accounts (Unsecured Loans)	13	12-24
Finance Companies—Operating Under State Small-Loan Laws	30	24-48
Pawn Shops—Under State Laws or Municipal Ordinances	36	30-40
Illegal Lenders—Often Called "Loan Sharks"	?	42-1,200
REVOLVING CHARGE CREDIT		
Commercial Banks—General-Purpose Credit Cards	15	15-24
Department Store and Other Special-Purpose Cards	15	15-24
INSTALLMENT CREDIT AGREEMENTS		
In States with Laws Governing Rates:		
New Cars	12	10-24
Used Cars Under Two Years Old	22	18-31
Used Cars Over Two Years Old	24	18-43
In States Without Rate Legislation:		
Appliances	?	40-120
New Cars	?	25-120
Used Cars	?	45-275

Source: U.S. Department of Agriculture's Home Economics Research Report Number 21, adapted and updated

"What is a credit union?" asked Billy, who had been study-ing the chart.

"Credit unions were started by groups of workingmen more than a hundred years ago—in the days when banks sel-dom lent money to people of ordinary means," his father ex-plained. "Men in the same shop, or in the same trade, would pool their spare money and make small loans to help out a needy 'brother.' Today, people who belong to an organization with a credit union find that it is a fine place to go shopping for a loan."

Borrowing at the bank

"Debbie's father took out a bank loan last month when he bought a car," said Marilyn. "He said it was cheaper than get-ting a loan from a finance company."

"He was perfectly right," said Mrs. Stewart, who had ma-jored in economics and who now handled most of the family's business affairs. "Bank loans are fairly inexpensive, even though ordinary people don't get the prime—or lowest—in-terest rate.

"But even bank loans cost a lot more than many people real-ize. Bankers still tend to quote rates at so many per cent a year with interest either added on or discounted. If you bor-rowed $100 at 8 percent with add-on interest and kept the money a whole year, you would receive $100 and repay $108.

"If you borrowed that same $100 for a year but the interest was discounted—that is, taken out ahead of time—you would receive $92 and pay back $100. Discount loans are both more expensive and more common than add-on loans.

"Actually, most bank loans are set up in an even more cost-ly way. While you borrow the $100 at 8 percent discounted, you must repay the loan in equal monthly installments. This is called amortizing the loan."

Mrs. Stewart went to the den and returned with two of her economic texts. "Here you can see it for yourselves," she said as the children gathered around (see the table on page 102).

"If the loan were to be repaid over a longer period of time, the cost of borrowing would be even higher," Mrs. Stewart said.

The True Cost of Interest When a Loan Is Repaid in 12 Equal Installments

If the quoted rate is:	The annual percentage rate is:	
	Add-On	Discount
4% per year	7.4%	7.7%
6% per year	11.1%	11.8%
8% per year	14.8%	16.1%
10% per year	18.5%	20.5%
12% per year	22.2%	25.2%

Source: *The Yearbook of Agriculture 1965*

She then turned to another page (see table on page 103). "Now this table shows the dollar cost of credit on a debt of $1,000 at different interest rates. You can see how the cost mounts up as you take longer to pay off a debt. Look at the second line. If the interest were $8 per $100 and if you repaid the loan in twelve monthly installments, the charge for credit would be $80. But you would pay $240 in interest if you took thirty-six months to pay off an 8 percent loan. If you were paying interest at 20 percent a year—that is $20 per $100 borrowed—your cost would be $200 for a one year's loan and $600 if the loan ran for thirty-six months."

"I had no idea it cost so much to borrow money," said Marilyn. "I guess I'll never borrow to buy anything as long as I live."

"Sometimes borrowing is a sensible thing to do," replied her father. "You might need cash for a new car at a time when it would be best not to sell your stocks and bonds. You might need a new refrigerator while your cash reserves were low. Just remember to borrow as little as possible and pay back the money as fast as you can. It's long-term debt that devours dollars."

"For very important purchases, people can safely assume even a large long-term debt, as long as they know just how they'll pay it back. You might have to borrow to complete your education. You might someday want to buy a house," Mrs.

Stewart said and reached for another book (see the table on page 104).

"The interest on a mortgage that runs for twenty to twenty-five years can add up to more than the sum you originally borrowed—and you have to repay the original sum as well. Still, if you love your home and you budget for the monthly payments, it's a good feeling to own the roof over your head."

Billy turned to his father. "Dad, how do you get a loan at the bank?"

"Most bankers offer personal loans only to people who have good collateral—something like bonds, shares of stock, a title to a new car, or some real estate against which they can place a lien. Unsecured loans—loans without collateral—are rare, unless the borrower has an exceptionally high credit rating or can persuade a relative or friend to cosign the note with him.

"Now hear this," said Mr. Stewart, wagging a forefinger for emphasis. "Never cosign a note or an installment sales contract for anyone—and I mean anyone—unless you are entirely prepared to lose every cent of your money. You wouldn't be asked to cosign if the buyer were a good credit

The Dollar Cost of Credit on a $1,000 Loan

When the Add-on Interest Rate Is:	The Interest in Dollars Over Various Numbers of Months Is:				
	12	18	24	30	36
6%	$ 60	$ 90	$120	$150	$180
8%	80	120	160	200	240
10%	100	150	200	250	300
12%	120	180	240	300	360
14%	140	210	280	350	420
16%	160	240	320	400	480
18%	180	270	360	450	540
20%	200	300	400	500	600

Source: *The Yearbook of Agriculture 1965*

Interest Paid per $10,000
Borrowed on a Mortgage

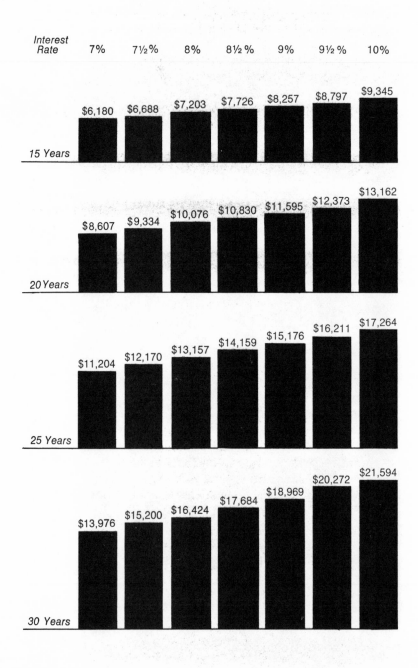

Interest Rate	7%	7½%	8%	8½%	9%	9½%	10%
15 Years	$6,180	$6,688	$7,203	$7,726	$8,257	$8,797	$9,345
20 Years	$8,607	$9,334	$10,076	$10,830	$11,595	$12,373	$13,162
25 Years	$11,204	$12,170	$13,157	$14,159	$15,176	$16,211	$17,264
30 Years	$13,976	$15,200	$16,424	$17,684	$18,969	$20,272	$21,594

risk. And once you've signed another person's note, you are just as liable for the repayment of the debt as if you, yourself, had received the money or the goods."

"That should go on my list of things to remember about credit," said Marilyn, picking up her pencil and pad.

"The best place to start looking for a bank loan," Mr. Stewart went on, "is at the bank in which you have a savings or checking account. The rate of interest will depend on the condition of the money market, your credit rating, and the length of time you will tie up the bank's cash. Short-term loans are the easiest loans to get. Your purpose in borrowing is important, too. If you wanted the money for a trip to Europe, you'd be less likely to get the loan than if you wanted it for college tuition. When money is scarce, bank loans are hard to come by for even the worthiest of purposes.

"The banker will ask you all kinds of questions about yourself, your education, your job, past residences, other debts, and how you expect to repay the money. Before you go to see him, it is best to write a sort of résumé. Then be patient. It usually takes several days to check up on your credit status, even when you offer plenty of collateral to back up the loan."

Establishing credit

"It's not easy for young adults to get credit," said Mrs. Stewart, "even when they have a job. Until you have borrowed money from some credit institution, no one has ever fed your name into one of the big credit bureau computers. The lender can't get an instant printout of your character, background, financial position, and reputation. He has to look you up in the telephone book, call your employer, maybe check with the head of the school you attended, and so forth.

"Older people who belong to the 'cash-and-carry set' have the same problem. Some years ago, I was told that I didn't have any 'credit experience.' I felt like telling that banker that I had too much experience with credit to use it very much— but, of course, I didn't. It pays to act civil and dress conservatively when you are trying to establish credit."

Mr. Stewart nodded. "Once you have a job and some tangible property, it's a good idea to establish credit whether you need it or not. Ask your local banker to lend you a few hundred dollars. When he's checked out everything about you except your fingerprints, he'll probably let you have the money for two or three months.

"Put the money in a savings account where it will earn something towards the interest you'll have to pay the bank. Meet every payment when it comes due. Then, a few months later, get another small loan from the bank. By that time you'll be entered in the computers as a good credit risk, so that someday when you do need ready cash, you can go to the bank and get service with a smile.

"And once you get a good credit rating, hold on to it. In a money-based society like ours, having credit within reach is of the utmost importance. Knowing when to reach for it is equally important."

Marilyn finished scribbling down her father's last remark. "If I can just remember everything you and Mother have told us tonight, someday I'll have the best credit rating in town!"

Mrs. Stewart smiled at her daughter. "Not long ago, Marilyn, women couldn't get credit in their own names. I know of cases where a woman's father would have to cosign a note if she wanted to borrow money; or her charge account would have to be made out in his name, even when he was old and on Social Security and she was a well-paid executive. And if a woman was married, no matter how much money she had of her own, the charge account was in her husband's name.

"Legislation passed by the federal government has made it illegal for lenders to refuse to give credit to a financially independent woman just because of her sex or marital status. But, I'm afraid, young women of your generation will have to reeducate many a lender before he will accept a woman as a good credit risk. The way to insure your own 'credit-ability' is to buy only those things you can pay for. In other words, use credit responsibly."

Borrowing on a charge account

Billy was beginning to fidget. He wanted to get the conversation back to ways of borrowing money. "What is a 'ready credit account,' Dad?" he asked.

"Some banks now offer their customers ways to charge money at the bank just as they charge merchandise at a store. When you take out a 'debit checking acount,' or a 'revolving cash account,' or a 'ready credit account,' you are really setting up a quick loan agreement. When you want to borrow money, you write a check-like document. It isn't a check, but a sort of I.O.U. promising to repay the bank so many dollars with interest.

"Seems like an easy way to get a loan, doesn't it? But if you read the fine print, you discover that, unless you make the repayments on specified dates, the bank can take you to court. It's entirely too easy to borrow when you merely have to write your name on a piece of paper; you can get into serious trouble before you know it. And if a husband and wife sign a 'ready credit' agreement, either one can run up debts that both are responsible for. Only a very careful person with a large and steady income should open a 'ready credit account.' I'd rather stick to a good old-fashioned savings account for emergency cash."

Finance companies, pawnbrokers, and loan sharks
Billy took another look at the table comparing the costs of consumer credit. "The annual percentage rate is a lot higher if you borrow from a finance company or a pawnbroker. Why does anybody go to them for a loan?"

"Well, son," replied Mr. Stewart, "finance companies lend people cash more freely than banks do. If you can't get a bank loan when you want money for a car or a television set or whatever, you pay what the finance company asks. Some finance companies are responsible lending organizations. Others give their customers trick contracts to sign, or they just wait for the buyer to be late with a single payment so that they can snatch away whatever he put up as collateral for the loan.

"If you are about to deal with a finance company—and when you buy on the installment plan, you will be dealing with a finance company because nearly all merchants sell their installment contracts to a finance company—be sure to read all the fine print and understand it. Then never be late with a single payment. As Mother and I always say, if you buy for cash, you run less risk of being swindled."

"I saw a pawnshop once on Tenth Avenue," said Billy. "It had lots of old jewelry in the window and some statues, and inside I saw a rack of overcoats in all different sizes. It didn't look like a place to borrow money."

"Pawnbrokers lend money to people whose credit isn't good enough for banks and finance companies of the better type. They lend about 40 percent of the value of the article brought in as collateral, and they hold the article for the term of the loan. Although their interest rates are high, as you can see, there is a limit to their charges because legitimate pawnshops operate under state laws or municipal ordinances. Unfortunately, many borrowers can't save up the money to repay their loan. Then the jewelry, coat, or whatever they left to secure the loan is sold. Although the poor person loses the article he put up as collateral, that's all he loses. People who use the more modern forms of credit run the risk of losing their purchases, their down payments, other possessions on which a lien has been placed, and, in some cases, even their homes because they failed to pay a modest debt.

"By far the most dangerous way to borrow cash is to go to a loan shark," Mr. Stewart warned. "These money-lenders prowl the streets in poor neighborhoods offering money to ignorant and desperate people at fantastic rates of interest. The pathetic victims of the loan sharks only see the $100 they need and don't realize that they will be hounded and threatened with bodily harm for years until they repay not only the $100 but also interest that runs anywhere from $42 to $1,200! The best defense against such financial disaster is a passbook to a savings account."

"Marilyn, when you finish your composition about credit, I want to read it," said Billy. "No loan shark's ever going to put the bite on me."

Credit with a card

People who would think long and hard before taking out a loan for nonessential travel, or clothing, or audio equipment scarcely realize that they are borrowing when they use a credit card. Oil-company cards, retail-store cards, travel-and-entertainment cards, and general-purpose bank credit cards —nearly half a billion of these plastic rectangles—offer instant credit to over half of the adults in America.

So new is credit with a card that many needed laws to safeguard card-holders have yet to be written. Some dangers are evident. The easier credit is to get, the easier it is for thoughtless people to slip into financial difficulties. Whereas handing over a crisp twenty-dollar bill gives every buyer a moment's pause, having the name and number of a credit card stamped on a sales check has no emotional impact at all until the day when the monthly bill arrives. In tomorrow's cashless, checkless society, incautious people will lose all touch with the reality of money. They will buy more lavishly, pay a larger fraction of their income for interest charges, and walk the narrow line between solvency and bankruptcy.

Credit cards are vulnerable to loss or theft. Even though federal law now limits to $50 the cardholder's liability, the loss of several cards at one time could prove a serious financial burden.

Credit-card billing depends on computers; and computers can make mistakes. If the computer bills more than it should and the cardholder refuses to pay, it may take months of anguished telephone calls and registered letters to get the matter straightened out. Computers do not read letters or answer the telephone.

Worse yet, the local credit bureau computer may file away in its little electronic brain a bad credit report on the individual who refuses to pay an unjust bill and then relay this message to the big computers in the regional credit bureaus. Thereafter, the cardholder may find himself with an unfavorable credit rating that travels with him wherever he goes. This problem became so acute in 1973 that Congress began considering ways to force credit bureaus to correct computer errors and to remove the black mark from the name of a person whose credit rating has improved.

One danger inherent in the growing web of local, regional, and national credit bureaus is the invasion of privacy of the individual citizen. To operate a nationwide credit system, it is necessary to have up-to-the-minute credit data on every person who has access to credit. A cardholder's background, education, work record, family composition, personality, health, and credit status must be on file in huge regional computers which can be tapped by any merchant before he extends credit to the cardholder.

The FBI recently sought to connect its computers to the credit files in various states. Some governors objected on the grounds of invasion of privacy of the states' citizens.

Many people feel that the value of using credit information to capture criminals is offset by the ease with which the private lives of innocent people could be invaded by government officials on any pretext whatsoever. These citizens support their stand by citing the guarantee in the Fourth Amendment of the Constitution of the United States which establishes "the right of the people to be secure in their persons, houses, papers, and effects, against unreasonable searches and seizures."

Revolving charge accounts

Hand in hand with credit cards goes a relatively new form of borrowing: the revolving charge account. The revolving charge account may be used like the older thirty-day charge account to give the shopper free credit until his monthly bill comes due. At the shopper's option, it becomes a source of long-term credit at a fairly high annual percentage rate (see table on page 111).

The store cannot quote a dollar finance charge on fluctuating balances, so, in the case of revolving charge credit, the cost is quoted as a monthly percent of the unpaid balance. These small fractions seem so unimportant that customers are likely to overlook the cost of revolving credit or confuse it with credit quoted on an annual basis.

The cost of revolving credit is often much higher than the annual percentage rates indicate. Many stores apply these rates to the balance due at the end of the previous month. For example, a customer's debit balance on July 31 is used to calculate credit charges for his bill dated September 1. Even if he returned the merchandise or paid

Annual Percentage Rates When Interest
Is Charged on the Unpaid Balance

If the Quoted Rate Per Month Is:	The Annual Percentage Rate Is:
½ of 1%	6%
¾ of 1%	9%
1%	12%
1¼%	15%
1½%	18%
1¾%	21%
2%	24%
2¼%	27%
2½%	30%
2¾%	33%
3%	36%

his bill of $300 in full on August 1, he would still be charged interest as if he owed $300 for the month of August. Department stores also make a minimum charge on unpaid balances. If the balance is very small, say only one dollar, and the minimum finance charge is seventy-five cents, the rate would be 75 percent. It is important, therefore, not to leave small unpaid balances in the account.

Safeguarding credit cards

Despite their drawbacks, revolving charge accounts and credit cards are here to stay. If credit with a card is handled conservatively, it is vastly useful in this credit-oriented world. Every teen-ager should know these safeguards for credit cards:

Upon receiving a credit card, make a note of the serial

number and the full name, address, and telephone number of the issuing company. Keep this record in a safe but accessible place. Should a card ever be mislaid or stolen, call the company immediately and ask that a stop be placed on the account. Follow this call with a certified letter that carries a return receipt.

Keep in your wallet or purse only those cards for which there is an immediate need. When not in use, credit cards should be stored in a locked desk or bureau drawer. People who are careless, or who, like college girls and businesswomen, have occasion to leave pocketbooks in unlocked rooms, ought not to carry credit cards at all. Instead, they should take with them only a list of the account numbers and the initials of the stores. If they have the account number and some personal identification, credit will be extended although there may be a short delay while the account is being verified.

Finally, the teen-ager with a credit card must learn to tailor spending to income. Even if parents are lenient with an overspender, credit bureaus are not. A credit rating, like a person's good name, is easy to lose and very hard to regain.

Credit charged with dynamite

One day Mrs. Stewart read an article about installment buying that began: "Your signature is your passport to security or to trouble. You can give away your past, present, and future with a few squiggles of your fountain pen."

The article went on to say that since the end of World War II, increasing numbers of automobiles, household appliances, and home furnishings had been sold on the installment plan. In the past decade or so, even impermanent items, such as jewelry, clothing, and vacations have been increasingly bought "on time."

Mrs. Stewart began to worry lest some day her children might be beguiled into buying things they did not absolutely need with money they did not have without realizing the grave dangers built into the installment contract. So that evening she said to her family, "You know, we never did talk about installment credit. I read that, besides being costly, installment contracts may be full of tricks to trap the unwary buyer. For over twenty-five years, important things—like household appliances and automobiles—have been bought by means of installment contracts; but now more and more luxury items are also being bought with this dangerous form of credit."

"What's an installment contract?" asked Billy.

"An installment contract is an agreement between a buyer and a seller in which the buyer promises to make a predetermined number of payments of a given size on specified dates. These payments cover the price of the article, the cost of setting up the loan, interest at a high rate, and enough insurance on the life of the purchaser to pay off the debt if he dies before doing so. Buying on the installment plan—or buying on time, as it is called—can be an expensive and hazardous way to purchase things."

"Expensive and risky, indeed," said Mr. Stewart thoughtfully. "I imagine that most people who sign installment contracts have no idea of the serious nature of the legal agreements they are signing. At best, they are documents that favor the seller; at worst, they are a legalized form of thievery.

"First of all, the article bought on time remains the property of the holder of the contract until the last payment has been made. If the buyer fails to meet even one payment, he may lose the article and all the installments he has already paid.

"Secondly, the installment contract itself can be—and usually is—sold by the merchant to a finance company. To his surprise, the buyer finds that he is dealing with an unfamiliar lending institution interested only in collecting the monthly installments. This secondary creditor, *the holder in due course*, has, at the present time, no responsibility if the goods prove defective. Should the buyer, hoping to have the goods replaced or repaired, delay making a single payment, he could lose his purchase, his previous payments, and even some of his other possessions."

Marilyn sighed. "You make it sound so complicated, when

all a person has to do is sign his name and get almost anything on time. It's really very simple."

"It's easy to sign your name—and easy to be swindled. There are many tricky clauses in installment contracts, and many tricks dishonest merchants pull on innocent buyers. That's why consumer groups and legislators are trying so hard to cut down the number of abuses associated with installment credit.

"Here are some tricks I know about. Maybe by the time you are on your own, these practices will be illegal. Still, if you understand what the fine print says, you are less likely to become the victim of a dishonest dealer.

"Many installment contracts have a wage-assignment clause. If such a clause were in the agreement, and if the buyer failed to meet a payment, the holder in due course could demand that the buyer's employer deduct the payments from the buyer's paycheck.

"Then there is the totally dishonest balloon clause that sometimes lies hidden in the fine print. Without realizing it, the buyer may have agreed to make a final payment more than twice as large as each of the other payments. If he couldn't scrape up the money for this outsized installment, the buyer would lose his purchase and all the earlier payments as well.

"In some states, installment contracts carry two clauses that can be ruinous to an individual's economic life. The first clause permits the creditor to place a lien on the buyer's personal property. Let's say that a woman cannot meet her payments on a refrigerator and that the store manager repossesses and resells it. Let's also say the resale price does not cover all the seller's costs and profits. When the installment contract contains a clause giving the seller a lien on the buyer's personal property, the seller may also seize some other property of the unfortunate buyer to pay off the rest of the debt.

"That's bad enough; that's dynamite. But a companion clause carries the fuse. This is the infamous confession-of-judgment clause. By signing a document bearing such a clause, the buyer gives up his right to defend himself in court.

He pleads guilty in advance to defaulting on his payments. When a buyer signs an installment contract containing both these clauses, the seller can, at any time he wishes, notify the sheriff to cart off the buyer's property and put it up at auction to satisfy whatever amount the seller says is owed him.

"Take that poor woman who owed money on her refrigerator. Let's say she signed a contract with a lien on her furniture and a confession-of-judgment clause. Say she had agreed to pay $250 for the refrigerator plus interest, insurance, and finance charges of 100 percent, making the total cost $500. She had paid off $350 of this sum before she lost her job. The store manager called soon after to say that late charges had been added and that now she owed $625. This, naturally, she couldn't pay; so the next day the store sent around a truck and took away not only the refrigerator but also her living-room furniture and her new rugs. Although she called a lawyer at the Legal Aid Society, he could do nothing to help her. She had already pleaded guilty to nonpayment of whatever sum the manager chose to name."

"But that's terribly unfair," said Marilyn. "Wasn't there anything she could do?"

"There was something she could have done the day she made the contract. She could have read those clauses and then refused to sign."

Marilyn asked, "Are there any other tricks that dishonest merchants play with installment contracts?"

"Unfortunately, yes," her father replied. "Sometimes blank spaces are left above a buyer's signature, and later these spaces are filled in with terms unfavorable to the buyer. Using a ball-point pen with indelible ink, you should cross out all blank spaces on the contract and on the carbon, too.

"Another trick is to have a duplicate contract that isn't a duplicate at all but another contract with less favorable terms. The salesman tries to get the customer to sign both copies and keeps the unfavorable version. To avoid this trick, a person should read both copies to be sure they are identical and then sign only one. If the salesman tries to make you sign a second time, tear up both contracts and walk away.

"Salesmen who divert a customer's attention by chattering,

or by offering 'free gifts,' are trying to stop the customer from studying the terms of the contract. If this tactic is ever used on you, refuse to sign the contract and head for the nearest exit.

"Make absolutely certain that the model number of the item you are buying appears on the contract and that it is identical to the number on the article you have selected. Many a car buyer has thought he was buying the automobile whose tires he'd been happily kicking, only to discover too late that the contract stated he had bought some less desirable vehicle.

"Make sure that the contract also states the total price and the amounts and due dates of each installment, along with the name and address of the person to whom the money should be sent. Make sure you understand exactly what the manufacturer guarantees to do in case the article proves defective. Finally, make sure that you can meet each payment the day before it's due. That's about it," Mr. Stewart said, and he began to fill his pipe.

Marilyn cupped her chin in her palm and thought for a while. Finally she said, "Buying on time isn't simple at all. It's expensive and dangerous—and one mistake could break your heart. It's one kind of credit I'll never want to use."

Saying good night, she went up to her room and began work on her paper for her consumer education class. She decided to call it "Don't Be Dollar Wise and Credit Foolish."

Two weeks later, Marilyn brought home the first five pages of her paper. A red "A" had been marked on the first page. The sixth page remained at school because her classmates wanted to pin it up on the bulletin board and memorize the good advice it contained (see page 117).

DON'T BE DOLLAR WISE AND CREDIT FOOLISH

Marilyn Stewart
Consumer Ed. 1
Rowland Senior High
April 14, 1974

As we have seen, people have to pay for the use of another person's money. Sometimes the cost of borrowing is fair; sometimes it is painfully high; and sometimes it is pure robbery. If you follow these rules, you can make credit your servant, not your master:

1. Live with credit, not on it. To stretch your dollars, pay cash or use cost-free 30-day credit accounts.

2. Whenever possible, save then spend. Don't borrow to buy.

3. Use extended credit sparingly. If you need all your income to live today, you'll need at least as much in the months to come.

4. Easy credit is never easy. The easier it is to get a loan, the harder it will be to pay it back.

5. If you must use credit, remember that annual percentage rates let you compare one credit deal with another.

6. Shop for credit carefully before you shop for the article you plan to buy with the borrowed money.

7. The longer you use credit, the higher the cost. Therefore, pay down as much as you can and pay off the balance as fast as you can.

8. Installment contracts are legal documents stacked against the buyer. Read the fine print and deal only with a firm you know to be reliable. Better yet, use some other form of credit.

9. Make sure that any credit agreement that you sign clearly states the dollar cost, the amount and date of each payment, and the name and address of the person to whom the payments must be made.

10. Beware the loan shark. If your credit is questionable and your cash limited, work or beg, but do not borrow.

11. Give thought to your credit rating. Your good name serves you well.

12. Buying on time means paying on time; so use only as much credit as you can readily repay.

Never ask of money spent
Where the spender thinks it went.
Nobody was ever meant
To remember or invent
What he did with every cent.

8

Records,
Checks,
and
Balances

In the course of a forty-year working life, a man or woman with an average income of $12,000 has almost half a million dollars to manage. The person whose income averages $20,000 handles well over three-quarters of a million. While most young people devote years to learning a trade or profession to provide this income, few learn the equally important skills of recording, preserving, and planning how to spend the money that they earn.

Accurate and accessible records are an essential part of sound money management. Records tell where money went so that nonessential spending can be decreased as prices of necessities rise. Records help in timing costly purchases such as cars, house furnishings, or home improvements. Records are required by the government to support deductions claimed on income tax returns and to explain the sources of nontaxable income such as inherited money, interest on municipal bonds, insurance repayments, or the allowable exclusion of dividends received from qualifying corporations. Taxpayers who keep good records often save substantially on income taxes.

People who buy on credit need extremely accurate records. Without ready records, they may overlook a payment and lose the merchandise. Or they may sign contracts for more installment purchases than they can afford. Records of prepaid mail orders and the expiration dates of magazine subscriptions may save both money and worry. By comparing a year-end statement of assets with a similar record from a previous year, it is easy to see whether an individual or a family is walking proudly through swirling inflation or sinking into the quicksands of debt.

There are other family records that are worth making and updating from time to time. Records of past illnesses, education, and jobs are of importance to teen-agers and adults alike. As time goes on, it becomes almost impossible to remember schools and dates attended, honors won, the names and addresses of employers, dates of employment, and supervisors; yet these facts are regularly demanded of students enrolling in college and persons seeking new employment.

Everyone will agree that a company has little chance of success if it has no bookkeeper, no method of keeping track of costs, sales, and profits, and no system of filing and retrieving information about past transactions. Thoughtful persons realize that managing family or personal finances is much like running a business with this single exception: success of a family is measured in happiness as well as in economic security.

Parents who keep an orderly office in their home usually find it easy to teach their children the habit of efficient personal record-keeping.

The making of a daybook

The basic record that every wage-earning individual or family group needs is a monthly account of income and expenditures. Whereas a budget is a spending plan apportioning anticipated income, a financial journal, or daybook, shows exactly how many dollars actually came in and how most of them were spent.

Just how accurate the record ought to be depends on the record-keeper's personality, and on the amount of income at his disposal. The tighter the budget, the more careful the records should be. Some people do not mind living dangerously; they are willing to balance on the brink of bankruptcy or at least to play hare-and-hounds with bill-collectors. But for people who like economic security blankets, none is better than a well-kept account book, or daybook, used from month to month and year to year.

What should a daybook look like? There is no single, proper shape or size, no right number of headings, no exact number of entries. Some people find a satisfactory twelve-column account book at the dime store for less than a dollar. Others, with larger handwriting or more active economic lives, prefer fourteen-by-seventeen-inch columnar sheets, which are sold in pads in stationery stores, and which can be folded and filed with paid bills to support claims on income tax returns. The book has the advantage of being more compact; its pages are less liable to be lost or misfiled.

Whatever the format, the journal, or daybook, must be easy to use and easy to locate for day-to-day entries. The headings must reflect the spending habits of the record-keeping family. Monthly sheets with well-thought-out headings and subheadings may take a little time to prepare; but because they increase the ease of making entries, they save time in the long run. They also make the monthly record more useful when comparisons with other years are required or when information is needed for income tax returns.

Mrs. Simpson's daybook

Mrs. Simpson had worked out a system of recording earnings and expenses that served her family well for over sixteen years. As the family's income and business affairs increased, more headings were added; still, the general setup of each monthly sheet remained the same. The book, clipped open to the current month, was kept in a kitchen drawer.

Sally, the Simpson's teen-aged daughter, wrote in the headings and subheadings for each month's record sheet. Mrs. Simpson had long ago decided that Sally would learn a great deal from this fifteen-minute monthly exercise and that she should be paid for her work because it saved her mother's time.

Familiar with the system, Sally and Mr. Simpson took a moment before dinner to jot down any cash expenditures beyond their personal allowances. Mrs. Simpson, who marketed only once or twice a week, copied the total from the register tape as she unpacked the groceries. On return from any shopping expedition, she also made it a habit to record in the proper columns money spent at the hardware store, the dime store, the car wash, and so on.

At the end of the month, Mrs. Simpson got out her checkbook and copied the amount of each check drawn during the month under the correct heading: mortgage, electricity, heat, telephone, car payments, medical bills, contributions, and all the rest. Since she wrote fewer than twenty-five checks as a rule, this did not take long. Using the family's electric adding machine, she quickly totaled the columns.

Mrs. Simpson's daybook sheet for April, 1974, appears on pages 124-126. It shows how the columns were set up to meet the needs of her family. It shows that by careful preparation of the sheet, entries are easy to write in and easy to find later. But it does not show how other families should apportion their money, as no two families have the same income or the same ideas about the way their income should be apportioned.

Moreover, as the cost of living continues to rise, the amounts listed in Mrs. Simpson's daybook may someday seem ridiculously low. Still, the principles of record-keeping shown here will continue to be valid and useful to those who study them thoughtfully.

The income side of the daybook

At the beginning of April, Mrs. Simpson had counted the travelers' checks kept on hand for emergency use and all the family cash except for allowances previously given to family members. She put the total cash on hand on the first line in the wide left-hand column headed "Cash Assets and Income Received." Next she copied the balances in the checking account, the regular savings account, and the special savings account. Since there were no outstanding loans or other amounts receivable, she added lines 1 through 5 and placed the total on line 6. These were the family's cash assets at the beginning of the month.

Investments such as securities, savings certificates, and real estate do not appear in the monthly account book with this exception: when money is withdrawn from the checking or savings accounts for investment purposes, the amount is listed in column IX and treated as an expenditure. How to keep records of stocks and bonds will be discussed in chapter ten.

Families who keep large sums in a regular savings account may prefer not to show this item in their daybooks. In such a case, additions made to the regular savings account would appear as money spent in column IX. Interest received on the account would be listed with other itemized income. Money transferred from the regular savings account into the checking account would reappear as "transfer from savings" under "Income Itemized."

A special savings account, quite separate from the regular savings account, is a necessary part of this particular system of family money management. Sums needed for such annual expenses as taxes, insurance, vacations, or Christmas giving, as well as amounts to be set aside for long-term goals such as a new car or college tuition for an adolescent son or daughter, should be estimated at the beginning of each year and divided into twelve equal parts. If one-twelfth of the total of these anticipated expenses is deposited in the special savings account each month, the family will always have money on hand to meet otherwise painfully large drains on income.

Earmarked funds should never be considered a part of the family's regular savings and investments. Once in the special account, the funds should be left untouched—just as if they were already spent—until an insurance premium is due, or a new car has been selected, or the travel agent asks for the payment on the approaching vacation cruise. At that time,

A Page from
Mrs. Simpson's Daybook

April 1974

Cash Assets and Income Received	I Food and Supplies	II Shelter and Services
1. 129.30 Cash and Travelers' Checks	32.18	Mortgage
2. 2,659.18 Balance Checking Account	6.49	Payment 260.00
3. 12,187.71 Balance Regular Savings	34.56	Electric-
4. 3,482.25 Balance Special Savings	1.66	ity 35.00
5. Other Amounts Receivable	Easter 38.13	Heat 66.92
6. 18,458.44 Cash Assets at Beginning	Dinner	Telephone 41.20
of the Month	Out 24.72	Water .00
	16.37	
Received in April:	27.99	
7. 1,421.80 Net Salary 2d & 16th	182.10	
8. 137.50 Interest (tax-free)		
9. 32.50 Dividend Income		
10. 67.34 Repayments		
11. 150.00 Other Income		
12. 20,267.58 April 30 Total Before	*Domestic*	*Essential*
Expenses	*Service*	*Home*
13. 18,565.97 Less Cash Assets May 1		*Repairs*
14. 1,701.61 Total Spent in April	Gross Wages 15.00	
	15.00	Plumber 19.65
April Income Itemized:	15.00	
710.90 Net Salary April 2	15.00	
710.90 Net Salary April 16	60.00	
137.50 Interest on Municipal	SS Tax	
Bond $5,000 Delaware Co.	(her share	
Pollution Control 5-1/2%	& mine) 7.02	
1997 (tax-free income)		
150.00 Mary Simpson: Garden Club	67.02	
Lectures (honorarium)		
32.50 Dividend: 50 Shares Sears		
67.34 Distribution on Veteran's		
Insurance		
(1,809.14) Total Income		
Summary:		
15. Total Spent in April 1,701.61		
(from line 14 above)		
16. Less Itemized Expendi- 1,694.82		
tures (Columns I-XI)		
17. Amount Spent But Not 6.79		
Accounted for		
18. Itemized Expenditures		
(Total of Columns		
I-XI) 1,694.82	Food 182.10	
	Service 67.02	422.77

A Page from
Mrs. Simpson's Daybook

(Continued)

III Furnishings and Improvements	IV Travel and Transportation	V Medical Expenses	VI Personal Allowances	VII Contributions and Personal Gifts	
Furnishings	Installment on car 82.30	Medical Insurance Premiums:	Mr. 70.00	Contributions With Check or Receipt	
Kitchen curtains 16.40	Car Repairs	John Han- cock Major			
Bathroom rug 8.48 24.88	Inspection 4.00 New tire 32.18 36.18	Medical for 1974 167.00	Mrs. 50.00	Am. Cancer Society 10.00 YWCA 15.00	
		Dr. Bates 15.00		Children's Hospital 5.00 30.00	
	Gas & Oil 5.25	Car mileage	Missy 35.00 Easter		
Garden Supplies	4.00 5.00 3.65	to go to doctor:	jacket 27.25 62.25	Other Cash Contributions	
Lawn food 32.99	4.10 22.00			Easter Fund for Handi- capped 3.00	
	Tolls & Parking .25	Cash fares to go to	Enter-	Sunshine Camp	
	.15 .10 .05	doctor:	tainment	Fund 3.00	
	.15 .10 .25		Opera 18.00 Books & maga-		
	3.65 .25		zines 9.50 Easter	Personal Gifts	
Major Improvements	4.95	Prescrip- tion	plant 6.05	Scarf to Aunt	
	Public Transporta-	Medicines 4.50 3.25		Kate 4.98 Grandma	
	tion	7.75		sweater 20.00 24.98	
	Commuter's ticket 24.00 Local bus 2.80 26.80				
57.87	172.23	192.55	Personal 182.25 Entertain. 33.55	Contrib. 36.00 Personal 24.98	

A Page from
Mrs. Simpson's Daybook

(Concluded)

VIII Taxes and Miscellaneous Deductibles	IX New Investments & Asset-Building	X Special Purpose Deposits	Savings Account XI Withdrawals
Taxes Paid Out-of- Pocket	Money Transferred To Savings Account	Vacation Fund 50.00	
		Christmas Fund 25.00	
		Insurance Funds:	
Interest Paid on Revolving Charge Accounts		Homeowner's policy 10.00	Paid for year 120.00
	Money from Checking Account Used to Buy Stocks	Life insurance 75.00	
Other Interest		Car policy 27.00	Paid 1/2 year to Oct. 6 162.00
Personal Property Tax	Money from Checking Account Used to Buy Bonds	Other Insurance (except Health)	
		College Fund 200.00	
Safe-Deposit Box Rental 16.50	Money from Checking Account Used for Other Investments	New Car Fund .00	

Legal and
Accountant
Fees
        25.00
		(Total Put
		in Special
		Account
		        387.00)	

41.50	.00		282.00

the necessary amount should be withdrawn from the special savings account and deposited in the checking account. The savings bank draft should never be endorsed and used as payment. Only by using a personal check will the family have a record of each important disbursement.

Although earmarked funds are usually deposited in the special savings account in a lump sum, it is a good idea to indicate in the daybook just how much has been set aside for each special project. Column X of Mrs. Simpson's account book shows the month's set-asides for several different purposes. Since this money has not been spent, column X is not totaled at the month's end. Withdrawals from the special savings account, on the other hand, are entered when made—as can be seen in column XI. These withdrawals are added up at the end of the month, and the sum at the foot of column XI is added to the total of columns I through IX. This grand—or ghastly—total is entered on lines 16 and 18, "Itemized Expenditures," at the lower left side of the page.

As income was received during the month, Mrs. Simpson—and occasionally Mr. Simpson—would jot down the source and amounts of the checks. At the end of each month, one of them would close the account for the month just passed and open to a new page for the following month.

This April 30, Mrs. Simpson entered the total net salary on line 7, all interest received on line 8, dividend income on line 9, repayments on line 10, and other income on line 11. By adding together lines 6 through 11, she had the month's-end total before expenses. As she wrote this total on line 12, she thought to herself, "How wonderful it would be if it didn't cost us anything to live!"

One final step remained. Heading a new sheet "May, 1974," Mrs. Simpson once more counted cash and travelers' checks, looked up bank balances, and totaled the cash assets at the beginning of May. Turning back to line 13 of the April sheet, she copied the cash assets on May 1, reminding herself to change the total if, when the bank statement came in, she discovered that the balance in her checkbook was incorrect.

By subtracting line 13 from line 12, she could write on line 14 the total spent in April. To finish the monthly accounting,

Mrs. Simpson glanced down the page to where the word "Summary" appeared. Here, on line 15, she repeated line 14, the total spent in April. Subtracting line 16, the itemized expenditures, she found out just how much had been spent but not accounted for (line 17). Pleased that the amount was so small, she put away the adding machine and took a coffee break.

The summary of annual spending

Sometimes, Mrs. Simpson reflected, expenditures exceeded income. This was nothing to be concerned about if the extra money had been previously deposited in the special savings account or if it had been used to buy securities or to swell the regular savings account. Mrs. Simpson knew she had nothing to worry about even when expenses really exceeded income for a month or two. Since this was a yearly, not a monthly, plan, the important thing was to ensure that during the course of the entire year income was greater than expenditure.

To make certain that the family was on firm financial ground, at the end of each year Mrs. Simpson summarized the year's spending. On a spare page of the old daybook, she set up a "Summary of Annual Spending" (see pages 129-131).

In the first column, she copied the total income received in each month and, with the help of her little adding machine, totaled the column.

To find out just what happened to all that money, she next listed any money invested in securities and itemized in column IX of each daybook page. To these assets she added the amount by which her regular savings account had increased over the previous year-end balance. She did not, however, include with these assets funds in the special savings account, as they were already earmarked for future expenses and thus were not savings or investments.

In the third column of the summary of spending, Mrs. Simpson put the twelve monthly amounts of money spent but not accounted for as they appeared on line 17 of the daybook pages. In similar fashion, she entered the monthly totals spent for food, services, shelter, travel, and all the rest. She

Summary of Annual Spending, 1974

	Total Income Less Withheld Taxes	Money Saved and Invested	Spent But Not Accounted For	Food and Supplies	Service: House and Grounds	
Jan.						
Feb.						
Mar.						
Apr.						
May						
June						
July						
Aug.						
Sept.						
Oct.						
Nov.						
Dec.						
Year's Total						
Summary 1974						
Total Income: (Less Withheld Taxes)	Total Outgo: Amount Spent: Amount Saved:					

Projected Annual Spending, 1975

Projected Income 1975	Money Saved and Invested	Spent But Not Accounted For	Food and Supplies	Service: House and Grounds	

Summary of Annual Spending 1974, Continued

Shelter: Running Costs & Improvements	Travel and Transportation	Personal Spending and Entertainment	Nondeductible Gifts to Friends	Medical Expenses

Projected Annual Spending 1975, Continued

Shelter: Running Costs & Improvements	Travel and Transportation	Personal Spending and Entertainment	Nondeductible Gifts to Friends	Medical Expenses

Summary of Annual Spending 1974, Concluded

	Deductible Interest Paid Out	Deductible Charitable Contributions	Miscellaneous Deductions	Out-of-Pocket Taxes

Projected Annual Spending 1975, Concluded

	Deductible Interest Paid Out	Deductible Charitable Contributions	Miscellaneous Deductions	Out-of-Pocket Taxes

headed the last five columns somewhat differently from the daybook columns. These five columns, carefully completed, would serve as a worksheet for the family's income tax return. Itemized deductions listed here would go on Schedule A of federal income tax Form 1040. Being, in all likelihood, much greater than the standard deduction, these itemized deductions might save several hundred dollars on income taxes.

When she had completed the columns, Mrs. Simpson totaled all of them except the first and placed the total beside the words "Total Outgo." By subtracting the total of the second column—"Money Saved and Invested"—from the total outgo, she found out just how much the family had really spent and how much had been used to build assets. The total outgo, of course, should match the total income (less taxes withheld, if any) ; but if, in all her computations, a slight difference appeared, she did not trouble herself about it.

To project the income and expenditures for the year ahead was now a simple matter. Mrs. Simpson merely copied the totals for 1974, making adjustments upwards of about 10 percent to allow for inflation and cutting down somewhat on optional expenses to keep the total projected spending within the total estimated income. She knew that if costs and income varied from the anticipated amounts, she could make other adjustments as the months went by. That is why she wrote the estimated budget in pencil.

Mrs. Simpson felt considerable satisfaction as she studied this summary page. She knew that now she and her husband could tell at a glance how much of their money became building blocks toward security. She knew also that her work would save her husband a great deal of effort when he began to prepare the income tax returns. She remembered how he had said, "I can't honestly say that the daybook makes doing the tax returns a pleasure ; but it sure makes the job a lot less painful."

The Henrys' "Penny Pincher"

Sally's newly wed cousin Hilda and her young husband had a much simpler economic life. Simon and Hilda Henry, both of whom held jobs, had a combined gross income of about

$14,500. They lived in a three-room apartment, were saving the money from Hilda's salary toward a down payment on a house, and hoped some day to afford a baby.

The Henrys' journal, which they jokingly called their "Penny Pincher," was far less complicated than Mrs. Simpson's. Yet it gave them a clear picture of what money came in and let them tell at a glance how fast their assets were growing. Although they planned to take the standard deduction on their income tax, they wanted to have all the facts at hand if it ever became profitable to itemize deductions or to claim a refund for overwithheld taxes.

One Saturday in May while Sally was visiting their apartment, she watched Hilda making entries in her account book. Sally studied the page and noticed that at the top of each column Hilda had written one-twelfth of the yearly estimate for each kind of expense. Sally asked Hilda why the amount spent on clothes that month was so much higher than her monthly clothing budget indicated.

Hilda explained: "A spending plan is a yearly, not a monthly, plan. Everybody knows that people buy most of their warm-weather threads in April and May and most of their fall outfits in September and October. As long as Simon and I don't go over our annual clothes budget, we buy what we want when we want it. Next month we'll pay a lot for life insurance; and in July, I guess, our extra money will go for a vacation."

"Oh," said Sally, brightening. "I thought a budget meant that you spend just so much every month and that the record book brought you up short if you spent a dime too much."

"A spending plan and a record book aren't policemen, after all," laughed Hilda. "They are just helpful friends. All they need is a little cooperation from you."

"How did you learn all this?" asked Sally after a thoughtful pause.

"Your mother started me thinking about ways to stretch a buck the summer I stayed with you at Ocean City. Then last fall Simon and I took an evening course in consumer ed at the community college. We found out that you win the money game if you plan ahead, spend less than you make, shop the sales, buy for cash or thirty-day credit, take care of the things you already own, and never expect to get something for nothing."

"If we follow all the rules," said Simon with a wink, "we'll be millionaires before we're thirty!" Sally noticed that he was busy making a handsome lamp out of an old brass candlestick.

"At least you'll be headed in the right direction," replied Sally, laughing.

Sally's "Monthly Monster"

On the way home Sally stopped at a dime store and paid eighty-four cents for a twelve-column account book.

Late in the afternoon of the last day of May, Mrs. Simpson found her daughter hard at work setting up her first monthly record. Peering over her shoulder, Mrs. Simpson was pleased to see how well the page was planned (see pages 136-137). She cleared her throat.

"I didn't hear you come in, Mom," said Sally, looking up. "I'm setting up my own daybook. I'm going to call it 'The Monthly Monster' because it's a monster of a job."

"Deciding on headings is half the battle," said Mrs. Simpson. "Luckily, headings need to be changed only once in a long while—when your income and way of life alter radically. But I do see one change that you might make right now."

"What's that?" asked Sally a trifle defensively.

"Put 200 before those zeros on the line called 'Checking Account'—there, in the assets column. I'm going to give you $200 and help you open your own checking account this very afternoon."

"Gee, Mom, that's terrific!" Beaming, Sally got up and hugged her mother. Then the glow flickered out. "Oh, darn! We can't do it today. The bank will be closed. It's nearly five o'clock."

"Banks are open late on Fridays. Let's go."

The challenge of the checkbook

"Young lady," said the bank manager as he put down his pen, "your printed checks will be mailed to you within a week. Just remember never to overdraw your account."

"Please see that Sally gets the larger size checkbook with three checks to a page and a separate register," said Mrs. Simpson. "Everyone needs space to list deposits, fill out check stubs, and do the necessary arithmetic to keep a checkbook in balance. Those little folding checkbooks are quite inadequate."

"And I'd prefer not to have my address printed on the checks," said Sally. "My cousin says an address on a check is an invitation to a forger to visit you under some pretext or other to get your signature. She says a person's name printed on the check is enough identification."

"You are perfectly right," replied the bank manager. "Forgery is a great and growing danger. Let me add a few other cautions. Always keep your checkbook in a safe place at home. Never use the glove compartment of your car as a storage place for your cash, checkbook, passbook, driver's license, or other valuables. Hundreds of thefts from locked glove compartments occur every day.

"Carry only one blank check in your wallet and guard that carefully. If a blank check is ever lost or stolen, notify the bank immediately. Never sign a blank check. Carrying around a signed blank check is just as dangerous as carrying around your whole bank deposit.

"Even at your desk at home make out each check completely before adding your signature. Moreover, never permit anyone to use one of your blank checks for any purpose whatsoever. No matter how carefully your account number may be scratched out, the computer will read the magnetic ink of the original number and charge the check to your account.

"Never give out a check with any numeral changed or written over. A poorly written check encourages the attention of a forger who might try to make a further alteration before cashing it. If your bank makes no charge for your checks, tear up a badly written check. If you have to pay for each check, destroy only the signature. When you have collected a few damaged checks, the bank will redeem them.

"You will receive a bank statement every month. Notify the bank if it does not arrive on time, because stealing canceled checks to copy signatures is a favorite trick of forgers.

Sally Simpson's "Monthly Monster"

June 1974

Assets and Income (Estimated Income $ 50.50)	Lunches + Snacks (Est. 10.00)	Travel + Carfare (Est. 3.50)
29.70 Cash on hand		
242.84 Savings Accounts		
.00 Checking Account		
1.50 Money lent to Pauline		
274.04 Assets June 1st		
. June Allowance		
. Baby-sitting for Jimmy James		Trip to Washington June 18th?
. Graduation Gift ?		
. Other Income		
. Total Before Expenses June 30th		
. Less Assets on July 1st		
. Actually Spent in June		
Summary:		
Actually Spent: .		
Less Itemized Exp: .		
Amount Unacc't: .		
Total Itemized Expenses: $. ←	.	.

Optional Spending (Est. $5.00)	Education (Est. 10.00)	Personal Expense (Est. 20.00)	Savings Account Put In (Est. 2.00)	Taken Out
Records:	School Supplies:	Clothes:		
Movies:		Cosmetics:		
Gifts:		Sports Equipment:		
			Deposited This Month	

Also notify me or one of the other bank officers if there seems to be any irregularity in your bank statement. Once in a while even the bank makes a mistake."

"I see I have a lot to learn about a checking account," said Sally. "I had no idea so many things could happen to a check."

"There is one thing more you ought to know," continued the bank manager. "Someday you may find it necessary to stop payment on a check that has been misplaced, lost in the mails, or handed to a seemingly dishonest person. To stop payment, telephone your bank and place a stop order. Then go to the bank immediately and fill out a form confirming that order. During the time a check is in transit—and this varies from a few hours to four or five days—your bank will try to track it down and refuse to honor it. But we cannot guarantee to do so.

"When you put a stop order on a check, wait a few days before issuing a duplicate. When you do reissue a check, write across the top: 'Duplicate of check stopped June 2, 1974,' or whatever the date might be. And, Miss Simpson, I am sure I need not remind you that it is dishonorable and dishonest to pay for something by check and then, without cause, to stop payment on the check. It is just as important to protect your reputation as it is to protect your money."

Left is right and right is wrong

When the register and pad of checks arrived, Sally was eager to write her first check. Later in the month her class was going on a three-day excursion to Washington, and interested students had to sign up and pay $122 before June 10. That evening Sally found her father in his study and asked, "Are there any tricks to writing a check?"

"No tricks, but a few things to remember. Bring in your checkbook and a ball-point pen."

When she was seated, he continued: "First you number the check to speed up the job of balancing your checkbook. Next you date it. The date makes the document legal and helps to identify the check. The date also protects you, for banks won't honor a check that is more than two months old.

"The name of the payee—the person to whom the check is

being written—should be started as far to the left as possible. You should keep parts of the name quite close together and draw a line following it so no other letters or names could be inserted by a forger. Forgers sometimes insert the words 'or bearer' after the name on a stolen check and then carry it to the bank and cash it. The figures following the dollar sign should also be plainly written and closely spaced. Amounts less than a dollar are written as fractions of one hundred in numerals half the regular size.

"On the far left of the next line, you write out the number of dollars you wish the bank to pay. Here, even more, left is right and right is wrong. Never write 'and' between the parts of the number. Write 'One hundred twenty-two,' not 'One hundred and twenty-two.' The word 'and' does appear between the dollars and cents, however. It is properly written on the diagonal so that no clever penman could readily turn it into the word 'thousand' without catching the bank teller's attention. Glance up to make sure the written number matches the numerals on the line above; then draw a firm line across any remaining blank space.

"Now write your signature carefully. Forgers have no trouble at all in copying those unreadable squiggles that some people make. And finally, make a note on the check itself stating what the check is for. Your check should state 'Washington trip, June 18.' Some future check might read 'Snorkle course at the Y.' Mother and I might write something like 'Invoice 16587' or 'Bill of June 20, Account #92403.' Notations like these help the payee make the proper credit to your account. They also protect you if the bill is presented again."

As Sally finished the check (see page 140), her father said, "That's perfect Sally. Just right."

"Not as easy as I thought it would be," murmured Sally.

"Like learning to dance or drive a car, handling your checkbook gets easier with practice. But you're off to a flying start."

Tool for living or instrument of torture?

Early in July, Sally's first bank statement arrived. With it came fourteen canceled checks.

A Check Correctly Drawn

THE FIDELITY BANK

PHILADELPHIA, PENNSYLVANIA

NO. *1*

$\frac{3-50}{310}$

June 7, 1974

PAY TO THE ORDER OF _Paoli High School_ $122 \frac{00}{100}$

One hundred twenty - Two $\frac{00}{100}$ ————— DOLLARS

Washington Trip
June 18ᵀᴴ

Sarah J. Simpson

Sarah J. Simpson

⑈0310⑈0050⑈ 123 456 7⑈

Published with permission of The Fidelity Bank

"What am I supposed to do with all this?" Sally asked her mother.

"Get your register of checks and I'll show you," Mrs. Simpson replied. She sorted the checks according to number as she awaited her daughter's return.

Looking over the register, Mrs. Simpson said, "I'm glad to see that you stubbed each check, putting down the number, the date, the name of the payee, the amount, and the purpose of each. I never tear a check out of my checkbook until I have made certain that all these facts are correctly entered on the stub."

Mrs. Simpson turned to the page with the latest entries. "It isn't hard to balance a checkbook, if you do it step by step. The work is done on the left side of the register of checks. First you add to the balance forward (see line 1 in illustration on pages 142-143) any deposit you may have made before the date of the bank statement (line 2) and bring down a subtotal (line 3).

"From this subtotal, you subtract the sum of the checks which appear on the page and which bear a date earlier than the date of the bank statement. Since your statement runs through June 30, you include all your June checks. These total $39.72 (line 4). By subtracting this amount from your subtotal, you get a tentative balance of $122.81 (line 5).

"Notice that I have drawn a double line to separate the checks written before the date of the bank statement from those written later. The later transactions will appear on your next bank statement and need not concern us now.

"From the tentative balance, you must subtract any service charges the bank may make (line 6) in order to arrive at your true balance (line 7). Since your account is a no-minimum balance, or special checking account, the bank deducts a small monthly service fee plus ten cents for every check you write. People who maintain large balances avoid these charges."

"But, Mother," said Sally, "the balance on the bank statement reads $125.78, not $120.51. I thought my balance had to match the balance on the bank's statement."

"When your balance and the bank's don't agree, you have to do a little detective work. It's called 'reconciling checkbook

A Register of Checks Showing
Month-End Balancing

	DEPOSITS		CHECKS ISSUED	AMOUNT	
(1) Balance Forward	112	53	NO. _13_ DATE _June 17_,19 _74_ PAY TO Betty's Bootery for shoes and sneakers	21 50	R
(2) June 19th Birthday Check	50	00			
(3) Subtotal	162	53	NO. _14_ DATE _June 20_,19 _74_ PAY TO Sears Roebuck for gray slacks	12 95	R
(4) Less checks drawn Through June 30th	− 39	72			
(5) Tentative Balance	122	81	NO. _15_ DATE _June 29_,19 _74_ PAY TO The Music Shop for records	5 27	o
(6) Less Bank's Service charge	− 2	30	Checks To Date of Bank Statement	39 72	
(7) True Balance July 1st	120	51	NO. _16_ DATE _July 3_,19 _74_ PAY TO Stevens Stationers for ring binder, paper, pen and other school supplies	7 69	
(8) OK					
			NO._____ DATE _____19___ PAY TO_____		
July 2nd Allowance	2d 35	00			
			NO._____ DATE _____19___ PAY TO_____		
TOTAL DEP			PAY TO_____		
LESS CKS DRAWN					
BAL. FOR.			TOTAL CHECKS DRAWN		

Reverse Side of Page from Register of Checks Showing Bank Statement Reconciled With Checkbook

DATE	DESCRIPTION	AMOUNT
(9)	July 1ˢᵗ Balance on Statement	125.78
(10)	Checks outstanding on July 1ˢᵗ:	
	# 15 The Music Shop	− 5.27
(11)	Adjusted Bank Balance, July 1ˢᵗ	120.51

and bank statement.' You start by looking for any outstanding checks. Checks numbered 1 through 14 have all been returned, so I put a tiny 'R' in the right-hand margin next to each. But check number 15 had not been presented to the bank for payment before the end of the statement period. Because the check is outstanding, I put a small 'O' in the margin.

"You should try to avoid writing checks during the last week of the statement period so that most, if not all, of your checks will 'clear' before the period ends. Of course, this isn't always possible.

"If you have an outstanding check or two, don't panic. On the reverse side of the page on which you have been working —or in the blank space above it—copy the balance that appears on the bank statement (line 9). Subtract from this balance any outstanding check or checks written before the close of the statement period (line 10). This gives you an adjusted bank balance—the balance you would have had if the outstanding check had been cashed before the statement period ended (line 11).

"This adjusted balance usually agrees to the penny with your true balance (line 7). If it does, mark it 'OK' (line 8) and be glad that your checkbook is in balance."

"What do you do if the adjusted balance and your true balance don't agree?" asked Sally.

"If your bank statement and checkbook still refuse to agree," replied Mrs. Simpson, "you have made a mistake in arithmetic, or you have forgotten to enter some deposit or service charge, or you have failed to stub some check. Go over your addition and subtraction for the entire statement period. If you don't find the error, hold each check beside its stub to make sure the figures match. Does the bank statement show a deposit of which you have no record? Did you neglect to deduct the service charge?

"If, after double-checking everything, you still can't reconcile your checkbook and bank balance, take them to your father or me, or to one of the bank's officers. Never go from month to month with some error in your checkbook; it won't disappear until it has been corrected, and the longer it runs, the harder it is to detect."

"I'm beginning to wonder whether a checkbook is a tool for living or an instrument of torture," said Sally with a rueful smile.

"A checkbook is a life-support system for careful money managers, Sally. With it you avoid the dangers of carrying large sums of money, and you have foolproof records of every payment you make. Few adults in a money-based society like ours could get along without a checkbook."

"I was only kidding," said Sally. "Most of the girls in my class just wish they had my problems!"

Wishing won't do it; saving will.

FOLK SAYING

CHAPTER 9

The Nest
and
the Egg

Many teen-agers find it difficult to think about the future. Much as they desire freedom from parental restraint, they become acutely uncomfortable at the thought that some day they will no longer live at home and enjoy parental emotional and financial support. Parents can help their children to develop the ability to see fifteen or twenty years into the future. Encourage the reading of science fiction. Talk to them about life a few years hence.

Newspapers and magazines give many hints of things to come. Medicine will conquer various diseases; people are likely to live longer. Supermarkets may have semiautomatic checkout systems and effortless ways to buy staples by means of picture-phones. Homes may have solar heating systems and video-telephones.

How small will cars become in order to stretch the world's

dwindling supply of energy? What about urban and inter-urban transportation—aerial monorail cars, moving side-walks, computer-programmed mini-taxis? What will govern-ments be like, and schools, and clothing?

And, more important, what will it feel like to be thirty-two years old instead of twelve, or thirty-seven instead of seven-teen? A teen-ager can more clearly visualize the years to come by writing a "future autobiography." He can pretend that fifteen or twenty years have gone by. Where is he living? What is his job? What kind of mate does he have? How many children? If a youngster pretends he owns his own home, how much money is invested in it and how is it financed? Assum-ing the price level to be much the same as today (and it is likely to be much higher because of continued inflation), he may need parental assistance to figure out what it costs to live at the scale he has envisaged.

Thinking about the future is by no means an idle specula-tion; for only when preteens and teens can ride a time-ma-chine forward ten, fifteen, or twenty years can they begin to comprehend the value of money in the bank or realize the importance of insurance in guarding them against the many problems and perils that life might bring.

Why build a cash reserve?

Saving is a defensive operation. Its purpose is to carry over some buying power from a time when it is not needed to a time when it is greatly desired. Ready money makes possible many things in our society. Ready money buys pleasure and satisfaction for the possessor or for somebody who is dear to him. Ready money buys opportunity—the chance to get some-thing at a bargain price, to obtain more education, or to make a sound investment. And ready money, left in the bank to earn interest, buys peace of mind and economic security.

So important is a cash reserve to personal and family wel-fare that many business organizations encourage their em-ployees to save through automatic payroll deductions. The employee specifies how much he wishes to set aside from each paycheck, and the company makes the deposit for him in a savings account. If the employee owns stock in the company, the management will often undertake to reinvest his dividends as they come due.

Some companies have developed long-range pension plans. Over 3,000 American companies even add part of the company's profits to every dollar saved. The federal government is taking an increasing interest in the pension plans of private industry in order to protect the rights of workers who have contributed to these plans. The government operates a generous pension plan for civil service workers. Realizing that self-employed individuals had no access to ordinary pension plans, Congress enacted legislation in 1962 to enable doctors, lawyers, shopkeepers, and others who work independently to build an estate for their retirement years.

When both business and government encourage people to save, it is evident that a cash emergency reserve is essential to personal financial security. The problem for the person who is starting a savings program is where and how to save.

Although funds for tomorrow's comfort and today's protection are still largely the responsibility of the wage-earning individual, a savings program is not for everyone. Newly married couples who are buying home furnishings and low-income families in times of rising prices have all they can do to stretch their dollars to cover present needs. Elderly people who live on fixed incomes should realize that these are the rainy days for which they prepared and should spend all their income to make their declining years as comfortable as possible. In emergencies, all these people must rely on borrowed money, gifts from family and friends, state unemployment insurance, federal aid, Medicare, or help from private social agencies.

Young adults who have both earnings and a limited responsibility for the welfare of others and heads of families who have above-average incomes are in quite a different situation. They have the means—actually the privilege—of building up the capital they need to shield themselves from adversity. These fortunate people need only goals impelling enough to offset the universal tendency to let money burn a hole in the pocket.

Goals in saving depend on the age and sophistication of the

builder of capital assets. For a tot, a valid goal might be hoarding a few nickels to buy a Mother's Day gift at the dime store. For a teen-ager, the goal might be a few hundred dollars set aside for a stereo system or $2,000 toward the purchase of a car. For the young adult who thinks big and who has a regular source of income, building a college fund or a second source of income are realistic goals. Whatever the goal, it must be strong enough to justify present sacrifices for future satisfactions.

The three Rs of saving and investment

The three Rs to remember when building a nest for a financial egg are readiness, risk, and return. Ideally, money set aside for future spending should be "liquid"—ready for use at all times. Risk should be avoided; the purchasing power of the set-aside dollar should remain constant so that it will buy the same amount of goods and services whenever it is spent. The return—the money the dollar earns while waiting to be used—should be generous.

Unfortunately, there is no way to have all of the three Rs at the same time. Cash in a safe-deposit box is ready and risk-free (except for the loss of purchasing power resulting from inflation), but it earns nothing. Money in savings certificates or bonds is comparatively risk-free, earns a good return, but cannot be counted on for emergency use. Stocks may earn a handsome dividend and increase in value, but they do not provide instant cash, nor are they risk-free. While they may rise in price faster than inflation erodes the value of the dollar, they may also fall so far that the entire investment is wiped out. Investing in land may someday prove astonishingly profitable; yet the cash so invested is anything but liquid, the risk is enormous for the inexperienced investor, and—instead of paying dividends—land costs the owner money for taxes and other assessments.

Knowing these facts, some people decide to act like the grasshopper in Aesop's fable of the grasshopper and the ant. They spend their money as fast as they get it, giving no thought to the stormy days of joblessness and ill health or to the winter of old age. They expect the neighborhood banker, friends, the government, or luck to help them out if expenses get out of hand. When disaster does strike, as it does in the life of nearly everyone, they usually find the help that they were counting on is too little and too late.

Be a piggy at the bank

For building and keeping the emergency reserve that everyone must have in order to be safe and self-sufficient, there are no better places than a mutual savings bank, where deposits up to $40,000 are protected by the Federal Deposit Insurance Corporation, or a savings and loan association, where savings are similarly protected by the Federal Savings and Loan Insurance Corporation.

Deposits in either type of savings institution are ready for instant withdrawal; they are risk-free (except as inflation chips away at the value of all money) ; and they earn a fairly good rate of return.

Large sums of money should never be squirreled away at home, carried in the glove compartment of a car, or toted about in a wallet—as an incredible number of people of all ages tend to do. The risk is 100 percent; the return, zero; and the cash is just as ready for the hand of the thief as it is for the hand of the owner.

Some relatively simple measures can be taken to insure a maximum return for every dollar in the emergency reserve. Avoid depositing savings in a commercial bank where the government-regulated interest rates are $1/4$ to $1/2$ percent lower than in the best-paying mutual savings or savings and loan associations. Shop for a convenient bank that pays the highest rates allowed by the government. The rates on passbook accounts are often advertised in local newspapers.

Choose a bank where the interest is computed on a daily, rather than on a semiannual, quarterly, monthly, or weekly basis; for the "yield"—the true annual interest rate—rises somewhat with the frequency with which interest is compounded.

As may be seen from the table on page 152, a 5.50 percent nominal annual interest rate becomes 5.576 percent when compounded semiannually but 5.654 percent when computed

The Effect on Annual Interest Rates
Of Frequency of Compounding

Nominal Rate	True Annual Rate When Interest Is Compounded			
	Semiannually	Quarterly	Monthly	Daily
5.25	5.319	5.354	5.378	5.390
5.50	5.576	5.614	5.641	5.654
5.75	5.833	5.875	5.904	5.918
6.00	6.090	6.136	6.168	6.183
6.25	6.348	6.398	6.432	6.449
6.50	6.606	6.660	6.697	6.715
6.75	6.864	6.923	6.963	6.982
7.00	7.123	7.186	7.229	7.250
7.25	7.381	7.450	7.496	7.519
7.50	7.641	7.714	7.763	7.788
7.75	7.900	7.978	8.031	8.057
8.00	8.160	8.243	8.300	8.328
8.25	8.420	8.509	8.569	8.599

daily. Thus a deposit of $1,000 at 5.50 percent interest, compounded semiannually, would earn $55.76, while the same deposit compounded on a daily basis would give the depositor $56.54 a year.

Finally, choose a bank where interest is figured from day of deposit to day of withdrawal. When other bookkeeping methods are in use, the depositor may lose a substantial amount of interest.

The egg in the nest

People who can afford to bank a fixed sum each month and allow the interest to accumulate year after year will be surprised to see how fast their capital grows.

Woody Walther's grandfather wanted his infant grandson to have a substantial cash reserve by the time he was through college. The grandfather was not a rich man, but he knew that small sums saved regularly could give the boy financial in-

How Savings of $15 a Month Will Grow
When Interest Is Compounded
Semiannually

At the End of:	4%	4½ %	5%	5½ %	6%
1 year	$ 182	$ 182	$ 182	$ 182	$ 183
2 years	371	372	374	375	377
3 years	568	571	575	578	582
4 years	772	779	786	793	800
5 years	985	997	1,008	1,020	1,032
10 years	2,187	2,242	2,299	2,358	2,418
15 years	3,651	3,798	3,951	4,112	4,282
20 years	5,436	5,741	6,006	6,414	6,786
25 years	7,612	8,168	8,774	9,432	10,152

Source: U.S. Department of Agriculture, Home Economics Research Report, Number 21

dependence. So every month he put $15 into a savings account in Woody's name. At that time interest was compounded only semiannually and 5 percent was a generous rate of return. Still, when Woody celebrates his twenty-fifth birthday next June, he will have nearly $9,000 in the bank (see table on this page). If, when he borrows from these funds, he saves up and replaces the money, the account will continue to shelter him as the years go by.

Ruth Roberts was twelve when she decided to save up enough money to furnish an apartment with style by the time she was twenty-seven. Luckily for Ruth, her mother, who had a full-time job as a legal secretary, paid her a generous wage for doing the housework after school.

One Friday evening, when all the banks in town were open late, Ruth asked her mother to drive her to the Savings Fund Society, where she had a small passbook account. Ruth's mother, mystified, followed along as her daughter asked the security guard to introduce her to Mr. Falkner, the manager.

"I am one of your depositors," said Ruth in her most grown-up voice, "and there is a question I would like to ask you."

"Yes, Miss Roberts," said Mr. Falkner after the visitors were seated beside his desk, "what can I do for you?"

"I'd like to know how much I would have to save each month in order to have $5,000 at the end of fifteen years. I may not always be able to deposit exactly the same amount each month; but if I could, how big would each deposit have to be?"

"Well," said Mr. Falkner, after he had recovered from his surprise, "very few of our young depositors—or any of our depositors, for that matter—think ahead like that. Fortunately, I have a chart that appeared in one of our advertisements some months ago. I think it will answer your question."

Mr. Falkner fished in his desk drawer. "You must understand that this chart was made up when interest rates on savings accounts were $5\frac{1}{4}$ percent calculated from day of deposit to day of withdrawal. If the rates were to rise or fall, the monthly deposit required would vary somewhat; but this gives you a pretty good idea."

Ruth eagerly scanned the chart he handed her (see page 155).

"If I put $18.10 in the bank each month for fifteen years, I'll have my $5,000."

"Absolutely right," said Mr. Falkner. "Would you like to keep the ad?"

Savings certificates and the teen-ager

As already noted, the interest on passbook accounts in mutual savings banks, savings and loan associations, and commercial banks is strictly limited by law. People who have built up a sizable emergency reserve in such an account can afford to trade some cash readiness for a higher rate of return on part of their savings.

Parents are probably in the best position to help a young person decide how large a contingency fund to keep in a passbook account before placing additional capital in less liquid situations. The size of this cushion against emergencies depends on individual needs and family responsibilities.

Heads of families need a generous contingency reserve. Ideally, it should approximate the wage earner's annual in-

Put Your Nest Egg in The Savings Fund Society

	Make these monthly deposits for			And your nest egg will be a nice, round number of dollars:
5 years	10 years	15 years	20 years	
$ 72.56	$ 31.48	$18.10	$11.64	$ 5,000
108.84	47.22	27.15	17.47	7,500
145.13	62.96	36.21	23.29	10,000
181.41	78.70	45.26	29.11	12,500
217.69	94.44	54.31	34.94	15,000
253.97	110.18	63.37	40.76	17,500
290.26	125.93	72.42	46.59	20,000
326.54	141.67	81.47	52.41	22,500
362.82	157.41	90.53	58.23	25,000

come. While the balance in a checking account may be counted as part of this essential cash reserve, the greater part should be kept in a passbook account in a savings bank where the money is instantly available.

Youngsters who can rely on parents or guardians for their major support and educational expenses may safely build a conservative investment program on a much smaller base of savings. Even so, they need a cash reserve large enough to insure protection against the unexpected—the breakdown of a car, an opportunity to travel, clothing and sports equipment, food and pocket money if their parents are detained away from home, and so forth.

Certainly, no long-term savings or investment program should be undertaken until there are at least $1,000 in the young person's savings account.

Once this goal has been achieved, the asset builder might be wise to seek risk-free ways of increasing the return on his capital. Certificates of deposit, popularly called savings certificates, are worth consideration.

In 1973, federal authorities, aware that high interest rates were luring large sums of money out of savings accounts, gave permission to mutual savings institutions and commercial banks to set up entirely new certificate-of-deposit accounts. No governmental limitation was placed on the rates that banks might offer, provided that the investor leave on deposit a minimum of $1,000 for four years.

The federal law did, however, provide for a stiff penalty if savings were withdrawn from a certificate account before the date of maturity. For an inconstant saver, the higher interest rate would be reduced to the bank's regular passbook rate and, in addition, three months' interest would be forfeited.

In 1974, long-term investors with $1,000 or more to salt away could obtain in a number of banks across the nation certificates of deposit with a nominal 7.50 percent rate of interest and an effective annual yield of about 7.90 percent. A very few banks topped this offer with rates of 8.25 percent or even 8.50 percent.

However, the demand for borrowed money might lessen or the supply increase to a point where certificate accounts no

longer earn such generous rates of interest. Then asset build-
ers might well study the comparative risks and returns associated with the stocks and bonds that are sold on the open
market.

Property has its duties as well as its rights.

DISRAELI

CHAPTER 10

Persons
of
Property

Many teen-agers are persons of property. Either through
their savings of Christmas and birthday gifts or through
their own hard work, these young people have accumulated
more money in the bank than they need for a cash reserve
against unforeseen expenses. If they do not wish to put their
spare money into certificates of deposit, they are faced with
the challenge of risking their capital in the uncertain field of
investments.

There is a great deal to be learned about the various types
of securities that are available to people with money to invest.
While few securities are as safe as money in the bank—and
this is not safe from the ravages of inflation—money invested
in the bond market or stock market sometimes compensates
for the higher risk by a higher rate of return on the investment or the chance of a capital gain.

Parents who are knowledgeable about investing in securities should teach their teen-agers as much as possible about the skills required by the conservative investor. Many of today's children will join the thirty million Americans who have at least a couple of bonds or a few shares of stock in their names. Parents who are themselves neophytes in the field of securities investment may find the following information of assistance.

Bonds and the young investor

Bonds are evidence of debt—the IOUs of city, state, and federal governments and of corporations, large and small. They represent a promise on the part of the issuer to pay the holder a stated sum of money (usually $1,000 per bond) on a certain date and, until that date, to pay a fixed amount of interest semiannually.

Bonds may sell a little above or considerably below their face value—the amount stated on the front of the bond. Whether or not a bond is a sound investment depends on the financial responsibility of the issuing organization.

Bonds may be secured by a lien or mortgage on specific property or unsecured, backed only by the general credit of the issuer. Unsecured bonds are called *debentures*. All bonds issued by the United States government and most bonds issued by American states, towns, and cities are debenture bonds, called *general obligation bonds*. They are usually safe investments because they are backed by governmental power to raise taxes to meet debts. Bonds of unstable foreign nations, on the other hand, are in the category of risky investments.

Some bonds are registered in the name of the owner, who then receives his interest by checks sent through the mail. Most bonds, however, are in bearer form. Attached to bearer bonds are small coupons. As the coupons come due, the owner has to clip them one by one and offer them at his bank for redemption, taking care not to lose them in the process. Because bearer bonds do not show the owner's name, the bonds are easily stolen. For this reason, bearer bonds not only should be kept in a safe-deposit box, like all securities, but also must be handled with extreme care when removed from the box for coupon-clipping.

Bonds issued by the federal government

There are three general classes of bonds: *U.S. government bonds,* the obligations of the federal government; *municipal bonds,* the obligations of states, townships, cities, turnpikes, pollution-control authorities, and bridge, tunnel, and port authorities; and *corporate bonds,* the obligations of business firms.

Because of the absolute safety of principal, bonds of the U.S. government return a relatively low rate of interest. Series E savings bonds—long popular with gift-giving uncles and aunts—are usually bought in denominations of $25, for which the buyer pays $18.75, and $100, for which the buyer pays $75. The interest is the difference between the cost and the face value. The government can raise or lower the interest rate by lessening or increasing the number of months that the bond must be held before it reaches maturity.

E bonds are not a particularly good choice for today's young investors. The investment is no safer than cash in a savings account in any bank where accounts are insured up to $40,000 by the Federal Deposit Insurance Corporation or the Federal Savings and Loan Insurance Corporation. E bonds usually pay less interest than can be obtained from a savings bank.

If E bonds are cashed before they mature, the rate of interest is sharply curtailed. The interest on E bonds does not become available to the investor until the bonds come due; then it is taxable all at once. While this tax angle is of small importance to investors with only a few E bonds, those holding large numbers of bonds with the same maturity date will find that they owe considerably increased income taxes in the year the bonds come due.

Bonds free of federal tax

Municipal bonds are usually issued in units of $1,000 and $5,000. They vary in quality, depending on the financial standing of the community whose promissory notes they are.

Municipal bonds rated *A* or above by Standard & Poor's Corporation or Moody's Investment Service are virtually certain to return the borrowed money when due. Bonds rated *B* or below are not recommended for the average investor.

Although the rate of return on municipal bonds tends to be moderate, the interest is entirely exempt from federal income taxes. This feature makes "municipals" valuable to persons with high taxable incomes, as is shown in the table on page 164.

Young investors, whose taxable income is usually very low or nonexistent, would ordinarily have little interest in municipal bonds. However, in times of tight money and high interest rates, when bonds bearing low interest rates sell at discounts of as much as twenty-five to thirty points below face value, certain municipal bonds might be very good buys indeed.

Consider, for example, a Pennsylvania General State Authority 2.7 percent bond, due July 15, 1975, bought in mid-1970 for $715. Five years after date of purchase, the bond was paid off at its face value of $1,000, a generous capital gain of $285. In addition, tax-free interest for five years at $27 a year added $135, making a total profit of $420 on the investment.

That same $715 deposited in a savings bank at 6 percent interest, compounded daily, would earn in the course of five years only $220.95. This interest, moreover, would be subject to federal income tax.

The successful investor, as any teen-ager can begin to see, must be aware of business conditions, and time his purchases and sales accordingly. Had the bond cost more, the overall profit might have decreased to the point where money in the bank would have been the wiser choice.

The bonds of business firms

Some corporations issue bonds when they wish to raise capital. Buyers of these bonds become creditors of the company and annually receive the amount of interest specified on the bond. In years when business is bad, bondholders are likely to receive their semiannual interest even though profits

Effective Rates of Return on Tax-Exempt Bonds

Rate of Interest on Tax-Exempt Bond	Equivalent Rate of Interest on Taxable Bond at Various Income Brackets				
	$8,000-$12,000	$12,000-$16,000	$16,000-$20,000	$20,000-$24,000	$24,000-$28,000
4.00%	5.27%	5.52%	5.78%	6.17%	6.62%
4.25%	5.61%	5.86%	6.14%	6.56%	7.04%
4.50%	5.94%	6.21%	6.50%	6.94%	7.45%
4.75%	6.27%	6.55%	6.86%	7.33%	7.86%
5.00%	6.60%	6.90%	7.23%	7.72%	8.27%
5.25%	6.93%	7.24%	7.58%	8.10%	8.69%
5.50%	7.26%	7.59%	7.95%	8.49%	9.11%
5.75%	7.59%	7.93%	8.31%	8.87%	9.52%
6.00%	7.92%	8.27%	8.67%	9.26%	9.93%
6.25%	8.25%	8.62%	9.03%	9.64%	10.35%
6.50%	8.57%	8.96%	9.39%	10.03%	10.76%

are insufficient to pay dividends to the stockholders. For this reason, bonds of sound companies are considered a more conservative investment than stocks.

If business ever becomes so bad that there is not enough money even to pay the interest on the bonds, the bonds are in default. Bondholders then have the right to sell the assets of the company, if necessary, to recover their principal plus the interest owed.

Corporate bonds are usually issued for periods of twenty years or more. During this time, the value of the bond might rise slightly above the amount stated on the face of the bond, or fall considerably below it. If the price exceeds the face value, the bond is said to sell at a *premium*. If the price falls below the face value, it sells at a *discount*.

When interest rates rise, borrowing companies have to offer their new bonds at higher rates of interest in order to attract the investing public. Older bonds carrying lower rates of interest sink in price until their yield—the annual return per dollar invested—approaches or exceeds the return on the new bonds.

In 1970, for example, interest rates on new corporate bonds rose above 8 percent. That May, Jersey Central Power & Light's 6.125 percent debentures, due August 1, 1996, sold for $760 instead of $1,000. This gave the buyer slightly more than an 8 percent return on his investment, as anyone who divides 6.125 by 760 can see.

Discounted bonds of well-regarded corporations, as in the case of discounted municipal bonds, can be good securities to own. Besides a regular, assured income, the holder knows exactly how much profit he is going to make. For, when any high-quality bond reaches maturity, it is going to be paid off at face value. Anyone who bought that Jersey Central Power & Light debenture for $760 can count on getting $1,000 in 1996.

How is a buyer going to recognize quality in a bond that is only a name to him? Two leading financial services, Moody's and Standard & Poor's, rate corporate bonds on the basis of quality. Although no system of rating securities is perfect, inexperienced investors will do well to limit their purchases of corporate bonds to those designated *Aaa, Aa,* or *A* by Moody's Investors Service and *A1+, A1,* or *A* by Standard & Poor's. Almost all commercial banks, brokerage houses, and many libraries subscribe to these services and make them available without charge to prospective security buyers.

A slice of the pie

Whereas a corporate bond is evidence of a company's debt, a stock certificate is evidence that the holder owns a part of the company itself. Although the *book value* of each share of stock depends on the value of the assets of the company divided by the number of shares outstanding, the *market price* of the stock is determined by the earning power of the company plus the judgment of investors about its future prospects.

To help your child understand what a share of stock represents, tell him to imagine that the stock company is a huge pie filled with a mixture of real estate, buildings, machinery, managerial personnel, various kinds of workers, piles of raw materials, shelves of finished goods, and a corps of salesmen. Each sliver of the pie—that is, each share of stock—gives the stockholder a tiny part of the physical plant, the labor of the employees, the company's reputation, and the profit on the product. Explain that the pie may be cut into many slices or few. Each sliver may be worth a couple of dollars or several hundred, depending on the quality of the ingredients in the pie, or on the stockholders' opinion of the quality of the ingredients.

When a number of people want a slice of a particular pie, they bid up the price. If the ingredients are excellent and the mix is right, the slices will have real value, and the cost of each slice will tend to remain steady or to increase. If, on the other hand, the pie is of poor quality, people will soon find out and try to sell their slices. Only nobody will want to buy them at the current price. After the price has dropped enough to tempt some venturesome investor, the slice will sell. But, unless there is real value in the business and its products, the price of the shares will continue to decline until eventually they become worthless.

To have and to hold

Owning shares of stock is always more risky than owning money in a bank account or the bonds of a solvent municipality or corporation. The price of stock in even the most conservative company can fall alarmingly in a single day or month and continue its downward trend for years. In times of business recession, the general level of stock prices recedes like an ebbing tide. Then, a young investor may wonder, why do people buy "securities" that prove to be "insecurities"? Why buy stocks at all?

There are several answers to these questions. Some people buy stocks to diversify their investments—to put their nest eggs in several different baskets. Some buy stocks to "own a piece of the action"—to risk their capital in the hope of making a big profit in a short period of time. Most investors who buy stocks hope to shield their hard-earned dollars from the ravages of inflation.

We live in a time of rapid inflation. The buying power of the 1973 dollar was only 73 percent as much as that of the 1967 dollar. The dollar of 1980 may be worth much less than today's dollar.

Because of inflation, the dollars put into a savings bank are likely to have less buying power when they are withdrawn. While everyone needs a generous emergency fund, people of property try to balance this erosion of their capital by buying assets that may increase in value as the value of the dollar sinks.

What kind of property acts as a hedge against inflation? People very knowledgeable in the field of art may start a collection of the paintings of young artists who may be tomorrow's greats. Others invest in gold coins, well-selected antiques, or in real estate.

None of these forms of investment is recommended for teen-agers unless they have knowledge or connections of a very specialized sort and a great deal of capital as well. The risks of such specialized investments tend to be very high. The capital so invested does not produce a regular annual income; it is not liquid—not readily exchangeable for cash. The most suitable form of investment for youthful capitalists is conservative common stocks.

All that money for a piece of paper

Each stock purchase is represented by an eight-by-twelve-inch certificate ornately printed in red, blue, green, yellow, pink, or purple. On it appears the owner's name, the date of issuance of the certificate, the number of shares represented, the certificate number, the par value (a meaningless figure), and the name of the transfer agent.

So many shares of so many companies are now being traded every business day that the paper work has been getting out of hand. In the near future, computers may take over the task of making stock transfers; and investors will receive only punched computer cards to prove their ownership of stock.

Large or small, handsomely colored or drab and full of com-

puter punches, stock certificates are valuable and should be
stored in a safe-deposit box.

A small safe-deposit box, which costs only a few dollars a
year, is a necessity for the person who owns even a single
stock certificate or one much-discounted bond. The Internal
Revenue Service recognizes this fact by allowing the taxpayer
to deduct as a business expense the cost of a box used for
this purpose.

Of shoes and ships and sealing-wax

There is as much variation in the types and qualities of
stock companies as in the colors on the certificates they issue.
Some companies are giants; others, midgets. Some manufac-
ture and sell a single type of article; others are conglomerates
—groups of subsidiary companies making and distributing
things as diverse as the "shoes and ships and sealing-wax"
talked of by the Walrus in *Alice in Wonderland*.

Some stock companies are over a hundred years old; others
are so new that the ink is scarcely dry on their incorporation
papers. Some are destined to march in the forefront of American business; some will merely plod along; and others will
fall by the wayside. The hope of investors, young and old, is
to pick some of the winners and none of the losers.

The common stocks most likely to be safe are the so-called
blue chips. These are the shares of nationally-known companies with a long record of stable profits and dividend payments. Because they tend to hold a good part of their value
in times when business is poor, blue chips may give a somewhat conservative return on the money invested.

The annual rate of return on these staid stocks may not
vary too much from the rate of return on money placed in a
savings bank. However, as the years go by, the industrial
giants are likely to develop new products, win new markets,
and improve their ways of doing business. Although the
prices of blue-chip stocks rise and fall with changes in business conditions and international economic developments, the
long-term investor tends to average 9 percent on dividends
plus capital appreciation. As inflation has been eroding the
value of the dollar by about 6 to 9 percent a year, investors

who buy and keep high-grade stocks are likely to hold inflation at bay.

Shareholders who want their spare dollars to earn a regular income, to increase moderately over the years, and to be as safe as money can be in any stock find that blue chips bought at the right time can be very sound investments. Well-known companies such as du Pont, General Electric, General Motors, Sears Roebuck, and Texaco are readily traded. American Telephone and Telegraph Company, the most widely held blue chip of them all, has over three million stockholders. All of these companies have a long record of regular dividend payments.

Nevertheless, no one can be certain that any stock will hold or increase its value. Highly regarded but ill-managed companies have gone into bankruptcy even in the most prosperous of times. The Penn Central railroad is a case in point.

The business cycle

There are many factors that influence the prices of even the best-managed and most stable companies. International crises, government regulations, lengthy strikes by the employees, new inventions and discoveries, a shortage of parts or energy, or public fads may bring about a slump in the prices of the stocks of affected firms and industries. Also, despite the long-term rise in prices resulting from inflation, stock prices are subject to the ebb and flow of commercial activity that is called the business cycle.

Since the beginning of the industrial revolution nearly 200 years ago, periods of brisk business activity have been followed by periods of decline. For a number of years there are jobs for everyone, factories are whirring, rates of interest are high, the nation's supply of money is fully invested, homes and office buildings seem to mushroom overnight, and people spend freely.

Then the tide turns. Consumers, saddled with debts, become tight-fisted, decrease their spending, and increase their savings. Products begin to pile up in warehouses. Merchants, faced with shrinking demand for goods and services, lay off sales help and office workers, and offer their merchandise for sale at bargain prices. Factories slow down. A recession sets in.

As business declines, so do the prices of stocks. People, who were once so eager to invest, sell their holdings—often at a great loss—and put their remaining money into bonds, banks, and safe-deposit boxes. If the decline in business activity and the market is painfully sharp, the recession is called a depression. The Great Depression of the 1930s caused so many people to lose their businesses, their jobs, their money, and their mortgaged homes that it is remembered to this day as a national disaster.

After a few bad months or years, business revives. The wheels of factories begin to turn, money comes out of hiding, new skyscrapers rise in the cities, and new houses dot the hillsides in suburbia. Investors, large and small, clamor to buy stocks in bustling new businesses and drive up stock market prices. A new inflationary period has begun.

These wavelike rises and drops in business and the market occur in all industrialized countries. So far, attempts of bankers and government officials to curb them have met with little success.

Because the business cycle is an economic fact of modern life, the sensible investor tries to invest his money when a new wave of business activity is gathering for an upward surge. He avoids the market when the wave seems about to crest and break. No one can count on perfect timing, since no two business cycles are identical; but timing can do much to increase the stockholder's chance for substantial capital gains when he does have occasion to buy or sell securities.

While the stocks of conservative companies decline in times of business recession, the decline is usually less severe than that experienced by companies which are less financially sound. Many a blue-chip company proudly boasts that it has not missed a dividend payment for fifty or a hundred years. For this reason, shareholders in such companies tend to keep the stocks for a generation or more and pass them on to their children or grandchildren.

To mature investors who have a steady income and a backlog of conservative securities, and to young investors who have sufficient family backing to forego present income in the hope of larger future gain, growth stocks can be very appealing.

Growth stocks are those of younger companies which show promise of vigorous expansion over a period of years. Rapidly growing concerns, such as Xerox and International Business Machines (IBM) in the 1960s and Reading & Bates in the early 1970s, plow most—or all—of their earnings back into the business. The dividends are small. The market price of such companies tends to swing more widely than the prices of older, more conservative companies. The stocks "trade up" —rise in price—when the management makes money or when future prospects appear especially bright. The stocks "trade down"—fall in price—when the companies are beset by problems or when they lose the favor of a fickle public.

What goes up may come down

Stocks of companies that are just getting started or that operate on a shoestring are called *speculative stocks*. On rare occasions one of these enterprises will develop some marvelous new product and grow into a respected industrial giant. Fortunes were made by the early investors in companies that produced shredded wheat, zippers, and Polaroid cameras.

Although every inexperienced investor dreams of buying stocks at $2 a share and riding them up to $100 a share, the chances of this kind of market success are extremely slight. While a few insiders may illegally push up the price of some high-risk security and make a "killing" when the stock is unloaded on a profit-hungry public, such artificially inflated stock is likely to collapse as fast as a punctured balloon. Ordinary investors, who cannot afford to lose every penny they put into the stock market, should never take a chance on speculative stocks.

The bulls and the bears

Some teen-agers may have spotted charts on which tiny bulls gallop up one side of a stock market rise while little bears coast down the other side. The bulls represent people who trade on a rising market; the bears, those who trade when stock prices fall. Less colorful, but equally valuable charts appear in many daily newspapers. Radio and television newscasters also broadcast daily comments on stock prices. The stock market is given this news coverage because millions of Americans own at least a few shares of stock, and millions more know that their jobs and economic security depend on the state of American business. All feel that the behavior of the stock market gives some indication of the health of our economy.

Actually, there is no single stock market. Stocks are traded in several different marketplaces. Our oldest stock exchange began operations in George Washington's time. In 1792, a group of New York merchants decided to meet under an old buttonwood tree that grew on Wall Street to buy and sell stocks in their companies. As the nation spread westward, more companies were formed and more stocks were bought and sold. The New York Stock Exchange (NYSE) became a formal organization and moved indoors. Today, in a huge hall not far from the old buttonwood tree, hundreds of traders buy and sell securities for people who live in every state of the nation.

The NYSE sells only those securities listed on its "Big Board." Because the shares of companies listed on the Big Board are so widely traded, investors who wish to buy more stock or sell out their holdings can usually do so within minutes of placing an order with their home-town broker.

As trades are made on the New York Stock Exchange, teletype machines tick out the latest prices. These prices go to thousands of brokerage houses throughout the United States. Anyone who writes to the New York Stock Exchange, 11 Wall Street, New York, New York 10005, will receive a great deal of free and fascinating information about the terms used by traders and investors and the operation of the NYSE.

Other trading posts

The second largest trading post in this country is the American Exchange. The auction rooms of this exchange, which is also based in New York, handle both seasoned securities and stocks of new corporations unable to meet the requirements for listing on the Big Board.

Although most stock trading takes place in New York, there are several smaller exchanges scattered throughout the country. The most active are the Midwest Stock Exchange, located in Chicago; the Pacific Coast Stock Exchange, in Los Angeles and San Francisco; and the Philadelphia, Baltimore, Washington Exchange.

Stocks traded over-the-counter

The stocks of some 50,000 companies are traded by direct negotiation between the broker for the buyer and the broker for the seller. Many U.S. government bonds, all municipal bonds, and most corporate bonds are also sold across this nonexistent counter.

While many over-the-counter stocks are perfectly sound investments, many others are the speculative stocks of unseasoned companies. It is best, therefore, for inexperienced investors to confine their first purchases to issues listed on the Big Board.

The buyer and the broker

All buying and selling of stock must be done through a registered representative of a brokerage firm. The stockbroker can act in one of two ways: he can accept and execute orders, no matter what he thinks of his client's selection, or he can—if requested—seek to give his client advice based upon his experience.

The broker makes no charge for his advice; the client need not take it. But if a person intends to act upon it, he had better act quickly. Market movements are as restless as the sea. A purchase that might be advantageous today might be a misfortune a couple of weeks from now.

Jeanine Jackson at fifteen had what her father called "a very good head for business." So he decided to take her into town during her Christmas vacation and introduce her to his stockbroker.

She had already become a successful entrepreneur. The delightful stuffed animals she created were snapped up by her friends and sold for astonishing prices at the local handicraft shop, The Hobby Corner.

Mr. Jackson telephoned for an appointment with Mr. Haight, one of the partners of Haight and Smith from whom he had been buying securities for several years.

"Mr. Haight gives sound advice," Mr. Jackson said, "and it costs no more to deal with the best man in the firm. Although commission rates are no longer fixed by the Securities and Exchange Commission—the SEC—small buyers of securities, like you and me, pay about the same at every brokerage house in town. Just make sure the broker is knowledgeable and that his firm is a member of the New York Stock Exchange because the exchange polices its member firms."

"But, Dad," said Jeanine thoughtfully, "when I'm grown-up, I might live far away from you. If I didn't know any stockbrokers in my new city, how would I be able to pick a really good one?"

"That's a good question, and I think I can answer it. Before any stockbroker can give you meaningful advice, he needs to know a great deal about you and your business affairs: how old you are; whether there are people dependent on you for their living; the state of your health; the kind of person you are; how much you earn; what other assets you have, such as savings accounts or insurance; and what future assets you can pretty much count on, such as a trust fund or money from your grandmother's estate."

"An economic checkup, the way Dr. Kerr gives us our physical checkups?" said Jeanine with a smile.

"That's right. Before going to a new broker you need to jot down all these facts and make a list of any securities you may own, with date of purchase and cost price of each. Only by comparing cost with current price can anyone decide whether it is better to hold or sell a security.

"By the way, people who refuse to divulge all their assets, or who pretend to have more than they really have, hurt no one but themselves. You see, nobody can help you check up on your present portfolio or indicate what sort of new investments are best for you unless he has a clear picture of your economic condition."

"But you haven't said how I can tell whether a new broker's advice is likely to be good, even when I give him all this information."

"I was coming to that," said Mr. Jackson. "Once you are aware of what a broker needs to know to give sound advice, you should wait for his questions. Any advice he may give you is suspect unless he first asks you a great many personal questions.

"If he appears hurried or uninterested during your first visit, thank him for his time and leave. Although he may have recommended a very fine stock, it might not be right for you unless it fits in with your goals and your present holdings.

"Go to another firm, if necessary, and repeat this simple experiment. Eventually, you will find a stockbroker in whom you can have confidence. Even then, don't lean on him entirely. In the world of finance, unexpected price changes can be brought about by new government regulations, shifts in public opinion, changes in taxation, unexpected scientific discoveries and inventions, galloping inflation, sudden acts of foreign governments, and countless other factors."

"Perhaps I should say 'thank you' to any broker and go away to think over his advice even when he seems to be doing a good job," said Jeanine uncertainly. "Or perhaps I should argue with him to make sure he believes what he suggests."

"Absolutely not," said Mr. Jackson. "Accept or disregard a broker's advice, but never argue with his suggestions. It would be unethical for a broker to try to convince you to take any course of action against your will. If you spend several days thinking things over, don't be surprised if the stock that was a good buy when you were told about it has risen in price to the point where it is no longer a bargain. Do not be angry with your broker for not forcing you to buy 'at the market.' After all, you are the person who has to make the final decision about how to invest your dollars."

Keeping an eye on the market
"It's all very well to say that the final decision is mine," said Jeanine, "but how can I make up my mind quickly when I don't know the prices of stocks?"

"The prices of many stocks are reported in the larger newspapers throughout the country," Mr. Jackson replied. "They are listed alphabetically under the headings 'New York Stock Exchange,' 'American Stock Exchange,' and 'Over -the-Counter Quotations.'

"In addition to these daily reports on individual stock prices, some newspapers publish graphs showing the general trend of the market as a whole. The best-known of these graphs are based on the Dow-Jones averages and Standard & Poor's 500-stock index. Not long ago, the New York Stock Exchange brought out its own composite index of common stocks, and the American Exchange has its index, too. So, as you can see, anyone who wants to follow the fortunes of a particular stock or keep up with market trends can easily do so."

Mr. Jackson picked up the *New York Times* for Sunday, December 16, 1973. Turning to the business section, he located the "New York Stock Exchange's Composite Index" for the week ended December 14, 1973 (see page 177). Jeanine was amazed to discover how much stock prices had risen and fallen in the course of two years.

High, low, and closing

That evening, determined to learn to read the stock market reports of daily prices, Jeanine joined her father as soon as he sank into his easy chair. Picking up the Friday *New York Times* before her brother used it for kindling the fire, she found the financial pages, located the heading "New York Stock Exchange Transactions," and tried to make sense out of the long columns of figures that paraded down the page (see page 179).

"I can't make head or tail out of this, Dad," she said.

Her father looked up from the book he was reading. "It isn't hard once you get the hang of it. Let's study the headings together.

"The first two columns, '1973 High and Low,' give the year's high and low prices for each stock on the list. The third column, 'Stocks and Dividends in Dollars,' names the stock in an abbreviated form and states the expected yearly dividend without the dollar sign.

New York Stock Exchange

WEEK ENDED DEC. 14, 1973

New York Stock Exchange's Composite Index

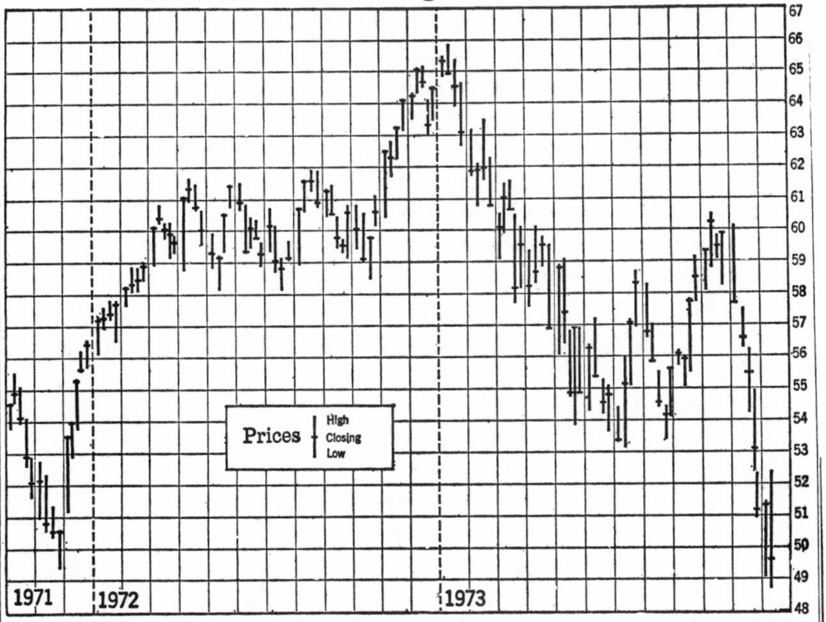

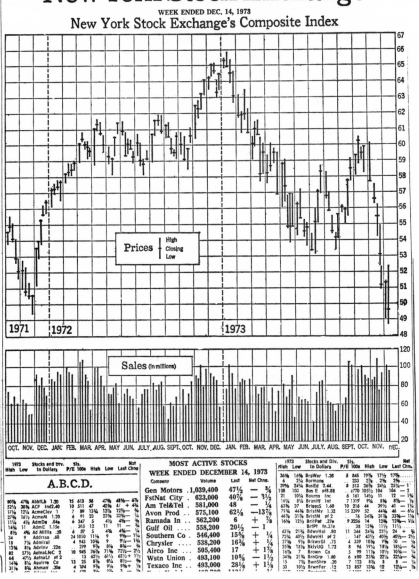

67
66
65
64
63
62
61
60
59
58
57
56
55
54
53
52
51
50
49
48
Prices
High
Closing
Low
1971
1972
1973

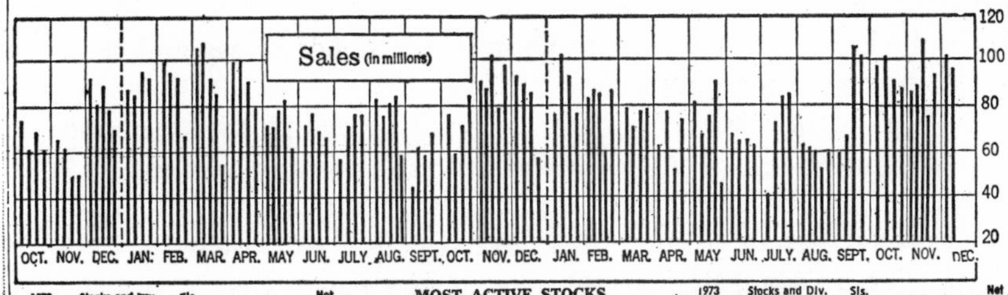

Sales (in millions)
120
100
80
60
40
20
OCT. NOV. DEC. JAN. FEB. MAR. APR. MAY JUN. JULY. AUG. SEPT. OCT. NOV. DEC. JAN. FEB. MAR. APR. MAY JUN. JULY. AUG. SEPT. OCT. NOV. DEC.

1973 High	1973 Low	Stocks and Div. in Dollars	P/E	Sls. 100s	High	Low	Last	Net Chng
		A.B.C.D.						
80⅞	47⅝	AbbtLb 1.20	15	613	56	47⅝	48⅜	— 6⅞
52½	38⅝	ACF Ind2.40	10	511	47	42¾	47	+ 4¾
17⅛	12¼	AcmeClev 1	7	89	13¾	12⅞	12⅞	— ⅝
27⅝	16½	AcmeM 1.20	6	91	23	22⅝	22¾	— ¼
11¼	4½	AdmDg .04e	6	347	5	4½	4⅝	— ⅜
14¾	11	AdmE 1.15e	..	315	12	11	11	— ¾
8½	4¾	Ad Millis .20	6	57	5	4¾	4¾	— ¼
34	9	Addrsso .60	24	1050	11⅛	9	9⅝	— 1¼
18	7¼	Admiral	4	943	10¾	9	9¼	— 1¾
13¾	8⅛	AdvInv .22d	..	299	9⅞	8⅛	8¾	— ¾
82	57½	AetnaLfeC 2	10	945	76⅞	71⅝	72½	— 2½
64	47½	AetnaLf pf 2	..	13	62½	61½	62½	+ 1½
14⅜	8¼	Aguirre Co	13	25	8⅞	8¼	8½	— ⅜
31⅛	8¾	Ahman .20e	4	194	9⅞	9⅛	9⅝	+ ⅛

MOST ACTIVE STOCKS

WEEK ENDED DECEMBER 14, 1973

Company	Volume	Last	Net Chng.
Gen Motors	1,039,400	47½	— ¾
FstNat City	623,000	40⅞	— 3½
Am Tel&Tel	581,000	48	— ¼
Avon Prod	575,100	62⅛	—13⅞
Ramada In	562,200	6	+ ⅞
Gulf Oil	558,200	20½	— 1
Southern Co	546,400	15⅝	+ ¼
Chrysler	538,200	16⅜	+ ¼
Airco Inc	505,400	17	+ 1⅞
Wstn Union	493,100	10⅝	— 1½
Texaco Inc	493,000	28⅛	+ 1⅛

1973 High	1973 Low	Stocks and Div. in Dollars	P/E	Sls. 100s	High	Low	Last	Net Chng.
36⅝	16⅝	BrgWar 1.35	5	845	19⅞	17½	17⅞	.....
6	2¼	Bormans	..	233	2⅞	2⅝	2⅝	.....
39⅝	24¼	BosEd 2.44	8	513	26⅞	24¼	25¼	— 1
118	103	Bos E pf8.88	..	z770	105½	104	104	— 2
21	10¼	Bourns Inc	6	161	14½	11	12	— 1¾
16¼	8¼	Braniff Int	7	1319	9¾	8⅜	8⅞	— ⅛
63⅝	37	BriggsS 1.60	10	216	44	39½	41	— 1¼
71¾	44⅜	BristMy 1.32	15	2399	52	44⅜	46	— 6¼
46⅞	31⅞	BristM pf 2	..	76	34⅞	31⅞	33⅜	— 1⅛
16⅛	12½	BritPet .37e	9	3236	14	12⅝	12⅝	— 1¼
.....	.....	BrtPt fn.37e	..	38	12⅝	11½	11½	.....
43⅛	21¾	BdwyHal .80	11	344	24¾	23½	24	+ ¾
72¾	40½	BdwyHl pf 2	..	147	43½	40½	40½	— 2½
27⅜	9⅛	BrkwyGl .75	4	339	10⅜	9⅝	10	— ⅛
25⅜	18⅛	BklyUG 1.72	8	96	19¼	18⅛	18¼	— ¾
16⅞	7	Brown Co	5	99	11⅛	10½	10¾	— ¼
34⅝	21¾	BrnGrp 1.60	6	x80	23¾	22¼	22¼	— ¾
15	7¾	BwnShrp .20	7	123	8¾	8	8	— ¼
33	10½	BrwnFer .12	13	857	13¾	12	12¼	— ⅞

© 1973 by The New York Times Company
Reprinted by permission

"The fourth column might be confusing. Under 'Sls,' meaning sales, you'll see 'P/E,' the symbol for the price-earnings ratio. If the price-earnings ratio is '10,' the stock is selling for only ten times this year's per-share earnings. If the price-earnings ratio is '25,' each share of stock sells for twenty-five times what it earned in a year. Some buyers choose only stocks with a low price-earnings ratio, and some investors give more weight to other considerations when selecting a stock.

"The '100s' indicate how many lots of 100 shares, called 'round lots,' were traded on this day. The columns headed 'High' and 'Low' give you the spread of prices for the day. The column headed 'Last' tells what the last buyer of the day paid for a 100-share lot just before the market closed. Odd lots—sales involving fewer than 100 shares—are not reported in the newspapers, but the buyer of an odd lot pays a fraction of a point more than the buyer of a round lot.

"The final column, 'Net Change,' compares the closing price of the day with the closing price of the preceding business day."

"All you'd ever want to know about stock prices and then some," said Jeanine.

"Now, how would you like to find General Motors common stock on the list and give me all the information about it?"

Jeanine hunted for a short time and then said, "I guess that's it—that 'GnMot 5.25e.' What does the 'e' mean?"

"There's a little box on one of the pages that gives the meaning of all the symbols used in the market reports. See, that 'e' means 'dividends declared or paid in the preceding twelve months.'"

"Oh," said Jeanine, "now I see how to read the line. To date in 1973, General Motors has sold as high as 84⅝ and as low as 44⅞. It paid dividends amounting to $5.25 a share. Its present price is only five times earnings, and 1,521 100-share lots were traded today. The highest price today was 49⅜ dollars a share; the lowest was 47⅛; and the last lot sold before closing went for 47⅜ a share. Finally, compared to the preceding trading day, the stock went down 1½ points, or $1.50 a share."

A Newspaper Report of Stocks Traded
On the New York Stock Exchange

THE NEW YORK TIMES, FRIDAY, DECEMBER 14, 1973

New York Stock Exchange Transactions

1973 High	Low	Stocks and Div. In Dollars	P/E	Sls. 100s	High	Low	Last	Net Chng

© by The New York Times Company
Reprinted by permission

Reading over-the-counter trading reports

Jeanine smiled at her father. "That was easy—almost."

Turning to another page, Mr. Jackson said, "Since you are such a smart girl, I'll show you something else. Over-the-counter stocks are reported in a different way, as you can see. Since these trades are essentially private transactions between two brokers, they report only the 'Bid,' the price at which someone is willing to buy the stock, the 'Asked,' the price asked by the seller, and the 'Bid Change,' the difference between the bid today and the bid on the preceding business day."

Jeanine looked hard at the over-the-counter stock quotations (see page 181). "I wonder which side gave in or whether the stocks were sold at all."

"That's something we shall never know," said her father.

Day of decision

On the first morning of Christmas vacation, Jeanine and her father arrived at Mr. Haight's office. They were seated beside his big desk. To open an account, he told her, she would have to give not only her name and address but also her Social Security number. This she promised to get from the nearest office of the Social Security Administration.

Then there was the matter of references. Mr. Haight explained: "No broker will buy stocks or bonds for a person whose financial standing is unknown or whose reputation for nonpayment of debts makes him a poor credit risk."

Fortunately for Jeanine, her father's standing with the firm was good enough to permit the opening of an account in her name.

"Now, Jeanine," said Mr. Haight solemnly, "once you have instructed a customer's representative to buy a security for your account and that order has been transmitted to any stock exchange or to another broker, you cannot change your mind and cancel the order. No matter how much you may regret your decision—no matter how much the stock may fall —you have to complete the purchase at the agreed-upon price.

"An oral contract is just as binding as a written one. If you should try to go back on your word, no brokerage house in

A Newspaper Listing of Stocks Traded Over-the-Counter

THE NEW YORK TIMES, FRIDAY, DECEMBER 14, 1973

Over-the-Counter Quotations

Most Active Stocks

Thursday, December 13, 1973

Day's Sales 6,459,300

Wednesday 6,889,500

Company	Volume	Bid	Asked	Net Chng.
Rank Organiz	322,200	7¼	7½	— 1¼
Penn Life	143,500	2½	2¾	— ⅛
Best Products	127,000	7⅞	8⅜	— 1⅜
Am Express	123,100	43¾	44¼	— 1⅞
Penn Offshore	102,700	8⅛	8⅜	+ ⅛
Oil Shale	71,000	7⅛	7⅜	— ⅜
Recognition Eq	56,600	2	2¼	— ⅜
First Mississippi	50,300	20	20½	— 1
Vaalreefs Exp A	49,400	31½	31⅞	+ 1
Data General	46,600	30½	31¼	— 1

A—B—C—D

	Sls in 100s	Bid	Asked	Bid Chg.
ACMAT Corp	94	3⅝	4⅛	— ½
AITS Inc	23	4⅜	4¾	— ¼
APS Inc .05e	10	10¾	11¾	—1¼
ASG Indust	5	3¾	4½	....
Abitibi Pap .12e	15	10½	11	— ½
Accelerator Inc	1	2	2⅜	....
Acushnet Co .52	3	12½	13½	....
Addisn Wesly .20	39	5⅛	5⅝	—1⅜
Adobe Bldg CnA	z40	3	3½	— ⅛
Advance Ross	13	3⅝	3⅞	— ⅛
Advanced Med Sc	7	7	7½	....
Advanced Mem	17	4	4¾	— ¼
Advancd Micr De	84	12	12½	— ½
Advent Corp	1	8	9	— ½
Ag Met Inc	31	11½	12¼	— ¾
Agnico Eagl Min	148	6⅞	7⅛	+ ¼
Aid Auto Strs	95	1¼	1⅝	— ¼
Ala Finl Grp .88	7	23	24	....
Albany Intl .56	22	23	23½	....
Alex & Alex .44a	88	19	19¾	— ¼
Alex Baldwin .60	27	11⅛	11⅝	— ⅝
Alico Ld Dv .10e	13	12	12¾	....
Alleghy Bev s	50	1½	1¾	....
Allergan Pharm	15	15¼	16¼	....
Allied Leisure	....	3¾	½	—⅛
Allied Teleph .28	3	15¾	16¼	+ ⅛
Alton Bx Bd .40r	z69	27	30	....
Amarex Inc	20	8⅞	9¼	+ ¼
Ambassadr Grp	....	4¼	5 ¼	....
Am Apprais .42e	15	4⅞	5⅜	....
Am Beef Packer	19	5⅜	5⅞	....
Am Bldgs .07e	1	7¼	8¼	....
Am Cnt Hm .05e	16	3⅛	3⅝	....
Am Express .52	1231	43¾	44¼	—1⅞
Am Exprs pf2.30	13	131	133	—5¾
Am Ex cv pf1.50	32	131	133	—5½
Am Filtrona .43	6	6⅜	6⅞	— ⅛
Am Finl Corp.04	118	12⅞	13¼	— ⅛
Am Furnit .28	14	5¼	5⅝	....
Am Greetgs.25	181	33¼	33	—1¼
Am La Frnc .07e	1	4⅝	5⅛	— ⅛
Am Marine Ltd	....	10	11	....
Am Micro Sys	285	16¾	17¼	— ½
Am Nuclear	26	3⅜	3¾	— ⅛
Am Quasr Petro	47	16¼	17	— ¼
Am Telecomm	23	9¼	9¾	+ ¼
Am Telev & Com	13	7½	8½	+ ¼
Am Weld M .80a	....	7½	8¼	....
Ammest Grp Inc	27	5⅛	5⅝	— ⅜
Analog Devices	16	7½	8	— ¼
Anaren Micrwve	12	1¼	1⅝	— ⅛
Andrsn Jacobs	39	1¾	2½	— ¼
Anheus Bush .60	465	35	35½	— ½
Anixter Bros	9	3¾	4	....
Anta Corp	30	2½	2⅝	....
Apexco Inc s	14	13	13¾	— ¾
Applebm Fd	2	2⅝	3⅛	....
Appld Dgtl Data	2	3	3⅜	....
Appld Material	36	7⅝	8⅛	— ⅜
Arden Mayfair	45	1⅜	1⅝	....
Argo Petroleum	123	14⅝	15⅛	+ ⅞
Ark Wstn Gs .78	49	13¾	14¼	....
Arlen Prop 1.74e	17	10	10¾	— ¼
Arpeja Cal .60	18	4	4⅜	....
Arrow Automtv	13	7½	9	....
Arrow Hart H 1	50	11½	12¼	— ½
Arts Way Mg .30	7	8½	9½	...
Arvida Corp	16	5⅝	6	....
Asso Cla Btl .27	10	12¼	13¼	— ¼
Assd Trk Ln .52a	5	9⅛	9⅝	....
Aspen Skiing Cp	z 1	8¼	9	....
Atlan GasLt 1.12	49	12⅛	12½	— ⅛

	Sls in 100s	Bid	Asked	Bid Chg.
Digicon Inc	10	5¼	6	....
Discn NY 4.90e	1	38½	40½	+ ½
Diversfd Earth s	5	2¼	3	....
Dixel Ind	1	3⅝	4	....
Docutel Corp	98	7⅛	7⅝	— ⅝
Dollar General	30	5⅛	5½	— ⅛
Domin Mtg 1.97e	6	14¼	15	— ¼
Donaldsn Inc .66	74	20¾	21¼	— ¼
Donbar Develop	9	3	3¾	— ¼
Donovan Cos .80	18	6½	7¼	....
Dorchester Gas	219	6½	6¾	....
Dow Jones 1	14	18½	19½	....
Dowdle Oil	37	9½	10	....
Doyle Dane B.96	29	8¼	9	— ¼
Duckwall Str .16	5	11	12	— ½
Ducommun Inc 1	3	11¼	12	...
Dunkin Donuts	47	1¾	2	....
Duriron Co .76	....	11¼	12	....
Durr Fill Md .12	2	5⅜	5⅞	....

E—F—G—H

	Sls in 100s	Bid	Asked	Bid Chg.
EDS Nuclear	3	13½	14½	...
Early Calif Ind	14	1⅝	1⅞	....
Earth Sciences	68	11	11½	+ ⅜
Eastmet Cp .60	60	14½	15½	— ½
Eatn Cp pf A2.30	2	29	30	— ¾
Econmic Lab .36	298	41	41½	— ¼
El Paso Elec .88	24	10⅞	11⅜	....
Elba Systems	28	2½	2⅞	....
Electro Nucleon	20	9⅝	10⅛	— ⅞
Elect PrAm .10e	20	7⅝	8⅛	..
Electron Array	70	4½	5	— ¼
Elizbet Wat 1.80	8	22¼	23¼	....
Ellis Bnkg .10r	15	12½	13	....
Elscint Ltd	39	3⅜	3⅞	— ⅝
Emersons Ltd	46	6⅝	7⅛	— ⅝
Energy Cnv Dev	30	6¾	7¼	— ¼
Energy Conv Un	6	8¼	9¼	— ¼
Energy Ventures	10	8	8¾	..
Envirodyne	3	5	6	— ¼

	Sls in 100s	Bid	Asked	Bid Chg.
Lane Co .52	2	15¾	16¾	....
Lawrys Fds .16	4	5	6	....
Lawson Prd .05h	41	21½	23	— ⅜
Lawter Chm .40	40	28	29½	— ⅜
Lazare Kaplan	....	8¾	9¾	....
Leader Nat .04a	....	10	11	....
Leadville Corp	12	5	6	....
Leeway Mot .32	12	10½	11½	— ¼
Legg Platt .28	15	10¾	11¼	+ ⅛
Leisr Lodges .23e	....	7⅞	8¼	...
Levingstn Ship	3	6½	7½	....
Lexitron Corp	6	6¾	7½	— ½
Liberty Homes	39	1⅜	1¾	...
Liberty Ntl 1.60b	2	32½	33½	....
Lil Champ Food	19	5⅝	6⅛	— ⅛
Limitd Strs .01e	3	11¾	12¾	....
Lin Broadcastg	66	3⅝	4	....
Linc Mtg In .82e	4	4	4½	....
Linc Pl Fd 1.12e	19	17¾	18¾	+ ¼
Lindberg Cp .60a	2	9¼	10	+ ¼
Lion Cntry Safri	5	1¼	1¾	....
Loctite Cp .07	236	38	38¾	— ⅛
Lone Str Br .80a	4	9¼	9¾	....
Longvw Fibre 6	....	120	125	....
LA Ld Off Ex B	141	7⅝	8	....
Lousv GE pf1.25	....	15¾	16¼	....
Louisv GE pf	....	24⅜	24⅞	....
Lowes Co .12	83	38½	40	....
Lynden Transp	7	7½	8½	....

M—N—O—P

	Sls in 100s	Bid	Asked	Bid Chg.
MB Assoc	32	1⅞	2¼	— ⅛
MCI Communct	194	3⅞	4⅛	+ ⅛
MLS Ind Inc	37	1⅞	2⅛	...
M&T Mtg 1.17e	2	7⅜	8⅜	...
MSI Data Corp	78	7½	8	— ⅛
Mac Dermid .52	1	10½	11½	....
Mack Strs .16e	6	4⅞	5⅜	+ ⅜
Mac Mill Bld 1a	9	30¼	31¼	—1½
Macrodata Cp	12	7¾	8¼	[illegible]

© by The New York Times Company
Reprinted by permission

your community would ever again do business with you."

"Does it work the other way, too?" asked Jeanine. "If the stock shoots up during the day on which it was bought, do I still pay the price it was the minute the trade was made?"

"Of course," replied Mr. Haight. "Moreover, we can execute an order either 'at the market,' meaning at whatever the price happens to be at the moment your order reaches the floor of the exchange, or at some limiting price named by you as the buyer. Putting a ceiling price on your order may save you a fraction of a point; or, in a rapidly rising market, it may cause you to lose the chance to buy the stock at all."

"What happens after the stock has been bought for my account?" asked Jeanine.

"Haight and Smith send you a notice—a confirmation slip —stating the exact number of shares bought, the exact price paid, the commission for our services, and the total amount that you owe the firm. You have five days from the date of purchase to pay the bill, unless you have previously deposited the full amount in your account with our firm.

"The transfer of title from the old owner to the new may take several weeks. Once we receive the certificate, we send it to you by registered mail. Then you should make a record of the transaction and put the certificate in your safe-deposit box. The company whose shares you own will send you your dividends four times a year."

Jeanine next asked, "What would I do if someday I wanted to sell my shares of stock?"

"You would bring the certificate into our office, sign it, and turn it over to us. Never sign a stock certificate in advance; that makes it as good as cash if it were lost or stolen. And never mail a signed stock certificate to your broker. If you cannot deliver it in person, send the certificate by certified mail. Then, in a separate envelope, mail a signed stock power —technically known as 'an assignment separate from certificate.' Once we receive both documents, our floor trader on the exchange will sell the shares. About five days later, our firm will credit your account with the proceeds, minus commission. You can then reinvest the money or ask to have a check for the amount sent to you.

"Now, have you any idea what stock you'd like to buy, young lady?"

"I think I'd like to own a few shares of General Motors, Mr. Haight. I plan to buy one of their new small cars in a year or two. Is this a good idea?" asked Jeanine.

"Not a bad choice," said Mr. Haight. "But just to verify our opinion, let's look at the December, 1973, stock report issued by Standard & Poor's. It will give a great deal of information about the company."

He obtained from his secretary a yellow sheet of paper covered with facts and figures (see pages 184-185).

"You can read the details at your leisure. The most important part is the recommendation that appears at the top of the page," he told Jeanine.

Jeanine saw that the report was favorable. "I have a little over $800 to invest. How many shares can I get for that?"

At a poke of Mr. Haight's finger, a small television-like screen sprang to life. "It's selling at 47½. Do you want to place an order at the market? You will get seventeen shares for your money."

Jeanine nodded. Mr. Haight filled out a form which his secretary carried to the trading department down the hall. Ten minutes later, the telephone rang.

Mr. Haight answered it and then turned to Jeanine. "Your stock has been bought at 48. You'll get a confirmation in a couple of days. You can deposit your money with us now or send us a check next week."

Jeanine decided to write the check for deposit in her brokerage account. Mr. Jackson, who had been sitting quietly during the transaction, smiled and said, "That about wraps it up. May I take my broker and my new stockholder to lunch?"

"No, indeed," replied Mr. Haight cheerfully. "On this memorable occasion, both my good clients shall have lunch as guests of the firm."

Nice work if you can get it

Two days later, the mailman delivered the promised confirmation. Jeanine's mother told her, "Confirmation slips must be kept indefinitely for income tax purposes. When that

A Stock Report Prepared by
Standard & Poor's Corporation

GM[1]

General Motors

978

Stock —	Price Dec. 13'73	Dividend	Yield
COMMON	47⅜	2__	2__
$5 PREFERRED.....................	70¼	$5.00	7.1%
$3.75 PREFERRED	52¼	3.75	7.2

RECOMMENDATION: This giant company normally accounts for slightly more than half of all the automobiles assembled in the U. S. Except in strike-distorted 1970, earnings have exceeded $5.50 a share in every year for more than a decade. Finances are strong, and a generous portion of profits is paid out as dividends. Although the gasoline shortage is an important negative consideration, the COMMON merits retention in investment portfolios for ultimate recovery. The PREFERREDS are high-grade income issues.

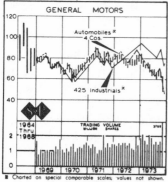

GENERAL MOTORS

Automobiles ˣ 4 Cos.

425 Industrials ˣ

1964 Thru 1968

TRADING VOLUME MILLION SHARES

■ Charted on special comparable scales; values not shown.

SALES (Million $)

Quarter:	1973	1972	1971	1970	1969
March	9,569	7,780	7,780	5,579	6,503
June.......	9,606	8,457	7,592	6,624	6,624
Sept.	7,608	5,378	5,624	3,592	5,031
Dec.		8,820	7,268	2,957	6,137

Sales for the nine months ended September 30, 1973 rose 24% from those in the same period of 1972 on an 18% gain in worldwide factory sales of cars and trucks. Deliveries were up 21% in the U. S., 29% in Canada, and 6% in other foreign countries. Dollar sales benefited from greater demand for optional equipment and somewhat higher average selling prices. In spite of the record unit volume and continuing gains in efficiency, margins were penalized by higher wage, materials, and other operating costs that were not nearly offset by price increases of December, 1972 and September, 1973. Pretax profits also advanced 24%. After taxes at 48.4%, against 49.2%, net income increased 26% to $6.54 a share, from $5.19.

[3]COMMON SHARE EARNINGS ($)

Quarter:	1973	1972	1971	1970	1969
March	2.84	2.26	2.12	1.21	1.82
June........	2.78	2.52	1.97	1.64	1.56
Sept.	0.92	0.41	0.75	d0.28	0.79
Dec.		2.32	1.88	d0.48	1.78

PROSPECTS

Near Term—Sales for 1973 are estimated in the vicinity of $36 billion, up from the peak $30.4 billion of 1972. Although December production schedules were cut by 79,000 cars to balance inventories, profits for 1973 should be reported at about $8.50 a share, well above 1972's record $7.51.

Sales for 1974 probably will decline from those of 1973. Demand for new cars could be some 10% or more below 1973's peak level, with the gasoline shortage a key contributing factor. The trend toward smaller-sized cars also will penalize dollar sales. Truck output may recede somewhat. Subject to sufficient availability of petroleum, foreign prospects appear favorable.

Rising operating costs and probable reduced U. S. automobile assemblies indicate lower profits for 1974, although December Cost of Living Council permission to raise 1974-model wholesale car and truck prices an average of $150 is beneficial. Including a $2.35 year-end payment and a $0.35 special dividend in June, dividends for 1973 totaled $5.25 a share. Payments for 1974 are unlikely to match those of 1973.

Long Term—Allowing for interim fluctuations, an outstanding trade position points to some long-range growth, assuming satisfactory gasoline supplies and prices.

RECENT DEVELOPMENTS

A three-year national pact with the UAW union was ratified in December; local plant agreements must be consummated.

GM plans to offer the Wankel rotary engine as an extra-cost option on its sub-compact Vega late in 1974, and is doing development work on the stratified charge engine.

DIVIDEND DATA

Payments in the past 12 months were:

Amt. of Divd. $	Date Decl.	Ex-divd. Date	Stock of Record	Payment Date
0.85...	Feb. 5	Feb. 8	Feb. 15	Mar.10'73
0.85...	May 7	May 11	May 17	Jun. 9'73
0.35Spl.	May 7	May 11	May 17	Jun. 9'73
0.85...	Aug. 6	Aug. 10	Aug. 16	Sep. 10'73
2.35Y-E	Nov. 5	Nov. 9	Nov. 15	Dec. 10'73

[1]Listed N.Y.S.E.; com. & $5 pfd. also listed Midwest, PBW & Pacific S.Es.; com. also listed Detroit S.E. & traded Boston & Cincinnati S.Es. [2]See text. [3]Based on avge. shs. d Deficit.

STANDARD N.Y.S.E. STOCK REPORTS   **STANDARD & POOR'S CORP.**
Reproduction in whole or in part without written permission is strictly prohibited. All rights reserved.
Published at Ephrata, Pa. Editorial & Executive Offices, 345 Hudson St., New York, N.Y. 10014

Vol. 40, No. 242   Wednesday, December 19, 1973   Sec. 9

Published by permission of Standard & Poor's Corporation

Reverse Side of a Stock Report

978 **GENERAL MOTORS CORPORATION**

[1]INCOME STATISTICS (Million $) AND PER SHARE ($) DATA

Year Ended Dec. 31	Net Sales	[3]% Op. Inc. of Sales	[3]Oper Inc.	Depr. Amort. & Obsol.	Net bef. Taxes	[4]Net Income	Common Share ($) Data: [4]Earns.	*Funds Generated	Divs. Paid	Price Range	Price-Earns. Ratios HI LO
1973--	-----	---	----	----	----	----	---	----	5.25	84⅝-44⅞	-----
1972--	30,435	16.3	4,960	912.4	4,223	2,163	7.51	10.36	4.45	84¾-71¼	11- 9
1971--	28,264	16.0	4,529	873.1	3,720	1,936	6.72	9.20	3.40	91⅛-73⅜	14-11
1970--	18,752	7.9	1,488	821.5	794	609	2.09	4.82	3.40	81⅜-59½	39-28
1969--	24,295	16.7	4,067	765.8	3,454	1,711	5.95	8.49	4.30	83⅜-65½	14-11
1968--	22,755	18.1	4,124	729.1	3,525	1,732	6.02	8.57	4.30	89⅞-72⅝	15-12
1967--	20,026	18.0	3,613	712.6	3,013	1,627	5.66	8.19	3.80	89⅜-67½	16-12
1966--	20,209	18.7	3,770	654.1	3,271	1,793	6.24	8.64	4.55	108¼-65⅝	17-11
1965--	20,734	21.6	4,483	556.7	4,092	2,126	7.41	9.47	5.25	113¾-91¼	15-12
1964--	16,997	21.3	3,615	494.8	3,284	1,735	6.05	7.88	4.45	102⅝-77¼	17-13
1963--	16,495	22.4	3,699	475.2	3,354	1,592	5.56	7.37	4.00	91⅜-57⅞	16-10

[1]PERTINENT BALANCE SHEET STATISTICS (Million $)

Dec. 31	Gross Prop.	[2]Capital Expend.	[5]Cash Items	Inventories	Receivables	Current Assets	Current [5]Liabs.	Net Workg. Cap.	Cur. Ratio Assets to Liabs.	Long *Term Debt	($) Book Val. Com. Sh.
1972--	15,469	940.0	2,946.9	4,200.2	2,806.2	10,538.5	4,973.7	5,564.8	2.1-1	790.88	39.85
1971--	14,939	1,013.0	3,342.1	3,991.6	2,724.2	10,536.7	6,006.3	4,530.4	1.8-1	615.62	36.70
1970--	14,528	1,134.2	394.1	4,115.1	1,725.7	6,491.9	3,224.4	3,267.6	2.0-1	281.22	33.39
1969--	13,211	1,043.8	1,824.4	3,760.5	2,112.7	7,697.6	3,345.6	4,352.0	2.3-1	316.99	34.64
1968--	12,422	860.2	1,898.2	3,423.3	2,013.9	7,335.4	3,105.2	4,230.3	2.4-1	284.28	32.96
1967--	11,761	912.6	1,802.5	3,210.4	1,833.6	6,846.5	2,840.1	4,006.4	2.4-1	344.83	31.17
1966--	11,012	1,188.1	1,951.0	3,103.3	1,657.5	6,711.8	3,105.8	3,606.0	2.2-1	287.46	29.27
1965--	9,982	1,322.0	1,387.2	2,986.5	1,538.7	5,912.5	2,227.6	3,684.9	2.7-1	231.66	27.47
1964--	8,865	929.6	1,390.5	2,677.8	1,387.2	5,455.5	1,804.5	3,651.0	3.0-1	231.98	25.22
1963--	7,967	647.2	1,890.7	2,221.2	1,250.6	5,362.6	1,635.2	3,727.4	3.3-1	260.46	23.53

[1]Consol. incl. all subs. engaged in mfg. or wholesale marketing opers.; does not incl. G.M. Acceptance Corp. & Yellow Mfg. Acceptance or their subs. · [2]Excl. additions for spec. tools. [3]Bef. depr., but aft. amort. of special tools & employee bonus. [4]Based on avge. shs. outstanding. [5]Aft. deducting gov't. sec. held for payment of taxes prior to 1966. [6]Note: During 1970 operations were affected by a 9 week strike.

*As computed by Standard & Poor's.

Fundamental Position

General Motors in 1972 derived 92.2% of U. S. sales from automotive products (including cars, trucks, buses, parts, and accessories), 6.6% from non-automotive products (including Frigidaire appliances, diesel and aircraft engines, locomotives, and earth-moving equipment), and 1.2% from defense and space work.

Chevrolet (including the Chevelle, Camaro, Nova, Monte Carlo, Corvette, and Vega), Buick (including the Century and Riviera), Cadillac (including the Eldorado), Oldsmobile (including the Cutlass and Toronado), and Pontiac (including the LeMans, Firebird, Grand Prix, and Ventura) accounted for 44.4% of total new U. S. registrations (including foreign-built cars) in 1972, compared with 45.2% in 1971 and with a strike-depressed 39.7% in 1970. Comparable figures for Chevrolet and GMC trucks are 39.1%, 39.7%, and 38.2%. General Motors has about 12,050 U. S. car dealers. Worldwide factory sales of cars and trucks in 1972 were 7,791,000 units, compared with 7,779,000 in 1971 and 5,308,000 in strike-depressed 1970. Domestic factory sales were 5,740,000, 5,767,000, and 3,591,000, respectively.

The company operates as a decentralized organization, with about 112 plants in 18 states, seven plants in Canada, and assembly, manufacturing, and warehousing operations in 24 other countries. In 1972 operations in the U. S. accounted for about 88% of worldwide profits before income taxes, equity income, and certain other items of a general corporate nature, those in Canada for 4%, and those elsewhere for 8% of the total Investments in non-consolidated subsidiaries, principally General Motors Acceptance Corp., totaled $1.142 billion at the end of 1972. GMAC earned $96.4 million in 1972, up from $88.8 million in 1971.

Dividends, paid since 1917, averaged 70% of available earnings in the five years through 1972. Employees (worldwide); 807,-882. Shareholders (common and preferred): 1,285,000.

Finances

Worldwide capital expenditures for 1974 may exceed $1.3 billion, of which about $1 billion would be spent in the U. S. and $300 million in Canada and other foreign countries. Worldwide outlays approximated $1.1 billion in 1973 and $940 million in 1972.

CAPITALIZATION

LONG TERM DEBT: $782,911,941, principally foreign subsidiary debt.

$5 CUM. PREFERRED STOCK: 1,835,644 shares (no par); redeemable at $120.

$3.75 CUM. PFD. STOCK: 1,000,000 shs. (no par); redeemable at $100.

COMMON STOCK: 285,989,305 shs. ($1 2/3 par).

Incorporated in Del. in 1916. **Office**—3044 W. Grand Blvd., Detroit, Mich. 48202. **Chairman & Chief Exec Officer**—R. C. Gerstenberg. **Pres**—E. N. Cole. **Secy**—C. Thomas. **Treas**—F. A. Smith. **Dirs**—R. C. Gerstenberg (Chrmn), S. D. Bechtel, Jr., E. N. Beesely, H. Branch, Jr., C. B. Cleary, E. N. Cole, J. T. Connor, F. G. Donner, E. M. Estes, W. A. Fallon, C. T. Fisher, III, H. Heltzer, J. R. Killian, Jr., O. A. Lundin, J. A. Mayer, W. E. McLaughlin, H. J. Morgens, T. A. Murphy, T. L. Perkins, J. M. Roche, G. Russell, G. A. Sivage, L. H. Sullivan, R. L. Terrell, C. Townes, H. G. Warner. **Transfer Offices**—Company's Office, 767 Fifth Ave., NYC; Wilmington Trust Co., Wilmington, Del.; Continental Illinois National Bank & Trust Co., Chicago; National Bank of Detroit; Bank of America, San Francisco; (Pfd.) National Bank of Detroit. **Registrars**—Chase Manhattan Bank, NYC; Bank of Delaware, Wilmington; Northern Trust Co., Chicago; Wells Fargo Bank, San Francisco; (Pfd.) Detroit Bank & Trust Co., Detroit.

Information has been obtained from sources believed to be reliable, but its accuracy and completeness, and that of the opinions based thereon, are not guaranteed. Printed in U S A

security is sold, you'll have to pay tax on the capital gains—
the difference between the cost and selling price. Of course,
the stock may fall in price. Then you are allowed to deduct
your losses to some extent."

"Let's staple the confirmation to the stock certificate when
it arrives and put both in the safe-deposit box. Then I'll always know where it is," said Jeanine.

"Not a bad idea," said Mrs. Jackson, "since you won't be
doing much trading. Still, it's time you had a letter-file box in
which to keep your savings account book, your statements
from the brokerage firm, and your own stock records."

"Do you mean I have to keep records, the way you do?"
asked Jeanine in dismay.

"I mean just that, my dear," said Mrs. Jackson. "As Disraeli said many years ago, 'Property has its duties as well as
its rights.' I'd put it more simply: keeping records of the
securities you own is nice work if you can get it.

"Well-kept stock and bond records are very informative.
You can see at a glance how much of each company you own,
when you bought the shares, and how much you paid for
them. By jotting down the income as it is received, you can
tell just how much the holding earned in each year. And if
you look in the newspaper two or three times a year, you can
keep a running record of the current value of your shares. In
fact, it would be impossible to be an informed investor without such records.

"Some people—and I am one of them—keep their stock
records on five-by-seven-inch cards held together with a large
elastic band or kept in a metal file box. Others prefer a loose-
leaf notebook. In either case, you need five manila dividers
marked 'Bonds,' 'Stocks,' 'Securities Sold,' 'Prepared Sheets,'
and 'Blanks.'

"I think I'll get you a notebook that will fit inside your
letter-file box. It will hold all your security records for years."

"I've got a spare notebook," said Jeanine. "But what do I
put on the sheet?"

"Let me show you a card covering the transactions on one
of your father's securities. He sold his Sears Roebuck stock
last week to take a year-end tax loss, and I've just completed

the record. See, he bought the Sears stock at two different times. It's a fine company, but because of the recent drop in stock prices, the shares are worth less today than when he bought them. By subtracting the sale price from the cost, the record shows just how much capital loss there was." Mrs. Jackson pointed to a card (see page 188).

"On the reverse side of the card, I had entered the certificate numbers so that if ever the stock certificates were mislaid, the company could look up the record of your father's ownership. On the right side, I listed the dividends as they were paid. Over on the left, I made occasional notations of current prices and the cash value of the holding. If a company is sound, it is not necessary to follow its ups and downs on a weekly or monthly basis.

"If you keep your stock records on the pages of a loose-leaf notebook, the sheet would look something like this," said Mrs. Jackson, taking the confirmation slip to her typewriter (see page 189).

"Thanks, Mom," said Jeanine, studying the completed record sheet. "Even keeping records isn't as hard as it sounds."

Tomorrow's persons of property

Students and young married couples who have no surplus money to invest at the moment often wish to prepare themselves for the day when they can invest in the stock market. There are several worthwhile things that they can do.

Every would-be investor needs a working knowledge of economics. If no course is available, a variety of economics textbooks can be found in school or public libraries.

Continuing reports on business developments are to be found in daily newspapers. To gain some perspective on the news, a business-oriented person should also subscribe to at least one weekly news magazine.

Tomorrow's investors can do more than study economics and keep up with the trends in business and the stock market. They can pretend to own stock in several well-chosen companies and follow the fortunes of "their" stocks as carefully as if the holdings were real instead of imaginary.

They should record the dates and buying prices of their

Front View of a Security Record Card

Shrs. Bt.	Bt. Date of Settlement	Per Sh. Cost	Gross Cost	Shrs. Sold	Sold Date of Settlement	Per Sh. Sale Pr.	Net Am't Received
25	2/ 4/'72	100⅛	2550.55	50	12/14/73	83¼	4104.14
25	5/ 9/'72	109⅛	2778.99				
50	Av. per Sh.	105	5329.54				

Sears Roebuck & Company

Listed on: Big Board

Cost 5329.54   Sale
Sale 4104.14   Cost _____
Loss - 1225.40   Gain +

Fill in left side at time of purchase. Make additions as needed. Complete right side after security has been sold. Retain completed card for reporting capital gains or losses on federal income tax return.

Reverse Side of a Security Record Card

Certificate # Ni-40384 (25 Sh.) and Ni-395365 (25 Sh.)

Dates Checked	Per Share Values	Cash Values	Dividends Paid .	Dividends Paid .	Dividends Paid
7/ 7/'72	109	5450.	April '72 8.75		
10/ 1/'72	109⅛	5500.	July '72 17.50		
4/ 9/'73	102	5100.	Oct. '72 17.50		
11/13/'73	89⅛	4500.	Total 43.75		
12/ 6/'73	83¼	4175.	Jan. '73 28.00		
			April '73 17.50		
			July '73 17.50		
			Oct. '73 17.50		
			Total 83.00		

Note certificate number for identification in case of loss. Record current value of holding two or three times a year. The broken line indicates that the number of shares held has been increased either by stock dividends or additional stock purchases.

Stock Record Page From Loose-Leaf Notebook

Description: 17 Sh. General Motors, Common
Date of Purchase;   Dec. 17, 1973
Date of Settlement: Dec. 24, 1973

Per Share Cost: 48
Gross Cost
  Including
    Commission $838.67
    $22.67:
Certificate #   K610 - 981

Number Shares Sold:
Date of Sale:
Date of Settlement:
Per Share Sale Price:
Net Sale Price
  Minus
  Commission:

Summary: Capital Loss   or Capital Gain
             Cost   Sale
             Sale   Price
              Price _____   Cost _____
             Loss -   Gain +

Dates Checked	Per Share Values	Cash Values	Dividends Paid

mythical purchases on stock record sheets or cards, make notations of the current price of their make-believe holdings, and concern themselves about the health of the industries to which their pretend companies belong. When they "sell" their imaginary holdings at a profit or a loss, they can figure out the capital gain or loss and "reinvest" the proceeds in some other company.

An even better introduction to security management is available to young people who can afford to invest a little money in a few shares of one or two growth stocks. It is true that a relatively high brokerage fee is charged for odd-lot purchases and that some stockbrokers do not want to be bothered with small transactions that cost the firm more than is earned by the commission. Still, many stockbrokers take a kindly interest in youthful investors who do not take up too much of their time.

As the owner of even one share of stock, the fledgling investor will receive the company's quarterly and annual reports. These statements and colorful brochures give valuable information about the work of the company, its future plans, and the state of its financial health. Any serious investor would do well to study these financial reports. The most important line to look for is the line comparing net earnings for two or more years. If, despite taxes and other costs, the net earnings continue to rise, the firm is probably sound. The dividends may be pleasing to note, but dividends offer little proof of the financial condition of the company. Many an incompetent board of directors has masked its inefficiency by declaring dividends that were paid out of working capital, not profits.

Every stockholder has the right to attend the annual stockholders' meeting. It is instructive to see the company officials in person and to question them about the company's affairs. After all, the quality of leadership has much to do with the success or failure of a business enterprise.

The competent investor

As any young person can see, intelligent investing demands an understanding of the nature of stocks and bonds, of the causes underlying fluctuations in stock prices, of quality, timing, and diversity of holdings, and of personal goals and expectations.

If the individual is unwilling to study economics and to follow the fortunes of business in general and his companies in particular, he is ill-equipped to defend his stock-invested dollars. For such a person, a well-stuffed bankbook, savings certificates, or a clutch of conservative bonds are less risky than the stock market.

If, on the other hand, a young person's imagination is fired by being a part of the business world, if he learns to take calculated risks to reap reasonable profits, and if he is willing to make efforts toward keeping his dollars at work, he is well on the way to becoming a competent investor.

*Whatever is worth doing at all is
worth doing well.*

CHESTERFIELD

CHAPTER 11

Cars
and
Common
Sense

To most Americans, an automobile is the prime status symbol. Nearly every sixteen-year-old dreams of owning a set of wheels; and when this dream comes true, most young car owners lavish love and wax on their vehicles.

Because car ownership—or the privilege of being the principal operator of a car—means so much to teen-agers, the business of financing, choosing, and maintaining an automobile gives parents a superb, perhaps the ultimate, opportunity to teach economic principles and shopping skills. Therefore, wise parents who can afford to give their sons or daughters a car, give them instead the experience of buying a car with parental help and guidance.

Wheeled vehicles started out as a helpful form of transportation. That is basically what they are today. Millions of dollars are spent each year on accessories, on newer cars when older cars still function, on costly finance charges, all because people let their emotions get tangled up with the economics of car buying. In thinking about a car, put first things first.

Safety is the most important feature to look for when considering a car. The vehicle must be sound, not the restored victim of a crash that might have weakened its frame. The car must have good brakes and tires. The wiring and rubber tubing must be in good condition. And in these days of fuel shortages, it must economize on gas.

The driver must also be sound. Knowing how to operate a motor vehicle is not enough. It is important to learn to drive defensively at all times, to master the local laws and the unwritten laws of the road, to know what to do in snow, on icy roads, in a downpour, at dusk, along expressways, on lonely roads at night. For this, a professional driver-training course is invaluable.

Parents or other family members can, of course, teach teenagers to drive safely; still, it is a rare parent who can do so without some anger, irritation, or criticism. And in the years when a youngster is seeking independence and identity, even the mildest criticism from parents or siblings is an affront to the ego. Moreover, a safe-driver certificate from a recognized driver-training school reduces the cost of insuring the young driver by about 10 percent.

Anger, fatigue, alcohol, or drugs have no place behind the wheel of a car. Cool judgment is required every inch of every mile that a car moves. Speeding, racing, tailgating, one-arm driving, running far below traffic speed, failing to use turn signals—these are just a few of the faulty judgments that lead to disastrous accidents. An accident may injure or kill the driver, his passengers, innocent motorists, or pedestrians. It may damage or destroy the vehicle. It may also wreak havoc on the economic and emotional life of the driver's family.

Planning the big purchase

After developing driving skills and a sense of responsibility, the future car owner—with the help of his family—should do some financial spadework. What kind of car can be bought with the money available? If part of the purchase price is to be financed, how big a monthly payment can be comfortably met? Where is the best place to go to get a low-cost car loan?

The very best way to purchase a car—or any other expensive article—is to save first and then buy for cash. Buying an automobile with borrowed money adds several hundred dollars to the price of the vehicle. As readers may recall from studying the table on page 103, the cost of installment credit on a loan of $1,000 at 14 percent add-on interest, would be $140 if the loan were repaid in one year, $280 if the loan were repaid in two years, and $420 if the borrower took three years to pay off his debt.

If the car were over two years old, the interest rate might rise to 20 percent or more. Installment credit on a $1,000 loan at 20 percent would cost the borrower $200 if he repaid the loan in one year, $400 if he repaid it in two years, and $600 if he stretched out his payments over a three-year period.

Since every car buyer has to collect and hand over the entire cost price of the vehicle sooner or later, he can save hundreds of dollars if he defers his purchase until he has the money in the bank. Instead of paying out—wasting—hard-earned dollars on interest charges, the person who saves, then buys, receives interest on his savings while he is accumulating the necessary cash. Planning and patience are among the best dollar-stretchers anyone can have.

Buying a car on time

For people who have been unable or unwilling to save the purchase price of a car, borrowing is necessary. Borrowing money on favorable terms is a complicated business. It is wise to handle the financing of an automobile as a separate transaction from the negotiations about trade-in values, repairs, and accessories that are part of buying the car itself.

Smart buyers shop for credit before they even visit showrooms or car lots. If the buyer is a teen-ager without a regular job, credit is seldom available to him unless his parent or guardian cosigns the note. But while a first car may have to be financed with the help of a benign parent, or deferred until the money has been saved in full, nobody remains a teen-ager for long. Parents who must lend a hand with financing that never-to-be-forgotten first car, can nevertheless teach their sons or daughters the right way to set about financing an automobile, so that later, when they are self-supporting, they can finance a car without making a costly mistake.

The most economical way to finance a car, if finance one must, is to arrange a personal loan at a credit union or commercial bank. At a preliminary visit to the banker, the borrower fills out an application for credit, giving the model, year, and price of the desired vehicle. After a credit check has been made, the banker will notify the applicant whether he and his future car qualify for a loan, and how much he may borrow.

Banks and other lending institutions insist that the borrower have cash in hand—or cash plus trade-in value of an older car—equal to one-third of the cost of a new or slightly used car. Conservative car buyers pay down a larger proportion than this. They finance no more than 50 percent of the total cost and plan to clear up the debt within two years.

The older the car, the less generous are the terms of the loan. Banks rarely finance old cars; finance companies charge high interest rates and seldom allow more than eighteen months to pay off the balance. Very old cars are financed, if at all, at extremely high rates of interest, and payments may be demanded on a weekly rather than a monthly basis.

Remember that "the fastest loan on wheels" is the most expensive loan. Any lender who fails to study the borrower's financial situation and reputation for meeting his debts makes up for inevitable losses by charging all borrowers exorbitant rates. It is better not to buy a car at all than to be saddled with interest that runs two or three times the total amount of the loan.

Even when a young person has a steady job and the prospect of a substantial monthly income, and even when rates of interest are moderate, installment payments may prove extremely difficult to meet.

Dusty was a young engineer with a salary of $12,000 a year. He was unmarried, lived at home, and gave his parents a modest $100 a month for room, board, and laundry. When he asked to borrow $2,500 towards the cost of a Mercedes, his parents hesitated. His old car was handsome and in excellent shape; the new Mercedes was a luxury that had no justification. But the workmanship—the wonderful precision—made this car a jewel beyond price in Dusty's estimation.

At length his parents gave in. Cars were Dusty's weakness. He spent his waking hours adding accessories to the Mercedes, polishing it, and tuning the motor to perfection. He made some repayments on the loan, but the months rolled by with most of the debt unpaid. His parents were baffled. How could a young man with over $10,000 to spend as he wished be less than the best credit risk?

In time their question was answered: Dusty had found a lovely war widow with two small children in desperate need of his support. Within a year they were married—and the unpaid balance on the car became a wedding present to them. Despite the happy ending, the point of the story is clear. It is all too easy to contract for credit; it is never easy—and sometimes impossible—to meet the credit payments.

Because money is never easy to repay, it is best, whenever possible, to avoid installment buying. Knowing this, many parents help to pay for their children's first cars, or assume the burden of monthly repayments on the loan. If such generosity is beyond their means, they encourage their children to build up their savings accounts and set a realistic target date for the purchase.

Last but not least

Before doing any serious shopping for a car, the teen-ager and his parents should draw up a list of their specifications. Should the car be a sports coupe or a vehicle large enough to accommodate friends? Should it be a small foreign car with excellent gas mileage, or big "Detroit iron" that suffers less damage in an accident but costs more to run? Should it be an "oldie" with expensive maintenance for all but a do-it-yourselfer, or a comparatively new car with many miles of trouble-free operation ahead of it? Should it be a special vehicle such as a camper or bus, or should it be a type of automobile that the teen-ager can use throughout his early adult years?

The answers to these questions depend on the family's tastes and pocketbook and on the availability of gasoline; but the final choice should be adapted, as far as possible, to the desires of the person who is to become the principal driver.

Shopping for a new car

There seem to be two schools of thought among car buyers. Some prefer a new car that they can break in, maintain carefully, and drive for a number of years. Others, realizing that depreciation is greatest during the first year of a car's life, prefer to buy an automobile that has been used for a year or two. A family's decision about this depends on the amount of money available, the amount of long-distance driving the teen-ager will have to do, and personal preference about the style and appearance of the car.

If the family has the cash available and if the young driver is inexperienced as a mechanic, a new car has much going for it. Many thrifty souls look for "executive" cars—those which have been used for a few thousand miles but are sold with a new-car guarantee. The disadvantage of such cars is that they are loaded with options and accessories that run up the cost.

Some options are justifiable because they promote better, safer transportation. Opt for a set of oversized, belted bias or radial tires because they grip the road and last longer than the standard tires provided by the manufacturer. Consider power brakes if the automobile weighs over 4,000 pounds or if the driver might find ordinary brakes difficult to operate. Disc brakes are desirable (whether power-assisted or not) as they are less likely to throw the car into a sudden skid and seem to recover from fading a little faster than drum brakes.

Heavy-duty suspension costs very little extra and makes the car better able to carry large loads. Heavy-duty brakes, cooling system, and battery will prolong the life of any car that works for a living.

Several consumer magazines are available in the library of nearly every town. They report on new cars of various makes and models. Take time to consult these magazines to see whether weaknesses in design or workmanship have shown up in the models under consideration.

Thus armed with knowledge of financial resources, a list of requirements for safety, comfort, and appearance, and some awareness of the quality or lack of quality built into various vehicles, the future car owner and his parents are at last ready to sally forth in search of the automobile that promises most in service and pleasure.

Choose the dealer as well as the car

People of all ages tend to fall in love with one particular car, and, like all people in love, they are apt to lose their heads. So, when at last you find your dream car, take a long, hard look at the man who is selling it. It is quite as important to choose the right dealer as it is to choose the right vehicle. He must be a man who is known to make honest deals and who services his cars carefully while they are under warranty. It is better to pay a bit more to a neighborhood dealer than to save a few dollars buying from a dealer who proves uncomfortably far away when warranty work needs to be done. Remember that most new cars come off the assembly line with minor defects and that no guarantee has any value unless the manufacturer or the dealer honors it.

Mary Davis thought that she was being thrifty when she found a "bargain" in a new car three towns away. But she soon discovered a poorly fitted rear window through which the rain seeped and wet the carpet. Mary brought the car back to the shop, waited there several hours while the carpet was being dried, and took the car home. The following week it rained again, and again the carpet was soaked. She again drove twenty miles to the dealer. Again she waited. Once more she thought the window was repaired. But no! After the carpet had become so moldy that the stench was sickening, her parents contacted the district manger, who said that he had never been told about the difficulty. Months after the purchase, a proper window gasket and a new carpet were installed; but by that time Mary hated the car that had cost her so much in time and energy.

If ever a car dealer, or any other merchant, tries to evade the responsibilities clearly set forth on a guarantee or warranty, write to the district manager or to the president of the company telling him of the problem. Most public libraries have reference books, such as *Poor's Register of Corporations* and *Moody's Industrial Manual,* which list all major firms in the United States. A dealer who has a franchise from a reputable company and who regularly fails to make good on warranty work may lose his right to sell the product. At the very least, the home office will insist that he make the necessary corrections.

Horse trading

Haggling over prices in an automobile showroom is like bargaining in an Oriental bazaar. Except in the case of small foreign automobiles, for which a heavy demand exists in these days of ecological concern, "horse trading" is expected. Still, to bargain successfully, a person needs to know a thing or two. The buyer must never let the love-light shine in his eyes as he contemplates the car of his choice. A poker face is handy at this point; so is a pair of dark glasses. Even better is a businesslike parent who can say coolly, "We'll think about it. You may hear from us later."

To bargain intelligently, the buyer needs to gauge the lowest price the dealer is likely to accept. The price sticker on the new car is a handy point of reference. To calculate the dealer's cost, jot down the final figure on the sheet and subtract the transportation charge which is also listed. For a subcompact or compact car, multiply the difference by .85; for all intermediates and most full-sized cars, multiply by .815. Finally, add in the freight charge, and you will come very close to the dealer's cost.

To this estimated cost, it is necessary to add the dealer's profit. Depending on the time of year, general business conditions, and competition among local dealerships, markups will vary from a low of $150 to as much as 10 percent of the dealer's cost. If sales prove disappointing—as in the winter—or if next year's models are due—as in late summer—the dealer usually offers his cars at a big discount. If an old car is being traded, ask the price of the new vehicle without mentioning a trade; then ask the appraised value of the old car and compare it with the *NADA Official Used Car Guide,* published

monthly by the National Automobile Dealers Association. Every auto-insurance broker or bank manager has copies of this or similar price guides.

The dealer will try to find out if he is to arrange the financing for the new car, since he expects to make 2 or 3 percent of the amount of the loan when he sells the "paper" to a finance company. The wise buyer, however, arranges for credit in advance at a bank and pays cash for a car. By so doing, he pays the lowest rate of interest and chooses the institution with which he is going to do business. Still, avoid letting the dealer know that you are paying cash until the rock-bottom price has been negotiated.

Buying a used car

If buying a new car takes the skill of a horse trader, buying a used car takes two or three times as much. The trouble is that no two used cars are exactly alike. Since used cars vary from sturdy two-year-olds to nine-year-old jalopies, and since dealers range from good guys to con men, it is a wonder that anyone comes out of a used-car lot without losing his shirt. Yet, here as everywhere, knowledge is power and gives the buyer a sporting chance of success.

Ideally, the used car to buy is between one and two years old. Because depreciation erodes 30 percent of the value of a full-sized American car in the first year and 17 percent in the second, a two-year-old American-made car in good condition should cost about half its original price. The percentage of depreciation on compact and foreign cars would be far less.

The ideal used car should have traveled somewhere between 12,000 and 24,000 miles. Fortunately, in 1973, a federal law made it illegal for anyone to set back an odometer. This affords the consumer some protection, but not so much that he can let down his guard. What if the automobile had been part of a rental fleet or was used by a traveling salesman who drove it 110,000 miles before trading it in? The odometer would then read a mere 10,000 miles. Worn pedals and weak springs under the driver's seat, coupled with a low odometer reading, suggest that the odometer is on its second time around.

The ideal car should have had only one previous owner, a fact that may be ascertained in some states by checking the original title. No car should ever be considered if it shows signs of having been in a serious accident. A damaged frame or steering linkage could turn the car into a killer. To check for serious damage, study the car in broad daylight. Look for slight irregularities in the fenders and hood and unscratched paint of a slightly different shade. If the entire body of a car two years old or older appears unchipped and immaculate, the car may be sporting a new coat of paint after a major accident. To detect a new paint job, raise the hood and look closely at the fire panel that separates the motorist's knees from the engine block. Since that panel cannot be repainted with the engine in place, it will show the original color of the car.

The ideal used car will never be bargain-priced. Dealers know to the penny the book value of every car on their lots. Actually, there are three book values for every make, model, and year: "very clean," "clean," and "fair." Naturally, a very clean car has low mileage and very few signs of damage or wear. As the most desirable merchandise, it will carry a higher tag than a similar vehicle in average condition.

Of course, on occasion a sharp-eyed buyer may discover a car that is exceptionally well-priced. This "cream puff," as it is called in the trade, may lack a good radio and automatic transmission, or it may have been a model that proved unpopular with the public. Or the dealer might be pressed for cash at a time when cars are moving slowly. But do not count on paying less than the car is worth. Unless the buyer is a skilled mechanic or brings one with him (as many used-car buyers do), he is an amateur playing with pros.

Buyer beware!

Along with those dark glasses, bring a pad and pencil to the used-car lot. When you see a likely prospect, jot down the name of the agency, the car's make, model, year, and condition, and the asking price. Otherwise, after you have visited several lots, the car of your dreams may be like the proverbial needle in a haystack—lost forever.

If you have a car to trade, say nothing about it as you shop around. You already know the book value of your car. Any inflated trade-in value you might be offered would only be offset by a higher price on the car you are considering. Besides, these inflated prices make comparison shopping impossible. Ask for the rock-bottom price without any trade-in; then expect to do some negotiating later to cut this price down a bit.

Instead of merely kicking the tires and sitting behind the wheel, insist on taking the car for a test drive. Many imperfections show up clearly on a road test—poor brakes, rattles, grinding gears, and so forth. It is an amazing fact that many people buy used cars without ever having driven them around the block.

Be wary of unknown "private owners." They are often car salesmen who are trying to unload a lemon. You get no guarantee from a private owner who sells his questionable merchandise on an "all sales final" basis.

Watch out for the bait-and-switch trick, which has been described in chapter six. If you go to a used-car lot after reading an advertisement about a fabulous car and find that the car has "just been sold" but that some other car, at a higher price, "is really a much better buy," you will know that you have been the victim of a con game that is more than a thousand years old.

Dishonesty is rampant in the used-car business. Various tricks are practiced to hide for a while some serious defect in the machinery. Often buyers are high-pressured into buying when their good judgment tells them to stop and think things over. The salesman asks to appraise your old car and promptly "loses" the keys. He may keep you at his desk for hours while a relay of managers and appraisers talk incessantly to you. Here is a case where a smart parent can be of inestimable help. He can ask for the keys and threaten to call the police if they are not returned without delay.

When an agreement has been reached and blank forms filled in, a salesman may go to "get his boss's signature on the deal." Then he will return and say that he made a mistake but the car will cost only $40 more and the check you handed over will be enough for the down payment. If this happens to

you, grab that check, tear it up, and stalk out, no matter how much you thought you wanted the automobile. It is proof positive that you are dealing with a dishonest firm.

There are other dangers to guard against. Before signing the sales contract, make sure that the serial number on the paper is the same as that on the car you intend to buy. Henry was so relieved when the bargaining was over, that he signed without checking and found that he had bought quite a different car from the one he had selected; and the used-car dealer would not do a thing about it.

Leave no blank space between your signature and the last typed line above it. Mary signed at the bottom of the page where the salesman told her to and found that a number of options she had not wanted later appeared on her bill.

Analee had an even worse experience. The salesman gave her a rather poor pen with which to sign. Then he said that her name did not appear on the second copy of the contract and asked her to sign that too. Later she discovered that this "second copy" was worded differently from the contract she had read; but because it had her name on it, the firm held her to the less favorable terms of the second contract.

These are but a few of the many tricks that are played in automobile agencies and used-car lots. When the buyer also allows the car salesman to arrange the financing, the opportunity for sharp practices is greatly increased. The safest way to buy a car is to pay cash. Taking out a bank loan with a car as collateral involves considerable cost and some financial risk. But by far the most dangerous way to finance a car is by signing an installment contract in the car dealer's office.

Pitfalls of financing

As you already know from the chapter on credit, installment contracts are legal documents that at best favor the seller and at worst contain clauses that might destroy the signer's economic life. A dealer who sets up an installment credit contract for the buyer to sign sells that contract to some finance company at a discount of 2 or 3 percent. The discount represents the salesman's fee for acting as an agent for the finance company.

The unsuspecting buyer may discover all too soon that his monthly installments must be paid to a company which has no interest in his problems with the merchandise and which may eagerly await a delayed installment in order to demand full payment of the debt.

Some dishonest finance companies do not even wait for the buyer to make a mistake in meeting his installments. Jake signed a contract, made his first payment, and drove off in his new car. A week later, the finance company sent a man around to repossess the vehicle. When he called a lawyer, Jake discovered that the contract he had signed contained a *confession-of-judgment* clause, in which he had "confessed" in advance to defaulting on his payments. The dishonest company knew that, by signing this clause, Jake had given up his right to defend himself at law and so had to stand by while his property was snatched away.

Although not all installment contracts fall into the hands of dishonest companies, every buyer who finances his car through the dealer must realize that he is really making two contracts: first, an agreement to buy a piece of merchandise as it stands, unless specific improvements are written into the sales contract; second, an agreement to pay so many dollars on so many specified dates, regardless of his dissatisfaction with his purchase or of the seller's failure to meet the obligations listed in the sales contract.

Many a buyer who has a legitimate complaint has withheld a monthly payment because of work not performed by the dealer who sold him the car, only to discover that the finance company has no connection with the dealer and cares only about receiving the payments as they come due.

While the federal government has recently passed a law to make the *holder in due course*, as the finance company is called, responsible for the car dealer's mistreatment of customers whose complaints are just, smart car buyers will continue to arrange their financing at a bank. If they cannot get a loan at a bank or at some responsible finance company because they, or their parents, lack a high enough credit rating, knowledgeable teen-agers defer buying a car until they have increased their savings.

The costs of car ownership

Anyone planning to buy a car must remember that, new or old, a car costs money to maintain and operate. To the original cost, add a state sales tax, which can run to several hundred dollars on an expensive vehicle. Then there are the costs of license tags and, in many states, of a semiannual compulsory inspection. For the driver who runs his car an average of 10,000 miles a year, gasoline and oil will add at least $600 more. Even if gas is not rationed, its use may be discouraged by high prices and taxes.

A young driver must also pay for adequate automobile insurance. No sane person would move a car one yard without insurance if he realized that in so doing he jeopardized every cent he had in the world and nearly every dollar he would earn for years to come. Yet uninformed motorists run this risk every day.

There are three kinds of automobile insurance. Nearly every car owner carries *comprehensive coverage* against fire, theft, vandalism, windstorm, and so forth. Owners of new cars are likely to take out *collision insurance* to help meet the cost of repairs should the vehicle suffer damage. Any car on which installment payments are due or which is serving as collateral for a personal loan almost certainly carries both coverages. In fact, lenders often insist that the borrower also carry a special life insurance policy to cover the loan in case he dies or becomes disabled.

But the most important type of insurance for every car owner is of no concern to a bank or finance company. This is *liability insurance*—coverage for damage the vehicle may cause to people or property. Each year well over two million persons are either injured or killed in automobile accidents. Juries are likely to award to the injured, or to their survivors, sums that may run as high as $300,000. Even more frequent are accidents that destroy or damage valuable property, and an above-average number of these accidents occur when young drivers—persons under twenty-five years of age—are at the wheel. A slight accident can involve a bill of several hundred dollars payable by the driver who appears to be in the wrong; a serious accident can cost an uninsured motorist all his savings and a part of his income for years. Only liability insurance can give a car owner sure protection against this constant threat to his economic security.

Liability insurance is expensive. Young male drivers pay the highest rates of all. Many parents and young drivers old enough to vote are therefore urging their legislators to enact no-fault insurance, as the cost of liability coverage drops when no-fault laws are in effect.

No-fault is a fairly new concept in liability insurance which allows accident cases to be settled by payments made to the insured by his own—instead of by the other driver's—insurance company. Under no-fault laws, a driver involved in an accident does not have to establish his innocence and the other driver's negligence. Payments for medical expenses and car repairs can therefore be made without years of legal arguments and court delays. No-fault laws also prevent huge and often unrealistic awards for damages being made to some accident victims while other victims, equally maimed, get little or nothing.

Car owners who carry liability insurance must learn to use it properly. If, for example, a very slight accident occurs and no apparent damage has been done to either car, many insured motorists forget the whole business. This is a grave mistake. Unless a full report is made to the insurance company promptly, the company may deny insurance protection on the ground that their right to gather evidence to prosecute a case has been breached. While it is never pleasant to have to admit to one's family and the insurance company that a negligible accident took place, it must always be remembered that the other party to the accident can—and often does—sue on the flimsiest of grounds.

Another mistake insured motorists make involves the use to which the car is put. If a liability policy has been issued for business and pleasure driving only and the insured takes a job that involves the constant use of his car, he must immediately inform the company and pay an additional premium. Unless this is done, no protection would be given the driver should an accident occur.

Insurance companies, moreover, have rules against picking

up hitchhikers. Carrying such a person may seem a simple act of kindness to the young driver, but the insurance company believes it vastly increases the risks. Stopping to pick up a hitchhiker may cause a rear-end accident. The stranger may steal something from the car or even force the driver out and drive off with the vehicle. If he is injured while a passenger in a car, a hitchhiker might sue for damages. For these reasons, the insured driver who breaks the rules by carrying a hitchhiker will not be covered if an accident takes place.

Every driver should carry a card—or leave it in the car—giving the name, address, and telephone number of the agent of the company that insures the automobile. With these facts and the policy number and date of expiration, the driver will be protected should he need bail or a tow car after an accident.

Outwit the repair racketeers

To the costs of operating and insuring a vehicle, must be added the cost of repairs. Unless the owner is a mechanic with a workshop in his home garage, the cost of maintenance rises fast as a car reaches its fourth year. The rackets practiced in repair shops have become a national scandal. Usable parts are thrown away to save the mechanic a few minutes' time; needless work is performed; secondhand parts are installed although new parts are billed. Because of these practices, repair shops and the mechanics who work in them may soon have to be licensed so that those who deal unfairly with the public can be put out of business.

What can a young car owner do to protect purse or wallet from dishonest repair costs? Girls and boys should learn how to make small adjustments and simple repairs on their cars. When the job needs a hydraulic lift or a more experienced hand, they should patronize a small garage where family or friends personally know the management and regularly receive good service at fair prices.

It is especially important to avoid having repair work done while traveling away from home. Before starting on a trip, have the car checked and the tank filled to reduce the need for service along the road. Even in your home neighborhood, carry some cash when going out in your car, plus a blank check from your own checking account, in case a tire blows or some other emergency develops.

Be sure to have your operator's license at all times. The owner's card may be carried with you; however, when several family members operate the car, it is best to tape a small envelope containing the card in the trunk where it can be reached if needed. It is unwise to leave it in the glove compartment as this might encourage theft of the vehicle.

Be a wheel within your wheels

Attaining the legal age for operating a motor vehicle is a milestone on the road to maturity. A car can be a valued means of transportation or a lethal weapon. Which it becomes depends on the driver.

Parents who help youngsters to achieve mobility deserve to know at all times that their sons and daughters are driving responsibly. They also deserve to know where their children are and when they will return home. A collect call costs the caller nothing and may save his family hours of concern.

When Gerry was sixteen, he received a green Mustang as a growing-up present. He drove it for five years with neither accident nor traffic violation. Best of all, his parents never had to worry when he was delayed along the road or out for a longer time than planned. He is twenty-two now and still the best driver in town.

Education is an ornament in prosperity
and a refuge in adversity.

ARISTOTLE

12

Cash
for
the
Campus

A college education has long been a part of The Great American Dream. Going to college is not for everyone, as a rapidly rising enrollment in vocational schools amply proves. Still, no young person with academic inclinations and an ability to profit from college life should be denied the opportunity because of financial pressures.

In 1977 the estimated annual overall expenses of a resident student in one private university was $6,800: for tuition and fees, $3,000; for room and board, $3,000; for books, $200; and for clothing, laundry, travel, and spending money, $600. Day students there must expect to pay approximately $3,000 a year. While the charges of this school are above the average, some colleges charge more, and the median cost for private colleges and universities is $4,200 for all expenses of the resident student and $2,600 for the student who lives at home.

For those who can enter public colleges and universities in their home state, costs are much lower. Tuition, room, and board cost in the neighborhood of $2,300. To this must be added the cost of books, clothing, transportation, and so forth, making a total of about $2,900. By far the best buy in education—if price alone is to be considered—is achieved by attending a nearby public college as a day student. Here the basic tuition runs around $900; including lunches, clothes, books, and transportation, it approaches $2,000.

To the cost of attending college should be added the cost of choosing a college. As with all expensive things—and higher education is one of the most expensive things a family ever buys—it is essential to shop before spending. Before applying for admission, high-school students should visit the colleges in which they are most interested. Parents, who would never think of buying a house or a car without inspecting it carefully, all too often let their sons or daughters enter unexplored colleges which turn out to be ill-suited to their needs.

Smart parents take their high-school juniors to visit several campuses. They arrange for an interview with the admissions officer before setting out. Even if this is not required, a young person stands a far better chance of being admitted if he makes a good impression while he asks about the school. The parents must be prepared to cool their heels in the outer office while the student and the dean of admissions go elsewhere for a conference. Nothing a parent can say or do at that time will be of any help to his child. In fact, a talkative, self-assertive parent has spoiled many a student's chances of admittance to a desirable college by dominating the conversation during a visit to the campus.

To the $300 or so that visits to colleges may cost, parents must add the cost of five or six applications at about $20 each. It is wise to apply to one or two schools that are outstanding but hard to get into, one or two to which admission is almost assured, and one or two others at which the student could feel at home. Although these preliminary expenditures may seem high, compared to the overall cost of a resident college education, now running between $16,000 and $32,000, they are dollars well spent.

Long-range financial planning for college

With college costs so high and likely to go higher, planning ahead is a must. Parents who can afford to put $50 or $60 a month into a savings account at compound interest from the time their child is a toddler will have accumulated almost all the money needed for a college education before the child becomes a freshman. Because of the effect of compound interest, the earlier they start to build the fund, the less money they will have to provide.

In some families, the mother of school-age children takes a job and sets aside her extra income towards their college education. As the children grow older and begin to earn money, they, themselves, may be able to add to their own college funds.

Parents or grandparents of substantial means can do much toward building up a child's college fund while saving on taxes. At the present time, an individual is allowed to make an annual gift of cash or securities up to $3,000, free of federal gift tax, to each of his children, grandchildren, or other persons or organizations, as long as these gifts are made three years prior to the donor's death. If gifts to minors are placed in a custodian account in accordance with state law, the income is taxed by the federal government at the recipient's lower rate, not at the donor's higher rate.

There is a further tax advantage. While the child is a full-time student and dependent on his parents for the major part of his expenses, he not only may be claimed as a dependent on his parents' federal income tax return but also may deduct the personal exemption on his own federal tax return. Thus, a few thousand dollars given to a child when he is very young and left to gather interest and dividends over the years will reduce the parents' current taxes and help to lift the financial burden of college costs.

The role of insurance

Insurance may also be used to further college plans. Policies may be bought that will provide a large sum of money for college expenses should the wage earner die or become disabled.

Some families use life insurance policies as collateral for low-interest loans to finance a college education. The danger of using life insurance as a basis for borrowing is discussed in chapter fourteen.

Borrowing for college

For those who were unable to set aside money for higher education, borrowing may become a necessity. Some families find it convenient to refinance the mortgages on their homes to obtain money, if interest rates are favorable at the time. However, when parents face long-term illness or early retirement with the attendant shrinkage of income, increasing the mortgage obligation can entail real hardship and may endanger the family's welfare.

If the family has a backlog of securities or similar assets to offer as collateral, the head of the household may be able to get a regular bank loan at current rates of interest. Such loans run from one to three years, with monthly repayment of a part of the principal along with monthly interest. The annual percentage rates run from 11.5 percent for a one-year loan to 13.4 percent for a three-year loan. Amortization of principal plus such high rates of interest could seriously deplete the available living-expense money of families that tend to spend to the limit of their income or that have more than one child in college at the same time.

Before 1973 middle-income families could participate in the federal government's Guaranteed Student Loan Program. In mid-1974, after a fifteen-month experiment with a "means test" that sharply reduced the subsidized college loans available to most families with incomes over $15,000, the Guaranteed Student Loan Program was once more opened to families with incomes up to about $25,000.

According to the newly revised rules, any student whose family has an adjusted family income under $25,000 is eligible for a subsidy on a loan up to $2,500 a year. "Adjusted family income" is defined as adjusted gross income on the federal income tax Form 1040, less a deduction of 10 percent, less the total of the family's personal tax exemptions. For example, a family of four whose 1976 tax return showed an adjusted gross income of $25,000 could deduct $2,500, plus the sum of four $750 exemptions and arrive at an adjusted family income of $19,500.

An eligible student applies for his subsidized loan at a bank or through his college. The government pays all the interest on the loan until nine months after the student leaves college. Then he must assume the interest obligation and begin to repay the loan.

Students whose family income exceeds $25,000 also face a means test. Unless there are special circumstances, such as family illness, disability, or several children in college at the same time, the family is not granted a subsidized loan. Even for the children of wealthy families, however, the government now guarantees loans, sets the rate of interest that the lender may charge, and pays all interest in excess of 7 percent.

How these liberalized rules will work out for middle-income families remains to be seen. Student loans on which interest is not paid by the government tend to be unattractive to lending institutions because they have to bill individual borrowers, and this raises the cost of servicing the loans. Moreover, in times of tight money and soaring interest rates, private lenders do not want to tie up their money in loans on which principal repayments are deferred until the borrower has been out of school for almost a year.

Another source of funds for college students is the National Direct Student Loans. These loans, which are the successors of the National Defense Student Loans of the late 1950s, are no longer based on academic achievement. Instead, they are based entirely upon need as determined by the financial aid officer of the applicant's college, in accordance with guidelines laid down by the U.S. government's Office of Education. These loans can prove very valuable for students from families with incomes under $20,000.

Students who are eligible may borrow up to $5,000 during the first two years at vocational school or college; $7,500 during a four-year course leading to a degree; and $15,000 for a combined undergraduate and graduate academic career. Interest at the rate of 3 percent is charged when the ten-year repayment period begins nine months after graduation or after leaving school.

The concern of middle-income students and their families about obtaining student loans has not been lessened by the 1973 proposal of the Carnegie Commission on Higher Education. The commission recommends that families with incomes between $11,000 and $15,000 a year bear a larger proportion of the expenses of public postsecondary institutions and that the subsidies presently used to keep tuition low on state-supported campuses be used instead to further subsidize enrollments of low-income students. If, during the coming decade, this recommendation is accepted and the states close the gap between the costs of public and private colleges, middle-income families will more than ever be dependent on long-range savings programs or high-cost borrowing to meet the expenses of a college education.

Help from scholarships

Outright money grants, or scholarships, are today based almost entirely on financial need. Need is usually determined by an analysis of the Parents' Confidential Statement, a questionnaire provided by the College Scholarship Service of the College Entrance Examination Board, Box 176, Princeton, New Jersey. The detailed financial statements made therein are subject to check against the family's latest federal income tax return and any other relevant official documents. Unless special family circumstances exist—separated parents, grave family illness, a large number of children, or several children in college simultaneously—those in the economic middle class have slim chance of receiving scholarship aid.

For those who are eligible, money grants are available from several sources. The colleges themselves may have scholarships for students with special abilities, as in art, music, or athletics. Community organizations, such as PTAs, civic groups, alumni clubs, religious, ethnic, and professional associations, and so forth, may provide small scholarships for local students. Some labor unions and employers offer aid to the children of needy families. Corporations, working through colleges of their choice, may provide training programs coupled with money grants to students interested in special fields.

National Merit Scholarships are awarded to high-school seniors who attain high scores on national examinations. Although the prizes are geared to financial need and vary from full tuition to a token payment, all college-bound students should take these examinations. Test scores determine acceptance in highly competitive colleges and universities. They are also taken into account in planning the student's curriculum. Finally, they are considered by financial aid officers when granting assistance to needy students.

For students with exceptional need, the federal government's Basic Educational Opportunity Grants program offers scholarships that for the school year 1977-78 range from $200 to $1,400. These grants, designed to provide funds for economically deprived college students, young and older, are available to any needy person who has had no college courses before 1973. Under this rule, college seniors in the school year 1976-77 would be eligible for one of these grants.

In order to apply for a Basic Educational Opportunity Grant, a form similar to that of the College Scholarship Service must be completed (see pages 220-221). Forms may be obtained through high schools, colleges, the U.S. Postal Service, and state employment offices.

Finally, scholarship aid may be sought from the student's home state. Some grants depend on the results of competitive examinations. Others are based entirely on need. Still others are offered by some states to special groups, such as nursing scholarships or grants to the children of deceased or disabled war veterans. To find out what aid is available, a student should consult the principal or guidance counselor at his school, the financial aid officer at the college of his choice, or state and federal educational assistance officials. School and local libraries also have up-to-date information about newly legislated changes in student aid programs.

Earning while learning

A majority of the ten million students now attending colleges and vocational schools earn some part of their expenses.

Application Form for
Basic Educational Opportunity Grant

Important: You are only eligible for consideration under this program if you will be attending an eligible post-high school educational institution for the **first** time during the 1973-74 academic year. In addition, you must be enrolled on a **full-time basis.** **Do not** complete this application if you have attended a college, university, post-high school vocational or technical school at any time before July 1, 1973.

DEPARTMENT OF HEALTH, EDUCATION AND WELFARE
OFFICE OF EDUCATION

OMB NO. 51—RO961
APPROVAL EXPIRES: 6/30/75
FOR OFFICE OF EDUCATION USE ONLY

APPLICATION DEADLINE:
FEBRUARY 1, 1974

BASIC EDUCATIONAL OPPORTUNITY GRANT PROGRAM
APPLICATION FOR DETERMINATION OF FAMILY CONTRIBUTION FOR 1973-74 ACADEMIC YEAR

READ INSTRUCTIONS FIRST

A — APPLICANT INFORMATION

01 (1-2)

1. APPLICANT'S SOCIAL SECURITY NUMBER
(3-11)

2. APPLICANT'S NAME
(17-30) LAST NAME | FIRST NAME (31-39) | MIDDLE INITIAL (40)

3. APPLICANT'S SEX   FEMALE ☐   MALE ☐ (41)

4. APPLICANT'S BIRTH DATE (42-47)
MONTH | DAY | YEAR

5. APPLICANT'S PERMANENT MAILING ADDRESS:
NUMBER AND STREET (48-71) 02 (1-2)
SEE INSTRUCTIONS FOR LISTING OF STATE CODES
CITY (12-29)   (30-31) STATE   ZIP CODE (32-36)

6. APPLICANT'S MARITAL STATUS: (37)
1 ☐ SINGLE   2 ☐ MARRIED
3 ☐ DIVORCED, SEPARATED, WIDOWED

7. IF APPLICANT IS MARRIED OR HAS DEPENDENTS, ANSWER BOTH (a) AND (b) BELOW:
(a) Total size of Applicant's Household—Include applicant, spouse, dependent children, other dependents . . . . (38-39)
(b) Number of Members of Household (including applicant) to be in post-high school educational institutions in 1973-74. . (40-41)

8. Have you attended a college, university, post-high school vocational or technical school at any time before July 1, 1973?   ☐ YES   ☐ NO (42)

B — PARENT (GUARDIAN) INFORMATION

1. NAME OF PARENT OR GUARDIAN
LAST NAME | FIRST NAME | MIDDLE INITIAL
2. (43-44) AGE
3. SOCIAL SECURITY NUMBER

4. PERMANENT MAILING ADDRESS OF PARENT OR GUARDIAN
SEE INSTRUCTIONS FOR LISTING OF STATE CODES
NUMBER AND STREET: CITY   ZIP CODE

5. PARENTS' OR GUARDIAN'S STATUS:
1 ☐ MARRIED
2 ☐ DIVORCED, SEPARATED, WIDOWED, SINGLE
3 ☐ BOTH DECEASED (45)

6. TOTAL SIZE OF PARENTS' (GUARDIAN'S) HOUSEHOLD—Include applicant, parents (guardians), dependent children, other dependents . . . . (46-47)

7. NUMBER OF MEMBERS OF HOUSEHOLD (including applicant) TO BE IN POST-HIGH SCHOOL EDUCATIONAL INSTITUTIONS IN 1973-74 . . . . (48-49)

C — APPLICANT'S STATUS

YOU MUST ANSWER EACH OF THE FOLLOWING QUESTIONS FOR EACH YEAR

1. DID OR WILL APPLICANT LIVE WITH PARENTS OR GUARDIAN (except for brief holiday periods) DURING . . .

	1972	1973	1974
	1 ☐ YES	1 ☐ YES	1 ☐ YES
	(50) 2 ☐ NO	(51) 2 ☐ NO	(52) 2 ☐ NO

2. APPLICANT IS, WAS, OR WILL BE LISTED AS AN EXEMPTION ON PARENTS' OR GUARDIAN'S FEDERAL INCOME TAX RETURN DURING . . .

	1972	1973	1974
	1 ☐ YES	1 ☐ YES	1 ☐ YES
	(53) 2 ☐ NO	(54) 2 ☐ NO	(55) 2 ☐ NO

3. DID OR WILL APPLICANT RECEIVE $600 OR MORE IN FINANCIAL ASSISTANCE FROM PARENTS OR GUARDIAN DURING . . .

	1972	1973	1974
	1 ☐ YES	1 ☐ YES	1 ☐ YES
	(56) 2 ☐ NO	(57) 2 ☐ NO	(58) 2 ☐ NO

IF: YOU ANSWERED *YES* FOR *ANY* QUESTION FOR *ANY* YEAR IN SECTION C, COMPLETE ONLY SECTION D ON THE NEXT PAGE, AND SIGN.

OR: IF YOU ANSWERED *NO* FOR *ALL YEARS* AND *ALL QUESTIONS* IN SECTION C, COMPLETE ONLY SECTION E ON THE NEXT PAGE, AND SIGN.

Reverse Side of Application Form

D · PARENTS' FINANCIAL STATEMENT

PARENTS' INCOME AND EXPENSES

1. DID PARENTS FILE A *JOINT* FEDERAL INCOME TAX RETURN FOR 1972? ☐ YES ☐ NO
(59)

2. TOTAL NUMBER OF EXEMPTIONS CLAIMED ON 1972 FEDERAL INCOME TAX RETURN: ☐☐ (60-61)

3. ADJUSTED GROSS INCOME *(from line 17 of IRS form 1040, or line 14 of IRS form 1040A)* . . . . $☐☐☐☐ .00 1972
(62-66)

4. ENTER THAT PORTION OF ITEM 3 EARNED THROUGH EMPLOYMENT BY:

 a) Father . . . . $☐☐☐☐ .00
(67-71)

 b) Mother . . . . $☐☐☐☐ .00
(72-76)
 03 (1-2)

5. OTHER INCOME (Social Security, child support, tax-free bonds, capital gains, welfare, etc.). See Instructions $☐☐☐☐ .00
(17-21)

6. TOTAL FEDERAL INCOME TAX PAID *(from line 20 of IRS form 1040, or line 21 of 1040A)* . . . . . . $☐☐☐☐ .00
(22-26)

UNUSUAL EXPENSES *(See Instructions)*
7. MEDICAL and/or DENTAL . . . . $☐☐☐☐ .00
(27-31)

8. CASUALTY or THEFT LOSSES . . . . $☐☐☐☐ .00
(32-36)

PARENTS' ASSETS AND LIABILITIES

	PRESENT MARKET VALUE a)	UNPAID MORTGAGE OR DEBTS b)
9. HOME . . . . $	☐☐☐☐ .00 (37-48)	$☐☐☐☐ .00
10. INVESTMENTS AND REAL ESTATE *(See Instructions)* $	☐☐☐☐ .00 (49-60)	$☐☐☐☐ .00
11. OTHER ASSETS *(See Instructions)* $	☐☐☐☐ .00 (61-72)	$☐☐☐☐ .00
04 (1-2)		
12. BUSINESS . . . . $	☐☐☐☐ .00 (12-23)	$☐☐☐☐ .00
13. FARM . . . . $	☐☐☐☐ .00 (24-35)	$☐☐☐☐ .00 (36-40)
14. CASH, SAVINGS ACCOUNTS, CHECKING ACCOUNTS . . $	☐☐☐☐ .00	

APPLICANT'S SPECIAL EDUCATIONAL BENEFITS
(to be received between July 1, 1973 and June 30, 1974)

15. a) Social Security benefits PER MONTH . . . . $☐☐☐ .00
(41-43)

 b) NUMBER OF MONTHS . . . . ☐☐
(44-45)

16. a) Veteran's benefits PER MONTH *(G.I. Bill)* . . . . $☐☐☐ .00
(46-48)

 b) NUMBER OF MONTHS . . . . ☐☐
(49-50)

APPLICANT'S RESOURCES

17. SAVINGS . . . . $☐☐☐☐ .00
(51-55)

18. OTHER RESOURCES *(See Instructions)* . . . . . . $☐☐☐☐ .00
(56-60)

We certify that we have read this application and that it is accurate and complete to the best of our knowledge. We authorize the United States Commissioner of Education, or his representative, to obtain from the District Director of Internal Revenue with whom it was filed, a copy of the 1972 Federal Income Tax Return upon which the computation of expected family contribution is based. In order to verify information reported on this form we further agree to provide, if requested, any other documentation necessary to verify information reported on this form.

S I G N

▲ APPLICANT ▲ (61) DATE COMPLETED (62-67)

▲ FATHER OR MALE GUARDIAN ▲ (68) ▲ MOTHER OR FEMALE GUARDIAN ▲ (69)

OE FORM 255, 3/73

E · APPLICANT'S FINANCIAL STATEMENT

INCOME AND EXPENSES: APPLICANT/SPOUSE

1. DID APPLICANT FILE A *JOINT* FEDERAL INCOME TAX RETURN FOR 1972? ☐ YES ☐ NO
(59)

2. TOTAL NUMBER OF EXEMPTIONS CLAIMED ON 1972 FEDERAL INCOME TAX RETURN: ☐☐ (60-61)

3. ADJUSTED GROSS INCOME *(from line 17 of IRS form 1040, or line 14 of IRS form 1040A)* . . . . . . $☐☐☐☐ .00 1972
(62-66)

4. ENTER THAT PORTION OF ITEM 3 EARNED THROUGH EMPLOYMENT BY:

 a) Applicant . . . . $☐☐☐☐ .00
(67-71)

 b) Spouse . . . . $☐☐☐☐ .00
(72-76)
 05 (1-2)

5. OTHER INCOME (Social Security, child support, tax-free bonds, capital gains, welfare, etc.). See Instructions $☐☐☐☐ .00
(17-21)

6. TOTAL FEDERAL INCOME TAX PAID *(from line 20 of IRS form 1040, or line 21 of 1040A)* . . . . . $☐☐☐☐ .00
(22-26)

UNUSUAL EXPENSES *(See Instructions)*
7. MEDICAL and/or DENTAL . . . . $☐☐☐☐ .00
(27-31)

8. CASUALTY or THEFT LOSSES . . . . $☐☐☐☐ .00
(32-36)

ASSETS AND LIABILITIES: APPLICANT/SPOUSE

	PRESENT MARKET VALUE a)	UNPAID MORTGAGE OR DEBTS b)
9. HOME . . . . $	☐☐☐☐ .00 (37-48)	$☐☐☐☐ .00
10. INVESTMENTS AND REAL ESTATE *(See Instructions)* $	☐☐☐☐ .00 (49-60)	$☐☐☐☐ .00
11. OTHER ASSETS *(See Instructions)* $	☐☐☐☐ .00 (61-72)	$☐☐☐☐ .00
06 (1-2)		
12. BUSINESS . . . . . $	☐☐☐☐ .00 (12-23)	$☐☐☐☐ .00
13. FARM . . . . $	☐☐☐☐ .00 (24-35)	$☐☐☐☐ .00 (36-40)
14. CASH, SAVINGS ACCOUNTS, CHECKING ACCOUNTS . . $	☐☐☐☐ .00	

APPLICANT'S SPECIAL EDUCATIONAL BENEFITS
(to be received between July 1, 1973 and June 30, 1974)

15. a) Social Security benefits PER MONTH . . . . $☐☐☐ .00
(41-43)

 b) NUMBER OF MONTHS . . . . ☐☐
(44-45)

16. a) Veteran's benefits PER MONTH *(G.I. Bill)* . . . . $☐☐☐ .00
(46-48)

 b) NUMBER OF MONTHS . . . . ☐☐
(49-50)

I (We) certify that I (we) have read this application and that it is accurate and complete to the best of my (our) knowledge. I (we) authorize the United States Commissioner of Education, or his representative, to obtain from the District Director of Internal Revenue with whom it was filed, a copy of the 1972 Federal Income Tax Return upon which the computation of expected family contribution is based, in order to verify the foregoing statement. I (We) further agree to provide, if requested, any other documentation necessary to verify information reported on this form.

S I G N

▲ APPLICANT ▲ (51) ▲ APPLICANT'S SPOUSE ▲ (52) DATE COMPLETED (53-58)

WARNING: ANY PERSON WHO KNOWINGLY MAKES A FALSE STATEMENT OR MISREPRESENTATION ON THIS FORM SHALL BE SUBJECT TO A FINE, OR TO IMPRISONMENT, OR TO BOTH, UNDER PROVISIONS OF THE UNITED STATES CRIMINAL CODE

MAIL COMPLETED FORM TO:
BEOG
P.O. BOX B
IOWA CITY, IOWA 52240

Depending on age, experience, and opportunity, they may make as much as $2,500 a year. With the rising costs of education, the shrinking market for student loans, and the vanishing scholarship aid programs for middle-income students, more and more students must rely on their own earnings to pay their way through college.

Many college-bound high-school students take summer jobs. These jobs vary from the unskilled work usually available to teen-agers to work requiring special skills, such as clerk-typist, salesclerk, actor in summer stock, professor's assistant in laboratory or office, house-painter, librarian's assistant, and similar occupations for which some aptitude or experience is required. This is when hobbies and skills learned as a youngster begin to pay dividends.

College sophomores, juniors, and seniors often develop a particular field of interest which makes highly skilled work available to them. Sandy, who, as a freshman, spent almost too much time hanging around the college radio station playing records and filling awkward pauses with wry comments, found it easy to get a summer job as a news commentator in a small upstate television studio while the regular newsman went on an extended vacation.

The next winter Sandy held a part-time job at the area radio station. Every Sunday he sniffed out the local news and gave five newscasts which combined national news from the big wire services with happenings of particular interest to residents of the locality. To his surprise, several of his news tidbits were bought by the wire services. This radio experience not only netted him about $1,000 during the school year, but also gave him poise, facility in public speaking, and a very nice job reference to put on his application forms for permanent employment.

There are many go-getters like Sandy. They never tell a prospective employer that they "will do anything." This phrase is the kiss of death to any hope of employment because it suggests that the applicant has no particular interest, no special skill to offer. The clever applicant gauges what sort of job openings the employer is likely to have, decides he can handle the job, and then, wearing a mask of self-confidence he rarely feels, he assures the prospective boss of his delight at offering his valuable services. The boss may realize that the job-seeker's manner is 90 percent pure bluff; but self-confidence, real or assumed, is infectious. Success breeds success.

One such success story is worth remembering. Philip was slightly handicapped by a short-circuiting of the brain that made him awkward and somewhat slow in moving. He wanted to work during the summer before entering his senior year in high school and learned that there was an opening as chef in one of the snack shops in his home town. Since this was a fast-food operation, his family was apprehensive when they learned that he had been hired, but they wisely made no comment.

The first couple of days were hard for Philip. He came home exhausted and rolled into bed. As the week progressed, he brightened visibly. He had begun to make friends with the other teen-agers who staffed the drive-in food shop. His family was amazed when he demonstrated how he put ten hamburgers on the grill, flipped them over with precision timing, slipped them on plates, and covered them with a special sauce. This boy, who found moving so hard, kept up this high-speed operation hour after hour, made many friends, had a wonderful experience, and earned several hundred dollars as well.

Help for campus workers

Young people who find themselves in a new city as college students need help in locating jobs. Every college has an employment office and/or a student aid office to provide on-campus jobs, off-campus employment, and summer work.

Of primary concern are jobs for students who demonstrate dire financial need. For them there is a federally funded work-study program, handled by the financial aid office, through which federal money is paid as wages to students doing part-time, nonprofit work. On-campus work may be in the cafeteria, the library, or the laboratory. Off-campus work might include jobs at a hospital, public school, or governmental agency. Hours may run as high as forty per week; pay varies from the bare legal minimum to nearly twice that rate. In 1976 the annual compensation averaged about $700. In the past, 56.7 percent of the work-study jobs have gone to students from families with incomes of less than $7,000; those with incomes in excess of $10,000 have received 17.3 percent of the federally funded job opportunities.

Student aid offices are aware that students from middle-income families also need or want to work. Fortunately for them, there are usually plenty of job opportunities at the colleges or in nearby communities. Many merchants, corporate employers, and families offer jobs to students who are willing to take on part-time work during the school year. While the wages tend to cluster around the legal minimum, many a young person has gained valuable experience and garnered a reference that stands him in good stead when he seeks postgraduate employment.

One other work-study program, totally unrelated to need, also aids students. Approximately sixty colleges offer a cooperative education program under which students spend alternate terms in study and in paid employment. Drexel University in Philadelphia, one of the pioneers of this program, sends its students out to work in more than 850 approved companies and institutions in thirty-eight states. Many distinguished men and women credit their college educations to programs such as this. Details concerning this program are available from the National Commission for Cooperative Education, 8 West 40th Street, New York, New York 10018.

Those who would like to learn about every college or university that might suit their educational needs and pocketbooks can find up-to-date information in *Comparative Guide to American Colleges*, Cass & Birnbaum, publisher Harper & Row, 10 East Fifty-third Street, New York, New York 10022.

Help for those who help themselves

One college president said recently that the thrust of the thinking of educators and lawmakers is toward a sliding scale of student aid "packages." Future student aid, in his opinion, will still combine loans, grants, and work-study programs

tailored to fit the student's needs and abilities. The amount of such aid will, he believes, diminish as the family income rises until some point (probably around the $25,000 mark) is reached. After that, students and their families will be expected to meet their own college costs through savings, commercial loans, and extra jobs.

To many middle-income families—those with incomes between $23,000 and $26,000—this college president's forecast gives cold comfort. If they have just recently attained salaries in this range, if they have had to pay for years of private school education, or if they have had elderly relatives to support, they may not have been able to set aside much toward college tuition.

For many years large corporations have made unrestricted gifts to private and public educational institutions. Now corporate giving seems to be declining.

According to the chairman of the board of one large corporation, speaking before a group of business leaders and university presidents, corporate philanthropy to higher education is declining because businessmen disapprove of policy-making decisions influenced by the views of militant faculty members. He stated that many students are taught that all corporations are evil and that capitalism should be abolished.

The speaker went on to say that corporations should continue to support colleges and universities, but that they should direct their funds toward schools, departments, and programs "which contribute in some specific way to our individual companies or to the general welfare of our free enterprise system."

At least some of the listening college presidents must have had reservations about the concept of corporate control over funds that business gives to higher education. Still, if many corporations share the point of view expressed by this board chairman, they may, as time goes on, make more of their donations to colleges and universities compatible with the goals expressed by him.

Although freedom of speech and thought should not be curbed at the whim of any corporate donor, there is one legitimate way that large corporations might promote both their image and the free-enterprise system. Corporations could once again offer scholarships based not on dire necessity but on brilliance of mind and fineness of character and thus reduce the burden of college costs on numerous architects, doctors, accountants, engineers, writers, and other business and professional leaders of tomorrow.

Low-cost loans, summer work, and part-time, year-long jobs are other forms of student aid that corporations could direct toward middle-income young people whose student years are now difficult, or even curtailed, because they are not rich enough to pay their way entirely nor poor enough to have it paid for them.

Marry in haste; repent at leisure.

OLD PROVERB

13

Money
and
Marriage

No human being goes to sleep one night as a child and awakes as a full-fledged adult. The human body grows in fits and starts, part by part, as every gawky adolescent knows. Sometimes a gain in height outpaces heart growth, inducing weakness and fatigue. Or musculature falls behind bone growth, making a once well-coordinated individual temporarily inept and clumsy. Secondary sexual characteristics appear sooner in some individuals than in others, depending on hormonal changes in the glandular system.

For some unkown reason, the onset of puberty—the period of this hormonal changeover that marks the end of childhood —tends to take place earlier in today's young people. Although there is much variation in timing, puberty often occurs as early as eleven in girls and twelve in boys. As a result, adolescents just entering their teens become physically capable of reproduction years before their emotional transformation into adulthood has been completed.

Emotional development, like physical development, is a lengthy process. Growing away from childish dependence on parents occurs in fits and starts. Just as physical damage can occur at any stage, emotional development can be arrested somewhere along the line from infancy to adulthood.

Gaining emotional maturity—that is, outgrowing the need for parental control—cannot take place unless the child has emotionally sound and understanding parents to grow away from. Parents must help their children to grow up by slowly increasing juvenile responsibilities and by standing aside while their young acquire experience. They must avoid the twin pitfalls of being overly protective and of thrusting the young person too early and unprepared into the adult emotional world.

Children vary greatly in the timing of their emotional maturation. Parents vary greatly in their understanding of the growth process and their sensitivity to their children's changing emotional needs.

First thrive; then wive

In addition to the problems that arise as a result of the young person's physical and emotional development, parents and teen-agers have to cope with the important matter of economics.

In a highly organized, technological society such as ours, successful people need a much broader education than they would need if they tilled the soil, prospected for metals, cobbled shoes, built furniture, or followed the sea as most people did in George Washington's time. Modern education continues through adolescence and often well into the twenties and delays economic self-sufficiency as much as ten to fifteen years after the onset of puberty.

Young people who drop out of school at sixteen or seventeen in order to take a job that will emancipate them from their parents and allow them to marry, short-change themselves when it comes to long-term economic success. Although the tables on pages 231 and 233 may not reflect current wage

Lifetime Income Grows
As Education Levels Rise

Lifetime Income
For Men
Age 18 to Death

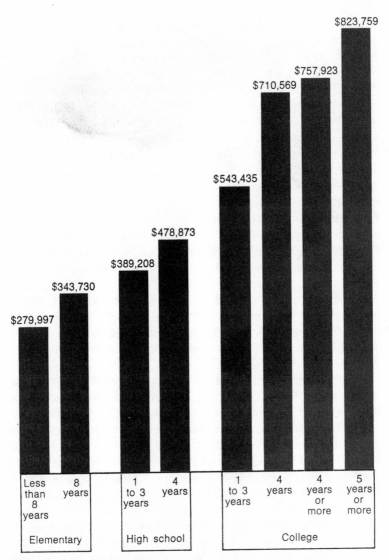

Note: Dollar figures are for 1972.
Source: U.S. Department of Commerce, Bureau of the Census

scales, they plainly show the comparative economic advantage of higher education, whether it be a college course leading to a bachelor's degree or vocational training insuring occupational skills.

Forward-looking, well-to-do parents sometimes support a married son and his young wife—or a married daughter and her student husband—during a long period of postgraduate training in order to ease the burden of these years of study. They understand the ultimate value of the extra education in terms of increased personal satisfactions and annual income. But few students have parents who are willing and financially able to give this assistance. Most young people must decide for themselves whether to continue their education or to marry and minimize the chance of economic success.

Two cannot live as cheaply as one

Young couples who decide to marry during, or shortly after, high school usually have to live on a shoestring. Although they may have handled allowances covering nearly all their teen-age expenses, they are likely to be shocked to discover how great are the costs of food, housing, clothing, personal care, medical aid, and transportation. To these basic costs of consumption must be added other essential expenses, including income taxes, Social Security payments, life insurance, and business expenses.

The table on page 235 indicates what it cost a young couple to live in 1975 just above the poverty level, at a moderate standard, and in an above-average manner.

The birth of two children would raise their costs of living to $7,404 for the lower budget, $12,032 for the intermediate budget, and $17,773 for the higher budget. For families on the lower standard, the annual cost of one child is about $1,010; on the intermediate standard, $1,530; and on the higher standard, $2,100.

These figures, derived from studies made by the Bureau of Labor Statistics, represent annual costs of living in an average urban community in the fall of 1975. While living costs vary to some extent from region to region, city to city, and

How Annual Income Climbs
With More Education

Average Annual Income
And Level of Education Completed

Men Aged	Grade School	High School	College 4 Years	5 Years or More
25-34	$7,755	$10,859	$13,274	$14,859
35-44	$9,776	$12,997	$20,085	$22,603
45-54	$9,693	$13,528	$22,307	$24,239
55-64	$8,873	$12,624	$19,765	$24,525
65 and over	$5,174	$ 7,768	$12,677	$15,013

Source: *U.S.News & World Report* Economic Unit figures
based on Census Bureau data

town to rural area, it must be remembered that the cost of living has risen sharply since these statistics were compiled. By mid-1977 inflation had raised the cost of living at least another 10 percent. It may require many more dollars to maintain these same standards of living a few years hence.

In addition to providing an income large enough to cover the cost of living, prospective brides and grooms must consider the expense of setting up housekeeping. To furnish a three-room apartment with new household goods of medium quality costs at least $5,200. Consider the bedroom. A queen-size bed with a superior mattress, box spring, and bedding costs around $500. Two bureaus of modest quality, two chairs, a night stand, two lamps, and an electric clock would cost at least an additional $630.

An above-average living-room sofa, one well-upholstered lounge chair, a straight chair, a coffee table, two end tables with lamps, and a dinette set consisting of six chairs and a table might well cost $1,850. A few kitchen utensils, toaster, vacuum cleaner plus a basic supply of canned goods and staples would easily require $400 more. Unless the landlord supplies the refrigerator—and many do not—another outlay of about $350 would have to be made.

Few young couples accustomed to comfortable living would consider their home furnished without rugs ($500 or more), curtains or draperies ($200 up), a color television set ($400 or more), a few pictures, ashtrays, and decorative accessories ($200 or so). A set of dishes, stainless steel flatware, glassware, and candlesticks would cost at least another $200. Fine furnishings, unless bought secondhand, could double or triple these prices.

While family and friends who attend a wedding usually give the bride many valuable and useful articles, young people who set up housekeeping after an elopement or a very quiet ceremony receive relatively few gifts. Some lucky couples can raid a grandmother's attic. Others hunt for bargains in thrift shops and auction houses. Still others are content to get along with half-furnished rooms for the first year or two of marriage while they save for their major furnishings. Still, even with luck, hard work, shopping know-how,

Annual Living Costs for Childless Couples Under 35 At Three Standards of Living
(Urban United States, Autumn 1975)

	Lower Budget	Inter-mediate Budget	Higher Budget
Consumption Costs			
Food, Housing, Household Operations, Transportation, Clothes, Personal Care, Medical Care, and Other	$3,820	$5,740	$7,910
Other Family Expenses			
Gifts, Contributions, Life Insurance, Entertainment, and Occupational Expenses	436	701	1,182
Social Security and Disability Payments	577	834	841
Personal Income Taxes	781	2,057	4,130
Total	$5,614	$9,332	$14,063

Source: Budgets of Bureau of Labor Statistics

and self-discipline in spending, it costs several thousand dollars to turn bare rooms into an attractive home.

Couples who are willing to wait a few years before getting married usually start housekeeping with much nicer things. If both hold skilled jobs for a while, they can bank quite a lot of money toward furnishings that will remain attractive and serviceable for years. While saving, they can stroll through showrooms and auction rooms, study styles of furniture, learn about quality, and collect good china, lamps, pictures, linens, and similar compact articles that will eventually be needed in their home.

In these days of costly sterling silver, some girls as young as thirteen or fourteen select a pattern of flatware and tell relatives and friends that they would appreciate a piece or two as birthday and Christmas presents. By the time these girls are twenty, they may have place settings for six or more and a few large serving pieces as well. Other young girls choose a pattern of fine crystal and collect goblets and wine glasses to use on their party tables in years to come.

The financial cost of having a baby

When teen-agers make a hasty marriage, they seldom give thought to the dollars-and-cents cost of having a baby. Yet, babies do come; and babies are expensive.

Prenatal care and hospital delivery cost at the present time $1,200 to $1,800. Low-cost health insurance plans rarely give subscribers maternity benefits until they have been members of the group insurance plan for approximately a year. At best, these benefits cover only part of the doctor and hospital costs.

Even minimal furnishings for an infant—a crib with a good mattress, bathinette, supplies of diapers, sheets, blankets, shirts, gowns, sweaters, and later a carriage, car carrier, high chair, and playpen—can amount to another $800, unless relatives and neighbors make generous donations or the articles are bought secondhand.

Then consider the space that all this equipment requires. A three-room apartment often is too small to accommodate all the things an infant needs—so much so that most young parents are forced to seek larger quarters. To compound this problem, many landlords refuse to accept tenants with young children. They claim that children are noisy, that they and their wheeled vehicles are destructive of interior walls and exterior plantings.

Young couples on tight budgets often find themselves in financial straits after the birth of an unexpected baby. In addition to the cost of maintaining a child, they may be forced to buy a house before they are in a position to undertake the risk and expense.

The emotional cost of having a baby

Emotionally mature individuals, who have taken time to establish a firm and loving relationship with a marital partner, and who realize that child-bearing and child-rearing are fraught with sacrifices as well as satisfactions, are likely to become first-class parents. On the other hand, immature people who are busy breaking away from dependence on their own parents, solving the problems of their own identity, completing their education, and establishing a workable economic existence, almost always find an unexpected baby a major disaster.

A teen-aged father faces at least eighteen years of child support—court ordered, if not volunteered. This economic burden can change a young man's whole future. Instead of being able to complete his college or vocational education, he may have to become an unskilled laborer whose job opportunities throughout life will be stringently curtailed. A brilliant medical student had to settle for work as an occupational therapist; an engineer-in-training became a garage mechanic; and there are thousands of similar personal tragedies every year.

Immature girls who rush into matrimony to achieve instant adulthood—or to gain the admiration of their friends —find teen-age wifehood, with or without motherhood, a bitter letdown from their romantic notions of life. Domestic bliss is not to be bought with dreams of chivalry and a few dollars a day.

Sandra Dee Brown wrote a letter (see page 238). Perhaps it will serve as a warning to other girls who need time to

Dear Dr. Sheffield,

I am writing you because I know you are good friends with my Aunt Martha and Uncle Freddie. They said you might be able to help me if I came to talk to you, and I need someone to help me now.

I am 17 and married to a fine man of 18. I am going to have his baby in a couple of months. I also have a year-old son. My parents helped me to get married but now will have nothing more to do with me.

I'm lonely with Bob away at high school all day. All I do is take care of Teddy in a garage apartment behind Aunt Martha's house. I'm not very good at housekeeping. When my girl-friends stop by to see me after school, they envy me with my own home and husband and baby. Big deal!

Doctor, I'm so miserable I could die! I'm just not ready to be a wife and mother. I don't even love my husband anymore. All I do is dream about the fun the other girls have - dates, swim parties, driving the family car, falling in love, vacation trips, that sort of thing. I'd give anything to be 14 again and back at good old Springfield Junior High.

Sometimes I am tempted to have the baby, then run away to another city and start life over again. Aunt Martha says no one can go back and start over. She says that in a few years I may learn to appreciate my family if I face the future and not the past. She thinks you could help me face the future. Please help me. Please.

Sincerely,

Sandra Dee Brown

Sandra Dee Brown

enjoy adolescence before taking on the responsibilities of womanhood.

Teen-agers who have children before they, themselves, have outgrown childish ways do more than hurt their own chances for personal financial success. The enormous and rapidly growing number of battered children attests to the dehumanizing effect of parenthood on immature persons. Unable to accept their reduced opportunities for earning a good living and the circumscribed pattern of their marital lives, immature parents often vent their anger on their helpless offspring.

Seen in this light, the cost of marriage without maturity can be staggering. Parents can protect their children, their wallets, and society if they teach their teen-agers that marriage is a civilized design for living which can be fully enjoyed only by responsible, financially independent, emotionally mature adults.

"In the days of my youth," Father William replied,
"I remembered that youth could not last;
I thought of the future, whatever I did,
That I never might grieve for the past."

CHAPTER 14

Insuring
the Future

Even the most forward-looking young person finds it nearly impossible to realize that someday he will need funds to finance a comfortable old age or will require insurance to protect himself and his family in case of injury, ill health, or death. Unpleasant as such thoughts may be, no sensible person can simply ignore them. It is, therefore, essential that young people learn the basic facts about life insurance, health insurance, and Social Security.

Insurance is a way of sharing life's risks. Those who escape injury and ill health help to pay the bills of those who are less fortunate. It is far less painful to pay for unused insurance than it is to need and receive it. But, if injury or illness does strike close to home, any feelings of annoyance about the expense of insurance payments are transformed into feelings of relief and gratitude for help in times of trouble.

Sometimes groups of people arrange for insurance coverage for every member of the group. Blue Cross, for example, writes health policies that cover all the people who work for a particular company. A growing number of group life insurance plans protect the families of employees, union members, or members of professional societies. The U.S. government administers life insurance and retirement pensions for military personnel, civilian employees, and employees of state and local governments.

Insurance companies also write many individual policies. The value of these contracts depends on the honesty of the insurer and the security of the funds from which policies are to be paid as they come due. It is, therefore, important to select an insurance company carefully. Beware of mail-order insurance policies. Many that appear to offer very generous terms hide serious limitations in the fine print. Deal only with a financially sound company and a local insurance agent in whom you can put your trust.

The ins and outs of life insurance

Life insurance pays a lump sum or a monthly income to the survivors—the beneficiaries—of the policyholder. The purpose is to provide financially for the widow, children, or other dependents of a breadwinner who is no longer here to care for them.

Most wage earners in America are underinsured. For one thing, life insurance can be expensive. Besides, even among adults, there are many who find the thought of death so depressing that they do not study their insurance needs. Moreover, even people who are willing to plan for the future find it hard to determine how much life insurance they ought to carry.

The table on page 243 shows the number of years various amounts of life insurance would last if the money were invested and earned 5¼ percent interest from the day of deposit to the day of withdrawal. For example, if the lump-sum insurance were $5,000 and the beneficiary used $95.11 a month, his capital would last for five years. If the insurance payment were $25,000 and the beneficiary spent $269.24 a

Life Insurance for Monthly Living Expenses

Amount Received From Life Insurance Policy & Invested at 5¼ %	Monthly Withdrawals Before Depletion Of Capital In			
	5 Years	10 Years	15 Years	20 Years
$ 5,000	$ 95.11	$ 53.84	$ 40.41	$ 33.92
10,000	190.22	107.69	80.82	67.85
15,000	285.45	161.54	121.23	101.77
20,000	380.45	215.39	161.64	135.70
25,000	475.56	269.24	202.06	169.62
30,000	570.68	323.09	242.47	203.55
35,000	665.79	376.93	282.88	237.47
40,000	760.91	430.78	323.29	271.40
45,000	856.02	484.63	363.71	305.32
50,000	951.13	538.48	404.12	339.25

Source: The Bowery Savings Bank, N.Y.C.

month, ten years would go by before the capital was entirely depleted. The same $25,000 spread out over fifteen years would give the beneficiary $202.06 a month.

How much is enough?

Before anyone can calculate how much life insurance a wage earner needs, certain facts about his family must be established. How many people are, or are likely to be, dependent on the insured? What is his income? What other assets does he have? Where does the family stand on the long curve of the family life cycle?

The life cycle of a family begins when a young couple marries; it may end about fifty years later when the surviving spouse is laid to rest. During the cycle, the family's insurance requirements vary with changes in the couple's financial responsibilities and standard of living.

Insurance salesmen from several large companies were asked to recommend the life insurance coverage that an upper-income family should have as they proceed from bride-and-groom days to the retirement years. Although there were large variations in the recommended amounts, all agreed that insurance needs follow the pattern described next. The amounts mentioned are an average of the coverages suggested by insurance salesmen.

A bride and groom in their mid-twenties, with an income of $12,000 to $15,000, no house, no children, and few other assets, need only enough insurance on the wage earner's life to pay funeral and legal expenses and to provide the widow with a year's income to give her a chance to rebuild her life.

A couple in their mid-thirties, with two or three children, an income of around $20,000, a house with a mortgage of $15,000, and savings and other assets totaling at least $10,-000, would require approximately $150,000 in life insurance to be adequately protected.

The need for insurance reaches its peak when the children begin their college education. The family headed by a forty-five-year-old man with an income of $30,000, a small mortgage on his home, and bank accounts plus securities totaling $45,000 to $50,000 should carry insurance coverage of around $200,000. Financing four years of college for two youngsters costs about $40,000; to support and educate three children comes close to $60,000. Families with large college funds need less insurance.

Eventually the children grow up and become self-supporting. The mortgage is paid off or very much reduced. In addition to owning their home, the upper-income family with a fifty-five-year-old breadwinner has probably set aside a considerable sum in savings or securities. If the family income should rise to $35,000 and the other assets total about $75,-000, insurance coverage could safely be reduced to something like $150,000 or $160,000 and still maintain the widow at her accustomed standard of living.

When the wage earner becomes sixty-five and Social Security provides a retirement or survivor's income, possibly supplemented by a pension, income from part-time work, and a return on personal investments, an elderly couple might carry just enough life insurance to cover costs of burial and legal fees for settling the estate. For this, the hypothetical family here described needs only about $25,000.

It is evident from the above that life insurance needs change with the size of the family unit, the age of the breadwinner, and the standard of living to which a family is accustomed.

Other factors also influence the amount of insurance a family needs. Increased Social Security benefits, generous company pensions with vested rights for faithful employees, and working wives who are economically independent lessen the need for large sums of insurance on the life of the family head. Inflation, on the other hand, may dictate increased coverage.

The best way to gauge insurance needs is to make up a usable budget based on present standards of living and current prices to which are added known expenses for the next three or four years plus about 20 percent to cover probable inflation. Then supplement savings and other assets, such as securities, with enough insurance coverage to make it possible for the surviving family members to live on that budget for their remaining years of dependency. If a new budget is made every three or four years and insurance coverage is reviewed at that time, a family's finances will be secure even after the sudden loss of its breadwinner.

This business of discovering income needs for the near future and estimating—as far as possible—income needs at a more distant time is called "estate planning." Insurance salesmen are not the best advisors when it comes to estate planning. At the time a couple draws up or reviews their wills, a lawyer can be of great help. Given a detailed picture of family assets, obligations, and prospects, and knowing something about the ages, personalities, and goals of the family members, he is in a good position to suggest ways to build an estate and to reduce as much as possible the costs of administering it.

The best costs least
The amounts of life insurance discussed above will stagger the imagination of most future wage earners until they realize that life insurance policies vary enormously in kind and in price.

To get the largest amount of life insurance for every premium dollar, it is necessary to understand the theory behind each of the three basic types of life insurance. It is also important to understand that the cost of similar policies differs greatly among the various life insurance companies. The buyer who knows the amount and kind of coverage he wishes to have is in a position to shop for the best terms available. Too many insured persons, being totally uninformed, are "sold" their policies. Prudent insurance buyers, having read a couple of good books on insurance, "buy" the policy that will provide them with the most protection for each insurance dollar.

The three basic types of life insurance are *term, whole life,* and *endowment* policies. The thousands of seemingly different policies offered by insurance agents are only combinations of these three basic types.

Term insurance buys protection and nothing else. If the insured person should die during the term—the period of time—that the policy is in force, the beneficiary receives the face value of the policy. Just as with fire insurance on a house or liability insurance on a car, if no disaster occurs during the years that the term policy is in force, no values remain when the policy expires. Because the policy builds up no cash values, a youthful buyer of term insurance gets large amounts of protection at the lowest possible rate. In 1974 a thirty-five-year-old man, for example, might buy $100,000 of renewable term insurance from a company known for its reasonable premiums for under $400 a year; whereas a whole-life policy from the same company would cost several times as much.

Whole life—often called *straight life* or *permanent life*—policies, once chosen, remain in force for the duration of the buyer's life if the premiums are paid on time. These policies combine protection against financial disaster following the death of the family breadwinner with a "cash value" feature. This is the amount the holder would receive if at any time he decided to cash in his policy. The cash value, which builds up at a snail-like pace as the years go by, can serve as collateral for a loan from the insurance company at low rates of interest. However, while the money is on loan, the face value of the policy is reduced by the amount of the loan. In

times of financial difficulty, the cash value may also be used
to pay current premiums.

Many buyers of whole-life policies do not realize that this
"savings feature"—so often stressed by insurance salesmen
—evaporates completely at the death of the policyholder. The
beneficiary receives only the face value of the policy. For the
privilege of a life-long level premium (a premium that remains the same year after year) and for the chance to build
up cash values that he might never want to use, the young
policyholder pays a far larger premium than he would pay
for term insurance.

Endowment policies—and the variant thirty-year paid-up
life policies—are a cross between term insurance and a savings plan. If the insured person dies before the maturity date
of the policy, his beneficiary receives the face value of the
policy. If the insured person is living on the maturity date,
he receives the face value of the policy. Endowment policies
are the most expensive form of life insurance. They are of
value only to people in very special circumstances and totally
unsuitable to the needs of young families trying to protect
themselves against loss of income at the untimely death of
the family breadwinner.

Coming to terms with term insurance

For the young family man whose insurance needs are on
the rise—in fact for a man of any age who has the self-con-
trol to bank some of his salary in order to build up an emergency reserve and capital assets—term insurance is the best
form of life insurance to buy. The money tucked into the
savings bank earns a far higher rate of interest than the part
of the premium retained by the insurance company as "cash
value." And money in the savings bank does not vanish if the
policyholder dies as do the cash values in a whole-life policy.

There are two kinds of term insurance. *Level-premium re-
newable term* is bought for a stated period—usually five
years. During that time, the annual premium is fixed. At the
end of the period of coverage, the policy may be renewed for
another five years at a higher premium without another
physical examination. As the policyholder ages, the premiums

rise sharply, and the insurance may be unavailable to persons who reach their sixties. The buyer of such a policy should pay the slightly higher premium that makes the policy *convertible* into whole-life insurance without a medical examination. Then, if poor health should make him uninsurable, he can retain at least the amount of coverage he has.

Decreasing term insurance works on another principle. For a fixed annual premium, the insured person may buy coverage that runs for ten, fifteen, twenty, or twenty-five years, possibly more. During this time, the value of the policy shrinks year by year. The premium payments usually stop a few years before the policy expires. Decreasing term, often referred to as "mortgage insurance" because many people carry at least enough of it to pay off the balance on a home mortgage in case of the wage earner's death, is the least expensive insurance of all. The death benefit can be paid as monthly income or as a lump sum.

In choosing insurance, the knowledgeable buyer makes certain that the policy contains a *waiver-of-premium clause*. Then, if he or she should become permanently disabled, the policy would remain in force without further premium payments.

Both level-premium and decreasing term insurance offer young families high coverage per premium dollar plus flexibility. As the need for protection grows, more policies may be added; as the need diminishes, policies may be allowed to expire. By buying only protection, the policyholder with foresight and common sense has money left over for savings and investment.

A package of insurance

Because the ill, the disabled, and the elderly do not always have the money they need in order to live, in 1936 the U.S. government set up a compulsory insurance program to which most working people now contribute. This program is called Social Security.

Under the Federal Insurance Contributions Act (FICA) as amended by Congress from time to time, employers and employees share equally in the FICA, or Social Security, tax on earned income. In 1977 incomes up to $16,500 were taxed 11.70 percent. Of this, 5.85 percent was deducted from the employee's paychecks while a matching amount was paid by the employer.

In future years, both the amount of earnings subject to the tax and the tax rate itself will be increased to cover automatic increases in benefits as consumer prices rise.

These compulsory contributions buy a great deal of protection. The Social Security system provides six basic benefits: a monthly retirement pension for an insured worker; a monthly pension for his or her dependents; survivors' benefits for the dependents of a worker who dies before or during retirement; a lump-sum death benefit to help cover funeral expenses; Medicare benefits to help pay hospital and doctors' bills; and disability benefits for a seriously disabled worker and his or her dependents.

Of particular interest to an adolescent are those benefits which would go into effect should one of his parents become eligible for retirement or disability payments or die while fully covered under Social Security. In such cases, a full-time student up to the age of twenty-two receives a monthly stipend so that he can continue his education. A young person who becomes disabled before reaching the age of twenty-two can get disability payments if either of his parents has Social Security coverage. Children supported by an eligible grandparent and some adopted children may also be eligible for monthly Social Security checks. Information about these and other possible benefits may be obtained at the nearest Social Security office.

The card and the coverage

Getting a Social Security card is a simple matter. Children and teen-agers who have started their own savings accounts or who own securities under a Uniform Gifts to Minors Act will have a Social Security card long before they begin their first summer job. Those who do not have a card need only go to a Social Security office to get the proper application form.

Once the card arrives, the owner should memorize the number, put the stub away in a safe-deposit box, and store the card itself in a safe place at home. If you lose your card, or if you change your name for any reason, apply for a new card bearing the old number. Should you ever find yourself with a second number, be sure to report it immediately and have all your credits transferred to the original number. This is important because the size of your retirement benefits depends on the amount of income that has been credited to your account over the years.

Every employed person must have a Social Security card on which appears his full name and the number that remains his alone as long as he lives. This card must be shown to each new employer, who is required by law to record the facts carefully and to send the employee's name, number, and the appropriate Social Security taxes to the Internal Revenue Service every three months. At the end of each year, or at the end of his period of employment, the worker receives a W-2 form stating how much he was paid, how much was withheld for income taxes, and how much went for his share of the FICA tax.

At least once every three years, every employed person should check with the Social Security Administration to make sure that all his earnings and tax payments were properly reported. If a mistake has been made, the worker must show his copy of the W-2 form and see that corrections are entered on his record. Corrections must be recorded within a period of three years, three months, and fifteen days or the credit for payments made will be lost. People who change jobs frequently should check their Social Security records every year. Checking is easily done by completing and mailing a postcard provided by the nearest Social Security office.

A worker's eligibility for some or all of the Social Security benefits depends on his status; and his status depends on the length of time he has worked in jobs covered by Social Security. To be fully insured, a worker must have a certain number of quarters of coverage. A person is credited with one quarter for every three-month period in which he earns at least $50 in non-farm employment. A farm worker or a self-employed person is credited with four quarters of coverage when he earns $400 in the course of a year.

Inexperienced workers may think it clever to go along with a dishonest employer who neither deducts his employee's tax from earned wages, nor pays his own half of the FICA tax. Evading the tax is not only illegal, it is shortsighted on the part of the worker. The dollars he forgoes each pay period will eventually give him a monthly pension, help for his dependents, an income if he becomes disabled, and health protection worth many times what he paid in taxes.

How health insurance works

Health insurance provides protection against costly hospital, medical, and surgical care and sometimes against loss of income resulting from the disability of the family breadwinner. No family can count on freedom from accidents and diseases; therefore no family can afford to ignore the need for insurance against ill health.

As the costs of medical care mount higher, the problem of how to meet them has become acute. Blue Shield and Blue Cross, a privately run low-cost form of group insurance, has since the 1930s helped many middle-income families meet their doctor and hospital bills. Families with the means to do so often buy from private insurance companies "major medical" policies that cover the astronomical expenses of extraordinary illnesses. But the poor have long had to go without care or rely on the charity of hospitals.

In an attempt to alleviate the sufferings of the elderly, in 1965 the federal government added Medicare, a health insurance program for the aged, to Social Security. Medicare, Part A, helps to pay for hospital care and certain follow-up services; Part B, a voluntary but inexpensive medical coverage, helps to pay doctor and other medical bills.

Medicare, however, has not paid for eye examinations, eyeglasses, hearing aids, dental services, drugs, and routine physical examinations. And, with the exception of coverage for persons suffering from acute kidney disease, Medicare does not provide free or inexpensive medical insurance to persons under sixty-five.

Plans for nationwide health insurance have been under consideration in Congress, and it is possible that low-cost health insurance may soon become available to every American.

Until a national health insurance plan goes into effect, people seeking protection from the financial hazards of severe illness or accident may be tempted to buy one of the many hospital insurance policies that are advertised by mail or by flyers tucked into Sunday newspapers. Such policies should be viewed with suspicion.

Mail-order insurance policies often offer benefits that have little worth. For example, some may cover hospital expenses "from the sixtieth to the hundred and fiftieth day," but give nothing before that time. The truth of the matter is that very few people are kept in a hospital for more than a few weeks. In most cases either the patient responds to treatment and goes home, or he dies. People with chronic illnesses are moved to nursing homes; those with remediable conditions are sent to rehabilitation centers. Moreover, a sound, reliable insurance company rarely offers an individual wide medical coverage without a careful investigation of his health and age. Only when large groups are insured together can a company afford to take such risks.

Protection for householders

Responsible householders can now buy homeowners' insurance. This single policy protects a person's house or apartment from fire and vandalism, windstorm and flood, and similar disasters. Such policies replace furnishings and other possessions that are damaged or stolen. If the policyholder has fine paintings, jewelry, furs, or a coin collection, these, too, can be covered for an additional premium.

Most homeowners' policies also include protection against damage suits that might be won by the mailman who was nipped by the householder's dog or by the old lady who tripped over a bicycle left on the sidewalk by the householder's child. Even when the accident does not result from negligence on the part of the policyholder and his family, homeowners' policies usually provide coverage for the medical expenses of individuals injured in the policyholder's home. Such insurance is well worth the annual premium.

Many other kinds of insurance can be written to protect

people against special hazards. Surgeons and musicians may insure their hands. Doctors usually insure themselves against malpractice suits brought by disgruntled patients. People in charge of costly outdoor gatherings often buy insurance against bad weather.

Nobody, of course, can foresee all the risks that might become realities. And this is fortunate. Sensible people consider the calamities that might befall them, insure themselves against the worst, and hope for the best.

*The world is his who has
the money to go over it.*

RALPH WALDO EMERSON

15

Travel
and the
Teen-Ager

More young Americans are on the move than ever, despite gasoline shortages and rising prices. Teen-agers travel to and from schools and colleges, to ski lodges, to summer jobs, to see the world. In order to make business travel or vacation jaunts memorable dreams instead of nightmares, some travel facts are worth remembering.

Door-to-door danger

Travel by car is cosy but costly. The per-mile cost of running a car—tires, repairs, depreciation, insurance, and gasoline—used to be estimated at twelve cents a mile. But that was in the days when gasoline was priced at less than fifty cents a gallon and readily available at any time of the day or night. Today's cost per mile is likely to be much, much higher.

Less predictable and more alarming are car costs of quite

another kind. For drivers and passengers of all ages, the chance of being killed on the road is ten to twenty times greater for travelers in a car than for travelers by plane, bus, or train. The chance of meeting death on the highway rises sharply when the driver of the car is under twenty-five years old. When more than two young people are in the car, the danger of a fatal accident soars even higher.

Since car pools are a necessity in these days of dwindling gasoline reserves, and since travel in a crowded car is the most hazardous form of transportation for teen-agers, young travelers would be well-advised to take a fresh look at public transportation.

Riding the blue sky

For trips of over 300 miles, especially when the element of time is important, airplanes have no parallel. But to assure happy landings, the air traveler needs to know a thing or two.

All air fares are approved by the Civil Aeronautics Board (CAB). A passenger must pay the fare in effect on the day he flies. If the fare has been increased since the ticket was purchased, the additional amount must be paid before boarding the plane. Although special youth fares have been eliminated, excursion and other special rates may be available at certain times of day or on certain days of the week. Travelers who qualify for such special rates may save sizable sums of money by asking for them.

Although airlines usually state that it is not necessary to reconfirm a reservation on most domestic flights, it is always wise to do so. Call the office of the airline about twenty-four hours before flight time, check that your reservation is in order, and give the company your telephone number just in case the flight should be canceled or delayed.

Experienced travelers arrive well in advance of flight time in order to be sure of a seat assignment. If the company suggests arrival half an hour before boarding time, add another fifteen minutes to avoid the rush. Last-minute passengers often find that even reconfirmed seats have been assigned and that they are destined to have a long, lonely wait for the next scheduled flight.

Upon arrival at the airport, worldly-wise travelers go directly to the check-in counter, deposit their bags, show their tickets, and get a seat assignment. Then they proceed to the boarding point, where they must be prepared to open all carry-on luggage and handbags and, if requested, to submit to a body search. Passengers who refuse to agree to security measures may be denied a boarding pass.

If, after a person has complied with all the airline's check-in requirements, he is denied a seat because the plane is overbooked, the company is obligated to find him a seat on another flight going to the same destination. On a domestic flight, the second plane must arrive within two hours of the original schedule; on an international flight, the delay must be less than four hours. When the airline cannot meet these conditions, it is required by law to offer the passenger compensation equal to the price of his ticket, but not less than $25 nor more than $200.

"Denied boarding compensation," as this payment is called, must be paid within twenty-four hours. The passenger who has been "bumped" should not leave the check-in area until he has received a written statement of the CAB rules and has been given the compensation for which he is eligible. After making a cash settlement, the airline's obligation does not end. The airline must offer the passenger assistance in reaching his destination.

Should the passenger not receive his denied boarding compensation promptly, he has ninety days in which to file a claim with the company. If the carrier fails to settle a claim— whether for denied boarding compensation or for damage to baggage—the passenger should contact the Office of Consumer Affairs, Civil Aeronautics Board, Washington, D.C. 20428. Airlines, operating in a competitive field, are anxious to provide satisfactory service and to avoid problems with the CAB.

Airlines, of course, cannot guarantee arrival or departure times. If, however, a passenger holding a confirmed reservation is delayed more than four hours, the airline must provide complimentary services. These services include limited communication with people at the traveler's home or at his destination, meals during normal meal hours, and hotel accommodations if the delay occurs during the night. Since some airlines do not seek out the waiting passenger to offer these services, the passenger should not hesitate to go to the counter and ask for the price of a meal or the room to which he is entitled.

Loss or damage to baggage is a frequent source of irritation to the plane passenger. If the air traveler waits in vain at the baggage claim area until all his fellow passengers have picked up their bags, he should immediately notify the airline's personnel. Possibly the plane is still on the ground and can be searched for the missing luggage.

No matter how great his hurry, a traveler should report the loss of a bag before leaving the airport. An official of the airline will fill out a form describing the bag and its contents, the date each item was bought, the cost, and the present value. Should the missing bag not turn up within three days, the company will mail claim forms which must be completed and returned to the airline so that the claim can be processed. As a rule, valid claims are settled within six weeks; but exaggerated claims are usually detected and denied. It is important to retain the baggage claim check until the bag has been found or compensation has been received.

To protect their possessions, seasoned travelers carry a sturdy bag and lock it before checking it. Even when staying at a hotel, it is a good idea to leave small and cherished objects in the suitcase and turn the key before leaving the room. While no baggage lock defies a determined thief, it deters the pilferer. And who wants the inconvenience of trying to replace essential items on a busy day in a strange city? Who wants to grieve over jewelry left on the side of a washbasin?

Knowing how rough baggage handlers are at airport and piers, experienced travelers often put a strap around a case that is heavy or tightly packed. A couple of inexpensive men's belts can be joined together to serve as a suitcase strap. Woven trunk straps can still be found by determined seekers. One young woman cut down an overly-long woven strap, whipped the raw end, then dyed it wine red to match the trim on her suitcase.

Luggage that is distinctive is less likely to be picked up by a fellow traveler who mistakes it for his own or by one of the suitcase thieves who operate around airport claim areas. Many smart travelers buy colored plastic adhesive tape at dime or stationery stores and decorate the sides and ends of each bag with their own "racing stripes" or such symbols as a triangle, a star, or a flower. A case with such a personalized design could be spotted half a block away, and this would not appeal to the fellow who snatches another person's suitcase at the baggage claim area or in a hotel lobby.

On highways and byways

A popular form of public transportation is the inter-city bus. Within a radius of 300 miles, travel by motor coach is as fast as by car and almost as rapid as travel by plane when the time spent going to and from the airport and waiting for takeoff is added to the time in flight. Bus seats are guaranteed without advance reservations; schedules are maintained despite stormy weather. Bus fares are less than half the cost of plane or car travel and approximately two-thirds the cost of a train ticket.

Even though bus depots leave much to be desired, once he has boarded the bus the passenger has a comfortable seat and a safe ride. Some bus lines offer weekend excursions, all-expense tours, and even month-long passes for unlimited travel. Many young people with more wanderlust than money have seen all parts of our nation through the wide windows of cross-country buses.

Your money or your life

Young travelers are often tempted to hitchhike in order to cut the cost of transportation. This is false economy. Thumbing a ride is frowned upon by parents, turnpike commissioners, and the police for several reasons. Many hitchhikers are injured on the roadside, particularly at dusk or dawn. Cars stopping to pick up or discharge passengers on busy roads are liable to be struck from behind by other vehicles. And not infrequently the teen-ager who rides in a stranger's car has a rapist, robber, or murderer as his driver.

Even when traveling in pairs, young people are not safe from these dangers. Until adolescents accept these facts and agree never to hitchhike, parents are well-advised to withhold the privilege of travel without supervision.

Riding the rails

For those who can afford to travel at leisure, few forms of transportation can match the comfort and pleasure of riding a crack cross-country train. Until the beginning of the 1960s, when passenger service between the east and west coasts of America was all but abandoned, well-to-do travelers enjoyed luxurious drawing-rooms, roomettes, or sleeping berths, ate in decorous dining-cars, walked carpeted corridors, or sat in glass-domed observation cars to view the towering Sierras or Rockies.

One of the few blessings of the energy shortage is the rebirth of public interest in railroading. The web of tracks, so long neglected, is being repaired. New rolling stock is on order for commuter runs and the "long lines." Innovations have already begun, among them free motion pictures to amuse those who have tired of the scenery, and flat cars to haul the automobiles of those who follow the wild geese south to their winter quarters.

In the coming years many Americans will rediscover the delights of the chattering rails and the mournful voice of the engine as it floats downwind to sing the traveler to sleep. A vacation by train is never to be forgotten. It can be a family treat or an adolescent's first adventure across the farmlands, rivers, deserts, and mountains that make up this land of ours. No history book, no text on economics can give so sure a grasp of America and its people as can a ten-day trip by train.

Footloose and fancy-free

Camping became very popular during the 1960s. What effect the shortage of gasoline may have on the future use of campers, trailers, and other gas-powered vehicles is unclear at the present time. Still, short camping trips and backpacking outings are possible without the extensive use of such recreational vehicles.

Some people like camping in areas with a minimum of facilities. Others prefer campgrounds furnished with easy-access roads, refuse cans, sanitary facilities, and drinking fountains. Still others dream of going into unspoiled back-country areas completely free from the sights, sounds, and restrictions of the human community.

Whatever his preferences, a person must give thought to collecting adequate, compact equipment and to planning his trip. There are numerous books on where to go and what to carry on camping trips of various kinds and lengths. The U.S. government offers a number of helpful manuals. One, *Camping in the National Park System*, lists the camping seasons, facilities at various sites, fees, services, and amusements at national parks across the country. By writing to the Superintendent of Documents, U.S. Printing Office, Washington, D.C. 20402, this and other booklets on camping may be readily obtained.

Dream trip or nightmare

Each year thousands of young Americans travel abroad for study, work, or fun. For those who lay careful plans, foreign travel can be a dream come true. For those who go unprepared or who break the rules, the dream trip can turn into a nightmare.

Knowledgeable parents can be of great help in making preparations for a safe and satisfying trip. Months in advance, they should check out various organizations that offer youth travel programs for vacation, study, or work abroad. Some are reputable and financially sound; others may be poorly run, charge exorbitant fees, or even leave the young traveler stranded penniless in a distant land.

Mr. Hanscome wanted his daughter Julia to tour Europe during the summer after she completed high school. One evening early in November, he sat down with Julia. They listed the key points to check about any organization or tour operator offering teen-agers a vacation trip. This is what they wrote:

1. *Check reputation of the organization:* Have any friends

of ours used it? If not, who in the neighborhood has traveled with it? What references may I contact? Who is the director? What does my school advise about this organization?

2. *If it is a study program,* what is the instructor's background? Will I receive credits? What subject matters does the course plan to cover? Discuss the organization and its program with the student advisor at school.

3. *What will the program cost?* Check to see that all costs are included. Be sure to read the fine print.

4. *Will the organization refund the money* if they cancel the trip? What if I have to cancel? Has the organization an office in the U.S. in case I have to take legal action against them?

5. *If the group is to use a charter flight,* make sure that a reliable airline is being used. Also make sure that return tickets have been bought before the tour begins. Many students have been stranded abroad because tour directors have failed to buy valid return tickets before leaving the United States.

The key to faraway places

"For most travel abroad, a person needs a valid passport," Mr. Hanscome reminded Julia. "It is true that you can make brief visits as a tourist to many countries in the Western Hemisphere as long as you have adequate proof of U.S. citizenship—such as a birth or naturalization certificate and, in some cases, a tourist card that costs a few dollars and can be obtained at the point of entry. But even in these countries, you are wise to have a passport; and a passport is a necessity if you plan a long stay."

"How do I get a passport, Dad?" asked Julia.

"You have to go to a U.S. State Department Passport Agency, or to a federal or state court, or to a Class I post office. Our local post office will tell you where to apply.

"When you apply for a passport, you will need proof of American citizenship—a birth certificate, a baptismal record, proof of naturalization, a census record, or an affidavit from someone who knows when and where you were born. You will also need identification—a driver's license, a document bearing your signature and picture, or someone who knows you.

And you'll need two recent, identical front-view photographs signed along the left side. They must be two and a half or three inches square."

"I know the kind you mean—photos with that 'Wanted by the FBI' look."

Mr. Hanscome chuckled. "Most passport pictures are anything but flattering. But no matter how it makes you look, your passport is a key that opens the door to far places and lets you come home again.

"You must always take care of that key. Sign your passport as soon as it arrives and fill in the information inside the front cover. Never alter it in any way; never lend it or give it as collateral for a loan. Never leave it in your hotel room or in an unattended pocketbook. In many countries, passports are stolen and sold. If ever you lose a passport in the United States, report it at once to the Passport Office in Washington, D.C. If you lose it while abroad, contact the nearest consulate. A replacement passport will be issued only after delays for investigation and then only for a limited time.

"In order to travel to some countries, you have to have a visa—an official stamp on your passport," continued Mr. Hanscome. "Visas are usually available through the local consulate or embassy of the country you plan to visit. To get this stamp of approval, you fill out whatever forms are necessary and send the required fee with your passport in a registered letter, enclosing a self-addressed, stamped envelope for its return. The Passport Office cannot help you to get visas; your travel agency may. The important thing to realize is that it takes time to get a passport and obtain visas from the consulates of the countries you intend to visit. It's best to start the procedure at least two months before you plan to go abroad."

How to use travelers' checks

"Smart travelers do not take much cash on a trip," Mrs. Hanscome said a few days before the tour took off. "Instead, they buy a supply of travelers' checks considerably larger than they intend to use. If the checks are not needed for an emergency during their trip, they will be handy back home some day when the banks are closed. Or they can be redeemed at the bank.

"I list the number of each check in a small pocket notebook; then as I spend each check, I jot down the date and name of the person to whom it was issued. Should my book of travelers' checks ever be lost or stolen, I could report each uncashed check to the company that issued it.

"This pocket notebook has many other uses. It can serve as a diary in which to note the happenings of each day. It can make it easy to keep track of expenditures. It can list the names and addresses of people to call in an emergency and of friends to whom cards might be sent.

"Several pages of the little notebook can be used for conversion tables—translating our nickels, dimes, quarters, and dollars into the coins and bills of each country to be visited." Mrs. Hanscome reached into a desk drawer and brought out a loose-leaf notebook with three-by-five-inch pages.

"The last time I visited Italy, the dollar was worth 625 lire. Of course, the foreign exchange rates may have changed by now—any bank will tell you the current rate. But this is how I made my conversion table and roughly how yours would look [see page 267].

"With lire on the left and dollar equivalents on the right of each column, you can instantly see how much to tip or how much an article costs. By making similar conversion tables for British pounds, French francs, or German marks and keeping these tables in the front of your notebook, you can handle foreign money almost like a native of the country you are in."

Julia asked, "Why have you underlined some of the numbers?"

"The underlined numbers indicate the coins or bills of the country. A 100-lire note, for example, was worth only 16 cents; a 500-lire note was worth 80 cents. If you wanted to tip a porter about 30 cents for carrying your bag, you'd give him 200 lire. If you bought something for 10,000 lire, you'd be paying around $16 for it."

"But how do I find out what coins each country has and what they look like?"

A Currency Conversion Table

Italian Lire

Coins
- 5 lire = ¾ ¢
- 10 lire = 1.5 ¢
- 20 lire = 3 ¢
- 50 lire = 7.5 ¢
- 100 lire = 16 ¢
- 625 lire = $1.00

£	$	£	$
10	.015	625	1.00
20	.03	700	1.12
30	.045	800	1.28
40	.06	900	1.44
50	.075	1,000	1.60
60	.09	1,250	2.00
70	.105	2,000	3.20
80	.12	3,000	4.80
90	.135	5,000	8.00
100	.16	6,000	9.60
150	.25	7,000	11.20
200	.32	8,000	12.80
312	.50	9,000	14.40
400	.64	10,000	16.00
500	.80	15,000	24.00

"Nowadays American banks sell packets of coins and bills for the countries to which large numbers of people travel. These packets, which cost around $10, contain a printed slip about the currency and give you a chance to study most of the coins of the country. Best of all, on arrival, you have usable cash for tips and taxis."

"What do I do with leftover money when the tour moves on to another country?" asked Julia.

"The coins of one country have no value in another; so unless you want to save them as souvenirs, you spend any coins you may have before leaving a country. Bills, on the other hand, may be exchanged either at a bank or by your hotel clerk. Both charge for this service, but banks charge less."

Forewarned is forearmed

Julia thought a moment. "Maybe I could trade money I no longer need for money someone else wants to get rid of. It would save the bank charges."

"Don't you ever exchange foreign money with a private individual!" Mrs. Hanscome's voice was sharp with concern. "Street-corner deals can lead to trouble. You may be stuck with counterfeit currency or involved in a swindle. Steer clear of anyone who offers you money at less than the going rate. Dealing on the black market often leads to jail. The people who offer to sell you cheap money or to buy it from you may be police informers who would gladly turn you in for a reward."

"Cool it, Mother," said Julia. "I was only thinking of a way to save a few dollars."

"Economy is a fine thing," said Mrs. Hanscome, "but not to the point where you defraud a bank, cheat a merchant, short-change a friend, buy stolen property, or disobey some other law. Even when you are an innocent bargain-hunter, you can get in trouble with the law. Many a young person who has bought an airline ticket 'at a discount' from a stranger has been prosecuted for accepting stolen goods."

Mr. Hanscome strolled into the room and said, "Also beware of people who offer to buy your possessions. Some countries restrict the purchase of certain luxury items, like cameras, watches, jewelry, or clothing. A visitor caught selling such things can get a stiff jail sentence; and even the American consulate can't get you out of jail.

"Some countries ask each entering traveler to declare travelers' checks, currency, and other valuables. When you leave, your travelers' checks and money will be compared with that early declaration. Undeclared currency and checks will be confiscated."

"How can they do such things to an American citizen?" Julia asked indignantly.

"Remember that you are governed solely by the laws of the country you are visiting. It's up to the visitor to conduct himself—or herself—within the framework of those laws. Right now over 900 young Americans are in foreign prisons for the possession of narcotics. In some countries, trafficking in or smoking marijuana draws the same penalties as the possession or use of heroin."

Julia grimaced. "Although no one I know uses any of that stuff, we all use money. I'm beginning to wish I hadn't signed up for the tour. I don't want to break some old law I know nothing about."

Mrs. Hanscome smiled. "People who behave sensibly and speak politely seldom run into trouble at home or abroad. Listen to the tour director, stay with the group, be your pleasant, intelligent self, and everything will be fine."

"I know you'll have a wonderful trip," said Mr. Hanscome.

"I sure hope so," replied Julia. "Now I've got to run or I'll be late for my own going-away party."

Use it up,
Wear it out,
Make it do,
Or do without.

NEW ENGLAND MAXIM

16

Money and the World of Tomorrow

Today's children—the adults of the 1980s and 1990s—will undoubtedly face a number of consumer problems about which present-day adults can only guess. Whereas, in the past, consumers have needed to know only how to buy wisely and how to make the most of personal and community resources, tomorrow's consumers will have to concern themselves with the social effects of their choices in the marketplace. They will have to tailor their consumption to society's need to survive, for ecological crises are already upon us.

Tomorrow's adult Americans are not going to have the cornucopia of foods, goods, and services that their parents enjoyed. Already fuel shortages have begun to reshape our lives. Our taste for pleasure driving, brightly lit homes, synthetic fabrics, and power-driven tools will have to be modified as the emerging nations continue to increase their need for coal, oil, and gas. Even if new sources of energy are discovered and harnessed, scarcities of fossil fuels and permanently higher prices are inevitable.

Air pollution in large cities is growing alarmingly. It will be only a matter of time—and a short time at that—before public transportation will have to replace daily automobile commuter traffic for this reason alone. The energy crunch of 1974 gave us a foretaste of a possible flight from the suburbs back to cities where people can manage quite well without cars.

The population explosion of the mid-twentieth century brought with it greater pressure on the world's food supplies and consequently higher and ever higher prices for groceries. Worse yet, we are faced with almost insoluble problems of trash and waste disposal. We have mountains of battered cars in automobile graveyards. Rivers and streams are fouled with tires, bottles, and detergents. Even the oceans can no longer handle the sewage that is being dumped into them day after day.

Strip mining is tearing up enormous areas of farm or timber land. Wild animals are dying out because the land on which they have lived is sprouting row after row of squat little houses. The cost of land is soaring because the number of plots of habitable land is finite.

What can be done about it?

If the remarkable technology which we have developed over the past 200 years is not to destroy us, each individual will have to make fewer demands on the natural resources of the small planet on which we live. Our children must learn to protect the ecology when they choose the things they buy. They must be helped to discover the satisfaction that comes from saving, fixing, and creating things, because Americans can no longer afford the luxury of national extravagance. We cannot afford to throw away almost new clothing because of rapidly changing styles. We cannot afford to abandon a motor because a screw is missing. We can no longer countenance the wasteful changes in models that make our cars old-fashioned and our appliances obsolete after a year or two.

The best way to teach is by example. Parents who practice thrift—repair possessions, recycle discarded items into useful and attractive articles, use tools and machines until they are no longer functional—provide valuable consumer education for their children. Parents can demonstrate responsible use of resources when they cook, shop, maintain their homes, and choose their leisure activities.

In some families, the teen-agers are teaching thoughtless parents how to protect the environment, how to promote the good things about American life, how to set about correcting the bad. And they have need to teach, for it is their world that is being shaped now.

An enduring monument

It has been said that money and immortality are the twin pursuits of most Americans. Whereas few of us can amass great fortunes, create great works of art, or turn the course of history, we all can do our part in passing on to future generations a green Earth where flowers bloom in the spring and birds sing. We can protect human and animal life by using no more than we need of Earth's resources. We can avoid waste even when we have the means to be extravagant. We can devote some effort to the conservation of land and sea against vandalism and pollution.

By caring for the world around us and by teaching our children that this planet—its plants, animals, and minerals—is the only source of wealth that they and their children's children are ever likely to have, each of us can achieve a touch of immortality. As Horace said, two thousand years ago, so we can say:

> I have wrought a monument more enduring than bronze, and loftier than the royal accumulation of the pyramids. Neither corrosive rain nor raging wind can destroy it, nor the innumerable sequence of years nor the flight of time. I shall not altogether die.

Many Americans are as wasteful of their personal resources as they are of the treasures of air, field, stream, and mine. Constantly stimulated by advertisements, they foolishly believe that "new" is synonymous with "better" and that "the latest thing" is unquestionably superior.

Advertisers use the whole range of human emotions—vanity, fear, embarrassment, desire for approval, unrealistic hope—to motivate mindless buying. No shampoo will make anyone popular overnight. No garment, however fine, will transform a Cinderella into a princess. No aftershave lotion will make a man irresistible. Not even a new car will make a motorist truly sought after. Every child should be told this:

The sum of all your buying choices makes up the person that you show to the world. But always the kind of human being you are inside—that bundle of attitudes, emotional reactions, and patterns of thought that is the real you—determines whether you will be lovable, popular, successful, and pleased with yourself.

Knowing these things, buy only what you truly want or need. Never buy to show off before your friends. Never buy because some article may not be available next month or next year. If it is not there, something else will be.

Remember that money in the bank is comforting. Remember that old things can be beautiful: polished leather, mellowed wood, a well-tended vintage car. Remember that no one ever has everything he wants. Remember that it is sometimes better to give than to receive.

Index

PHOTO CREDITS
Adams Studio, Inc.—83
Carlo Bavagnoli, Time/Life Picture Agency—263
Tom Nebbia, Black Star—19
James Pickerell—23, 32, 74
Irwin Rosen, Black Star—225
Marion S. Trikosko, *U.S.News & World Report*—160, 201, 205, 233
Doug Wilson, Black Star—261